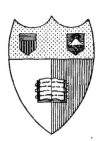

Date Due

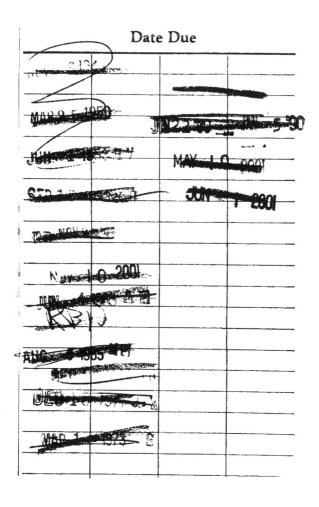

THE AMAZON.

A

MISSION TO GELELE,
KING OF DAHOME.

WITH NOTICES OF

THE SO CALLED "AMAZONS," THE GRAND CUSTOMS, THE
YEARLY CUSTOMS, THE HUMAN SACRIFICES, THE
PRESENT STATE OF THE SLAVE TRADE,

AND

THE NEGRO'S PLACE IN NATURE.

BY

RICHARD F. BURTON,

(LATE COMMISSIONER TO DAHOME,)
AUTHOR OF "A PILGRIMAGE TO EL MEDINAH AND MECCAH."

"If a man be ambitious to improve in knowledge and wisdom, he should travel into
foreign countries."—PHILOSTRATUS IN APOLL.

"Every kingdom, every province, should have its own monographer."
GILBERT WHITE.

IN TWO VOLUMES.

VOL. I.

LONDON:

TINSLEY BROTHERS, 18, CATHERINE STREET, STRAND,
1864.

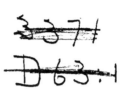
LONDON : .
BRADBURY AND EVANS, PRINTERS, WHITEFRIARS.

Dedicado

Á MIS AMIGOS ESPAÑOLES EN FERNANDO PÓO, ESPECIALMENTE A
LOS SEÑORES

BRIGADIER D. PANTALEON LOPEZ DE LA TORRE AYLLON,
(GOBERNADOR-GENERAL DE FERNANDO PÓO Y SUS DEPENDENCIAS);

D. ATILANO CALVO ITURBURU;

D. TEODOSIO NOELI Y WHITE;

D. FRANCISCO OSORIO Y D. CARLOS DE ROJAS;

EN PRUEBA DE AFECTUOSA AMISTAD.

PREFACE.

In the Preface affixed by an anonymous hand to "The History of Dahomy," published nearly three-fourths of a century ago,[*] we are told that the "short interval from Whydah beach to Abomey is perhaps the most beaten track, by Europeans, of any in Africa." The Author thereupon proceeds to show a difference of 104 miles between the maximum and minimum estimates of the distance, which is nearly doubled by the most correct.

In this Year of Grace, 1864, there is at least an equal amount of uncertainty concerning the "Land of the Amazons;" but it shows rather in things metaphy-

[*] "The History of Dahomy, an Inland Kingdom of Africa; compiled from authentic Memoirs; with an Introduction and Notes. By Archibald Dalzel, Esq., (Governor at Whydah, then) Governor at Cape Coast Castle, (and lastly Governor-in-Chief of the Company's Service)." London, 1793. 4to. Printed for the Author by T. Spilsbury and Son, Snowhill. In the following pages, whenever "The History" is alluded to, Dalzel's is to be understood.

PREFACE.

sical than physical. So well informed a journal as the
"Saturday Review" (July 4th, 1863), gravely informs
its readers that "The King of Dahome has lately
been indulging in a sacrifice of 2000 human beings,
simply in deference to a national prejudice (!), and to
keep up the good old customs of the country" (! !).

This complete miscomprehension of the subject,
coming from such a quarter, induces me to attempt
without fear so well worn a theme, and to bring up to
the present time a subject worthily handled by Snelgrave,* Smith,† Norris,‡ Dalzel, M'Leod,§ and Forbes.‖
And if, in depicting the manners and ceremonies of
this once celebrated military Empire, and in recounting
this black Epopæia, there has been a something of

* Captain William Snelgrave arrived off Whydah, in the Katherine
galley, in the latter end of March, 1726, three weeks after its capture
by Dahome. His book, "A Full Account of some Parts of Guinea and
the Slave-trade," appeared in 1734. 8vo.

† William Smith, Esq., was sent out as surveyor in 1726. His "New
Voyage to Guinea" is a posthumous work, published in 1744. 8vo.

‡ "Memoirs of the Reign of Bossa Ahadee: with an Account of a
Journey to Abomey in 1772, by Mr. Robert Norris." London, 1789.

§ "A Voyage to Africa; with some Account of the Manners and
Customs of the Dahomian People. By John M'Leod, M.D." London:
John Murray, 1820.

‖ "Dahomey and the Dahomans; being the Journals of Two Missions
to the King of Dahomey, and Residence at his Capital, in the years 1849
and 1850. By Frederick E. Forbes, Commander R.N.," &c. 2 Vols.,
8vo. London, Longmans, 1851.

excessive detail, and there shall appear much that is trifling and superfluous, the kindly reader will perhaps find for it a reason.

My principal object, it may be frankly owned, has been to show, in its true lights, the African kingdom best known by name to Europe. But in detailing its mixture of horrors and meanness, in this pitiless picture of its mingled puerility and brutality, of ferocity and politeness, I trust that none can rightfully charge me with exaggeration, and I can acquit myself of all malice. "*A nadie si elogia con mentira, ni se critica sin verdad.*"

So far back as 1861 I had volunteered, as the Blue Book shows, to visit Agbome. The measure not being then deemed advisable, I awaited till May—June, 1863, when an opportunity presented itself. In the meantime (December, 1862—January, 1863), Commodore Wilmot, R.N., Senior Officer of the Bights Division, accompanied by Captain Luce, R.N., and by Dr. Haran, of H. M. S. Brisk, devanced me, and that officer proved the feasibility of a visit to Dahome. Returning to Fernando Po, I soon received the gratifying intelligence that Her Majesty's Government had been pleased to choose me as the bearer of a friendly

message to King Gelele.   The official letters are, by
permission, given *in extenso* below.

FOREIGN OFFICE, August 20, 1863.

SIR,

You were informed by my Despatch of the 23rd of June
last, that you had been selected by Her Majesty's Government
to proceed on a Mission to the King of Dahomey, to confirm
the friendly sentiments expressed by Commodore Wilmot to the
King on the occasion of the visit which he made to that chief in
the months of December and January last.

I have accordingly to desire that as soon after the receipt of
this Despatch as it may be feasible to do so, you will proceed to
Dahomey, taking care first, by previous communication with the
King, to ascertain that a proper reception will be accorded to you.

You will, on your arrival, inform the King, that the many
important duties which devolve on Commodore Wilmot as the
Officer in command of Her Majesty's Naval Forces on the African
Coast, have prevented him returning in person to confirm the
good understanding which it is hoped has been established between the King and Her Majesty's Government by the Commodore's late visit.   You will state that the Commodore faithfully
reported all that passed between him and the King, and that he
correctly made known the wishes and feelings of Her Majesty's
Government on the several topics on which he addressed the King.

With regard to the question of the export of slaves from his
territories, you will not fail to impress upon the King the importance which Her Majesty's Government attach to the cessation
of this traffic.

Her Majesty's Government admit the difficulties which the
King may find in putting a stop to a trade that has so long existed

in his country, and from which his ancestors have derived so much profit, but his income from this source must be very small compared with that of former Kings, and it will be to his interest to find out some other source of revenue, before that which he now derives from the sale of his fellow-men to the slave dealers is entirely put a stop to. You will remind the King that he himself suggested to Commodore Wilmot that if we wished to put a stop to the slave trade, we should prevent white men from coming to buy them, and you will state that Her Majesty's Government, having determined that the traffic shall cease, will take steps to prevent effectually the export of slaves from his territories. You will add, in illustration of what you state, that Her Majesty's Government have concluded a treaty with the United States Government, which will prevent, for the future, any American vessels from coming to ship slaves.

With regard to human sacrifices, I rejoice to find from Commodore Wilmot's Report, that the number of victims at the King's customs has been exaggerated.

It is to be feared, however, that much difficulty will be experienced in prevailing upon the King to put a stop entirely to this barbarous practice, which prevails more or less openly, along the greater part of the Western Coast of Africa. But we must seek by whatever influence we may possess, or be able to attain, to mitigate, if we cannot at once prevent, the horrors of these customs, and I rely upon your using your best efforts for this purpose.

The King in his interview with Commodore Wilmot expressed a wish that English merchants should come and settle and make trade at Whydah, and he offered to help to repair the old English fort there, and to permit it to be garrisoned by English troops.

You will thank the King for this mark of his confidence, and you will at the same time state, that as he has promised to protect any British merchants who may settle at Whydah, Her Majesty's

Government put entire faith in his promises, and see no necessity for sending English soldiers to garrison the fort there. You will, however, add, that there is one thing needful in order that the King's wishes in regard to the settlement of English merchants at Whydah should be carried out, and that is, that there should be a sufficiency of lawful trade to induce them to do so.

English merchants cannot take slaves in return for their goods, they must have palm oil, ivory, cotton, and such other articles as the country is capable of producing. The King will see, therefore, that it must depend very much on his own exertions, and those of his subjects, whether it will be worth while for British merchants to settle at Whydah. Should however the King think fit to enter into an engagement with Her Majesty's Government to encourage lawful trade, and to promote, as far as lies in his power, the development of the resources of his country, Her Majesty's Government would be willing to appoint an agent at Whydah to be an organ of communication with the King and to assist in carrying out his views.

As an earnest of their friendly feelings, Her Majesty's Government have caused the presents, of which a list is inclosed, to be prepared and forwarded to you for presentation to the King. You will see that, as far as possible, the King's wishes as expressed to Commodore Wilmot, have been carried out in regard to the articles selected for presents, with the exception of the carriage and horses, and with respect to these, you will explain to the King, that in the first place it would be a difficult matter to get English horses out to the Coast, and even supposing they arrived safely at their destination, it would be very doubtful, from the nature of the country and climate, whether they would long survive their arrival.

If, however, our future relations with the King should be of a nature to warrant such a proceeding, Her Majesty's Government would not hesitate to endeavour to comply with his wishes, by sending him an English carriage and horses.

I have only in conclusion to add, that it has been suggested to Her Majesty's Government that among the King's captives there may still be some of the coloured Christian prisoners taken at Ishagga, and if on inquiry you should be able to ascertain that this is the case, you will state to the King that it would be taken by Her Majesty's Government as an earnest of his friendly feeling, and as shewing a desire to perform his promises to them, if he would restore these prisoners to liberty.

I am, Sir,

Your most obedient humble Servant,

(Signed)   Russell.

EXTRACT.

Foreign Office, August 20, 1863.

Sir,

With reference to my other Despatch of this day's date containing instructions for your guidance on proceeding to Dahomey, I have to state that you should, if possible, stipulate with the King before proceeding to Abomey, that there should be no human sacrifices during the time of your stay in his capital, and you will, under any circumstances, decline to sanction these sacrifices by your presence, if they should unfortunately take place whilst you are in the country.

The last packet from the West Coast brought reports of the King of Dahomey having died from the effects of a wound received in one of his slave-hunting expeditions. Should these reports be well founded, it will be advisable that you should ascertain something of the character of his successor before proceeding to the Dahomian capital, and I leave it to your discretion to proceed subsequently to Abomey, and to deliver the presents to the new King or not, as you may after due consideration deem advisable.

I have requested the Lords Commissioners of the Admiralty to give directions that you may be conveyed to and from Whydah in a ship of war, and I have also informed their lordships that it would be advisable that a medical officer should accompany you, if one can be spared from Her Majesty's ships for this purpose.

I am, Sir,

Your most obedient humble Servant,

(Signed)   RUSSELL.

FOREIGN OFFICE, July 23, 1863.

SIR,

     With reference to my Despatch of the 23rd ultimo, instructing you to hold yourself in readiness to proceed on a mission to the King of Dahomey, I have now to acquaint you that the presents with which you will be entrusted for the King, and the instructions for your guidance, will be forwarded to you by the packet which leaves Liverpool with the African mails on the 23rd of August, and you will therefore make your arrangements accordingly.

I am, Sir,

Your most obedient humble Servant,

(Signed)   RUSSELL.

LIST OF PRESENTS forwarded to CAPTAIN BURTON by packet of
the 24th August, 1863, for presentation to the KING OF DA-
HOMEY.

One forty feet circular crimson silk Damask Tent with Pole
complete (contained in two boxes).

One richly embossed silver Pipe with amber mouth-piece, in
morocco case. Two richly embossed silver Belts with Lion and
Crane in raised relief, in morocco cases. Two silver and partly
gilt Waiters, in oak case. One Coat of Mail and Gauntlets. (Contained in one deal case, addressed to Captain Burton, H. B. M.'s
Consul for the Bight of Biafra, West Coast of Africa.)

September, however, was hardly the month to be
preferred for crossing the Great Agrime Swamp, and
my health required a change of air before submitting
to the *peine forte et dure* of a visit to a West African
King. A few weeks upon the South Coast, in the
delicious " Caçimbo,"* soon brought me up to working
mark, and the following pages will tell the rest.

In Chapter XIX., I have taken the liberty of personally addressing my friend Dr. Hunt, author of " The
Negro's Place in Nature." He has called for the
results of my humble experience—I had written the
remarks before seeing his able and graphic paper—and
I have done my best to aid him in dispersing the mists

* The cloudy (but not rainy) season in Angola and on the Congo
River, lasting from May to September.

with which "mere rhetoric of a political and religious nature" has invested the subject.

Some excuse may be expected for the length of the Appendix : the object has been to supply the Public with as complete a picture of present Dahome as my materials, and my capability of using them, have permitted. The items are as follows :—

I. Itinerary, from Whydah to Agbome (corrected by Captain George, R.N., Royal Geographical Society of London).

II. List of expenses at Agbome. Mr. Bernasko's account current with Captain Burton, Her Majesty's Commissioner, Dahomey, from December 8th, 1863, to February 26th, 1864.

III. Reprints of previous modern notices.

A. Extract of a letter from the Reverend Peter W. Bernasko, Native Assistant Missionary, dated Whydah, November 29th, 1860, and describing the Grand Customs. ("Wesleyan Missionary Notices," February 25th, 1861).

B. Despatches from Commodore Wilmot respecting his visit to the King of Dahomey in December, 1862, and January, 1863, and describing the Platform Sacrifice.

C. Dahomy, its People and Customs, by M. Jules Gérard, describing the Oyo Custom of Kana.

IV. A Catalogue of the Dahoman Kings, with the dates of their various exploits, their "strong names," and the events of their reigns. It is merely produced as *documens pour servir:* I have not only analysed the several histories, but have gathered from the natives traditions and explanations of the royal titles. Moreover, I wish these volumes to be a picture rather of the present than of the past.

The Pages now offered to the Public are the result of a three months' personal study of Dahome, my work extending over the day, and often half through the night. I may venture to assert that, by comparing its results with the authors before cited, the labour expended upon this monogram will become apparent.

It only remains for me to apologise for the involuntary errors which will doubtless be found in the following volumes, and to hope that I may, at some future time, find an opportunity of correcting them.

BUENA VISTA, FERNANDO PO,
    April 20, 1864.

CONTENTS.

—•—

CHAPTER I.

CHAPTER VIII.

A MISSION TO GELELE,

KING OF DAHOME.

CHAPTER I.

I FALL IN LOVE WITH FERNANDO PO.

This fertile soil, which enjoys a perpetual spring, is considered a strong prison, as the land of spectres, the seat of disease, and the mansion of death.

Said of Bengal by its Moslem conquerors.

A Ilha Formosa, the lovely island of Fernando Po, has, like most beauties, two different, indeed two opposite, aspects.

About Christmas time she is in a state deeper than rest,—

A kind of sleepy Venus seemed Dudu.

Everything, in fact, appears enwrapped in the rapture of repose. As the ship glides from the rolling, blustering Bights into that wonderfully still water, men come on deck feeling they know not what; *çela porte à l'amour,* as the typical Frenchman remarks. The oil-like swell is too lazy to break upon the silent shore, the wind has hardly enough energy to sigh, the tallest trees nod and bend drowsily downwards, even the grass is, from idless, averse to wave : the sluggish clouds bask in the soft light of the sky, while the veiled sun seems in no hurry to run his course. Here no one would dream, as does our modern poet, of calling nature " sternly fair." If such be the day, conceive the cloister-like stillness of a night spent in the bosom of Clarence Cove. Briefly, Fernando Po, in the dry weather, is a Castle of Indolence, a Land of the Lotophagi, a City of the Living-Dead.

But as I saw her in November, 1863, and as she had been for the six months preceding, the charmer was not to be recognised by *that* portrait. A change had come over her Madonna-like face—as is sometimes witnessed in the " human organism." The rainy season had set in earlier than usual ; it had opened in May, and in November it was not ended. A heavy arch of nimbus, either from the north-east or the north-west, gathered like a frown on the forehead of the dull grey firmament. Presently the storm came down, raving like a jealous wife. In a few moments it burst with a flood of tears, a sheet of "solid water," rent and blown about by raging, roaring gusts, that seemed to hurry from every quarter in the very ecstasy of passion. Baleful gleams of red thready lightning flashed like the glances of fury in weeping eyes, and deafening peals of thunder crashed overhead, not with the steady rumble of a European tempest, but sharp, sudden, and incisive as claps of feminine objurgation between fits of sobbing. These lively scenes were enacted during half the day, and often throughout the night : they passed off in lady-like sulks, a windless fog or a brown-blue veil of cloud settling hopelessly over the face of heaven and earth, till the unappeased elements gathered strength for a fresh outburst.

Amidst this caprice, these coquetries of the " Beautiful Island," man found it hard to live, but uncommonly easy to die. Presently all that was altered, and the history of the metamorphosis deserves, I think, to be recorded.

The shrew was tamed by an inch and a half of barometric altitude. The dictum of the learned Dr. Waitz, the Anthropologist, no longer holds good.*

* " There are many districts in Africa where strangers, and especially Europeans, can neither live nor become acclimated, whilst the natives

When I first landed on this island (September, 1861), Sta. Isabel, *née* Clarence, the lowland town and harbour, was the only locality inhabited by the new Spanish colony. Pallid men were to be seen sitting or lolling languid in their verandahs, and occasionally crawling about the grass-grown streets, each with a cigarette hanging to his lower lip. They persistently disappeared in the dry season, whilst their example was followed by the coloured " liberateds" and the colonists during the " balance" of the year. H. B. M.'s Consulate is situated unpleasantly near a military hospital : breakfast and dinner were frequently enlivened by the spectacle of a something covered with a blanket being carried in, and after due time a something within a deal box being borne out on four ghastly men's shoulders. And strangers fled the place like a pestilence : sailors even from the monotonous " south coast," felt the *ennui* of Fernando Po to be deadly—grave-like.

At length Yellow Fever, the gift of the " Grand Bonny," which was well-nigh depopulated, stalked over

enjoy good health. Such is the case in some parts of the Darfur, the greater portion of Kordofan, *Fernando Po*, and Zanzibar."—Anthropology of Primitive Peoples, vol. i., excellently translated by J. Frederick Collingwood, Esq., F.A.S. London, Trübner and Co., 1863.

the main in March, 1862, and in two months he swept
off 78 out of a grand total of 250 white men.*

The "Beautiful Island" was now going too far.
Seeing that the fever did not abate, H. E. the Governor
de la Gandara determined to try the effects of altitude.
A kind of "quartelillo"—*infirmerie* or *baraque*—was
hastily run up in twelve days, beginning from June
22nd, 1862, by M. Tejero, Commandant of Military
Engineers. The site, a kind of shelf over the village
of Basile, about 400 mètres above sea-level, received
the name of Sta. Cecilia. On the day after its com-
pletion, July 6th, nineteen *pénitentiaires*, or political
prisoners, the survivors of some thirty men that had
died of yellow fever in the hulks, were transferred to
the new quarters ; two were lost by attacks of the
same disease contracted on the seaboard, the rest of
those condemned to *travaux forcés* kept their health,

* On Aug. 28, 1859, 155 white soldiers, young and picked men, who
had shipped at Cadiz, July 16, 1859, arrived at Fernando Po, under H.
E. the Governor de la Gandara, who is now fighting his country's bat-
tles in Santo Domingo.

On July 16, 1863, after concluding their three years' service, forty-
seven of these men returned to Spain. I have been unable to procure
statistics of their health or sickness since that period.

Of the 108 casualties, or more than two-thirds of the original number,
thirty-five men died, mostly during the first eighteen months : the other
seventy-three were sent home invalided.

and were returned to their homes in November, 1862.

This old *baraque* is now nearly always empty, being converted into a kind of lodging-house. Its dimensions are 11·50 mètres long, by 6 broad, and raised on piles 1·50 high ; the rooms are three in number, one large, of 6 mètres by 4·25, and the other two of 4·25 mètres by 3.

Seeing the excellent result of that experiment, H. E. Sr. D. Lopez de Ayllon, the present Governor, to whom these pages are respectfully inscribed, determined to increase operations. Major Osorio, of the Engineers, was directed to build a *maison caserne*, intended to accommodate white soldiers not wanted for duty at Sta. Isabel. It was begun March 22nd, finished September 5th, and opened November 30th, 1863. The *rez de chaussée* lodges forty men, the second story as many more, whilst the first stage has rooms for the Governor, his aide-de-camp, and four officers. Besides these two lumber houses, there are tolerable stables for horses and mules, good roads well bridged, and a channel of mountain water, which the white soldiers, who can work in the sun with the thinnest of caps, have derived from the upper levels. About thirty men were sent here. Their number has varied but little. During the five months from December, 1863, to April, 1864, though there have been sporadic local cases of simple intermittent fever—March, 1864, shows only one—and though dangerous diseases have been brought up from the lowlands, not a death has occurred.

Thus, then, the first sanitarium in Western Africa owes its existence to the Spanish Colony, that dates only from the middle of 1859. As far back as 1848, the late Captain Wm. Allen and Dr. Thompson, of the Niger Expedition, proposed a sanitary settlement at Victoria, on the seaboard below the Camaroons Mountain, a site far superior to Fernando Po. Since their time, the measure has been constantly advocated by the late Mr. M. Laird. *Eppur non si muove*—Britannia. She allows her "sentimental squadron" to droop and to die without opposing the least obstacle between it and climate. A few thousands spent at Camaroons or Fernando Po would, calculating merely the market value of seamen's lives, repay themselves in as many years. Yet not a word from the Great Mother !

When I compare St. Louis of Senegal with Sierra Leone, or Lagos with Fernando Po, it is my conviction that a temporary something is going wrong with the popular constitution at home. If not, whence this want of energy, this new-born apathy ? Dr. Watson assures us that disease in England has now assumed an asthenic and adynamic type. The French said of us in the Crimea that *Jean Boule* had shattered his nerves with too much tea. The Registrar-General suggests the filthy malaria of the overcrowded hodiernal English town as the *fomes malorum*. The vulgar opinion is, that since the days of the cholera the Englishman (physical) has become a different being from his proto-type of those fighting times when dinner-pills were necessary. And we all know that

C'est la constipation que rend l'homme rigoureux.

Whatever the cause may be, an Englishman's lot is at present not enviable, and his children have a Herculean task "cut and dry" before them.

Nothing can be more genial and healthful than the place where I am writing these lines, the frame or plank-house built by D. Pellon, of the Woods and Forests, now absent on private affairs in Spain. The aneroid shows 29 instead of 30·1—30·4 inches, and the altitude does not exceed 800 feet. Yet after sunrise the thermometer (F.) often stands at 68°,

reddening the hands and cheeks of the white man.
We can take exercise mentally and bodily without that
burst of perspiration which follows every movement in
the lowlands, and we can repose without the sensation
which the " Beebee " in India defined as " feeling like a
boiled cabbage." The view from the balcony facing
north is charming. On the right are the remnants of
a palm orchard ; to the left, an avenue of bananas
leads to a clump of tropical forest ; and on both sides
tumbles adown the basaltic rocks and stones a rivulet
of pure cold mountain water—most delightful of baths
—over which the birds sing loudly through the live-
long day. In front is a narrow ledge of cleared ground
bearing rose-trees two years old and fifteen feet high,
a pair of coffee shrubs, bowed with scarlet berries,
sundry cotton plants, by no means despicable, and a
cacao, showing what the island would have been but
for the curse of free labour.* Beyond the immediate

* " Without slaves," says Koeler (Notizen über Bonny), " the fertile
tropical valleys would be unproductive and deserted, as white men
cannot labour there in the open air." The question is, whether the
world has been sufficiently cleared to enable men to dispense with forced
labour ? At Fernando Po, the hire of a Kruman, who does about one-
fifth of an Englishman's work, amounts, all things included, to thirty
shillings a week. The expression in the text is not too strong. Mr.
Lee, Professor of Agricultural Chemistry in the university of Georgia,
estimates the manual requirements of the Southern States at one million

foreground there is a slope, hollowed in the centre, and densely covered with leek-green and yellow-green grasses of the Holcus kind now finding favour in England, and even here fragrant, when cut, as northern hay. The drop is sufficiently abrupt below to fall without imperceptible gradation into the rolling plain, thick and dark with domed and white-boled trees, which separate the mountain from the Ethiopic main. The white houses of Sta. Isabel glisten brightly on the marge ; beyond it the milky-blue expanse of streaked waters stretches to the bent bow of the horizon ; and on the right towers, in solitary majesty, a pyramid of Nature's handiwork, "Mongo ma Lobah," the Mount of Heaven,* now capped with indistinct cloud, then gemmed with snow,† and reflecting from its golden head the gorgeous tropical sunshine; whilst over all of earth and sea and sky there is that halo of atmosphere which is to landscape what the light of youth is to human loveliness.

of men for twenty years, and regards it as "providential that there should be so much unemployed power in human muscles in Western Africa."

* The topmost peak of the Camaroons Mountain, so called by the natives.

† To talk of snow so near the Line! The erudite Mr. Cooley will certainly swear it is dolomite.

And as night first glooms in the East, the view borrows fresh beauties from indistinctness. The varied tints make way for the different shades of the same colour that mark the several distances, and hardly can the eye distinguish in the offing land from sea. Broken lines of mist-rack rise amongst the trees of the basal plain, following the course of some streamlet, like a string of giant birds flushed from their roosts. The moon sleeps sweetly upon the rolling banks of foliage, and from under the shadowing trees issue weird fantastic figures, set off by the emerald light above. In the growing silence the tinkle of the two rivulets becomes an audible bass, the treble being the merry cricket and the frog praying lustily for rain, whilst the palms whisper mysterious things in their hoarse baritone. The stars shine bright, twinkling as if frost were in the air; we have eliminated the thick stratum of atmosphere that overhangs the lowlands, and behind us, in shadowy grandeur, neither blue nor brown nor pink, but with a blending of the three, and sometimes enwrapped in snowy woolpack so dense as to appear solid against the deep azure, the Pico Santa Isabel, the highest crater in the island, rises softly detached from the cirrus-flecked nocturnal sky.

Life, as an American missionary remarked, is somewhat primitive at Buena Vista, but it is not the less pleasant. An hour of work in my garden at sunrise and sunset, when the scenery is equally beautiful, hard reading during the day, and after dark a pipe and a new book of travels, this is the "*fallentis semita vitæ*" which makes one shudder before plunging once more into the cold and swirling waters of society—of civilization. My "niggers" are, as Krumen should be, employed all the day long in clearing, cutting, and planting—it is quite the counterpart of a landowner's existence in the Southern States. Nothing will prevent them calling themselves my "children," that is to say, my slaves; and indeed no white man who has lived long in the outer tropics can prevent feeling that he is *pro tempore* the lord, the master, and the proprietor of the black humanity placed under him. It is true the fellows have no overseer, consequently there is no whip; punishment resolves itself into retrenching rum and tobacco; moreover, they come and go as they please. But if a little "moral influence" were not applied to their lives, they would be dozing or quarrelling all day in their quarters, and twanging a native guitar half the night, much to their own discomfort and

more to their owner's.   Consequently I keep them to
their work.

At certain hours the bugle-call from Santa Cecilia
intimates that all about me is not savagery.   And
below where the smoke rises " a-twisten blue " from the
dense plantation of palms, lies a rich study for an
ethnologist—Basile, the Bubé village.   No white man
has lived long enough amongst this exceptional race
of Fernandians to describe them minutely, and, as a
rule, they have been grossly and unjustly abused.*
A few lines will show the peculiarities which distinguish
them from other African tribes.

The Bubé—who, as may be proved by language, is
an aborigine of the mainland—has forgotten his origin,

* Bosman (A New and Accurate Description of the Coast of Guinea,
translated into English, 1705) seems to have led the way, and others
have repeated him. " The island of Fernando Po is inhabited by a savage
and cruel sort of people, which he that deals with ought not to trust.   I
neither can nor will say more of them."

It is hard to discover whence was derived the word Adiyah or Eediyah,
which all writers have copied from the Niger Expedition of Messrs.
Allen and Thompson, and have applied to the Bubé race. The fact is, the
Fernandian, as might be expected, has no national name, for " adiyah "
is probably derived from adios, arios, aros, the salutation borrowed from
the old Spanish colony long extinct.   Bubé (not " bubi," or " booby,")
means, not " friend," but " man," a frequent address as the Castilian
hombre, and thus assumed by strangers as the popular appellation.   In
" High Bubé," " adyah " means " the moon," which in the vulgar is
" ballepo."

and he wisely gives himself no trouble about it. If you ask him whence he comes, he replies " from his mother ;" whither he goes, and he answers "to Drikhatta ra Busala 'be* if a bad man," and " to Lubakko 'pwa (the sky) if he has been a good Bubé." He has a conception of and a name for the Creator, Rupe or Erupe, but he does not perplex himself with questions of essence and attribute, personality and visibility. Perhaps in this point too he shows good sense. He is also, you may be sure, not without an evil principle, Busala 'be, who acts as it were chief of police.

Coming down from the things of heaven to those of earth, the Fernandian is " aristocratic," an out-and-out conservative ; no oldest Tory of the old school can pretend to rival him. But in many points his attachment to ancient ways results not from prejudice, but from a tradition founded upon sound instinct. He will not live near the sea for fear of being kidnapped, also because the over-soft air effeminates his frame. He refuses to build higher up the mountains than 2000 to 3000 feet, as his staff of life, the palm and the plantain, will not flourish in the raw air and rugged ground.

* Literally, kingdom (drikhatta) of the devil (bad ghost). So, the sky or heaven is also called Drikhatta ra Rupe, *i.e.*, Kingdom of God. Possibly these are European ideas grafted upon the African mind.

He confines himself therefore to the exact zone in which
the medical geographer of the present age would place
him—above the fatal fever level, and below the line
of dysentery and pneumonia. His farm is at a
distance from his cottage, to prevent domestic animals
finding their way into it ; his yam fields, which
supply the finest crops, are as pretty and as neatly
kept as vineyards in Burgundy, and he makes the
best " topi " or palm toddy in Western Africa. His
habitation is a mere shed without walls : he is a
Spartan in these matters. Nothing will persuade
him to wear, beyond the absolute requirements of
decency, anything warmer than a thin coat of palm oil :
near the summit of the mountain, 10,000 feet above sea
level, I have offered him a blanket, and he has preferred
the fire. His only remarkable, somewhat " fashionable "-
looking article of dress is an extensive wicker hat
covered with a monkey skin, but this is useful to prevent tree snakes falling upon his head. He insists
upon his wife preserving the same toilette, minus the
hat—oh, how wise ! If she does not come up to his
beau ideal of fidelity, he cuts off, first her left hand,
then her right, lastly, her throat ; a very just sequence.*

* In Northern Europe and America the injured husband kills the

He is not a slave nor will he keep slaves ; he holds them to be a vanity, and justly, because he can work for himself. He is no idler ; after labouring at his farm, he will toil for days to shoot a monkey, a "philantomba" (*alias* "fritamba"), or a flying squirrel. Besides being a sportsman, he has his manly games, and I should not advise every one to tackle him with quarter-staff; his *alpenstock* is a powerful and a well-wielded weapon. Though so highly conservative, he is not, as some might imagine, greatly destitute of intelligence : he pronounces our harsh and difficult English less incorrectly than any West African tribe, including the Sierra Leonite. Brightest of all is his moral character : you may safely deposit rum and tobacco—that is to say, gold and silver—in his street, and he will pay his debt as surely as the Bank of England.* And what caps his worldly wisdom, is his perfect and perpetual suspiciousness. He never will tell you his name, he never receives you

lover ; in Asia and Southern Europe he kills the wife. Which proceed- /ℓ ing is the more sensible ? Can any man in his senses believe in the seduction of a married woman ? *Credat Creswell Creswell !*

* I allude of course to the Bubé in his natural and unsophisticated state, not to him as corrupted by Europeans and Krumen. Mr. Winwood Reade, the author of an amusing and picturesque book, " Savage Africa," unfortunately visited only "Banapa," one of the worst specimens of a Bubé village. As a rule, the Fernandian has little of the ignoble appearance that characterizes the true Negro.

as a friend, he never trusts you, even when you bring gifts; he will turn out armed if you enter his village at an unseasonable hour, and if you are fond of collecting vocabularies, may the god of speech direct you! The fact is, that the plunderings and the kidnappings of bygone days are burned into his memory : he knows that such things have been, and he knows not when they may again be. So he confines himself to the society of his native hamlet, and he makes no other intimacies, even with the fellowmen whose village smoke he sees curling up from the neighbouring dell.*

*   *   *   *   *   *

After two years of constant quarrelling the beautiful

* Some of the kidnapping tales that still linger on this coast, show the straits into which, at times, men were driven for a cargo. At Annobom, where the people are Negro-Portuguese, they are ever looking forward to hearing mass from the mouth of a priest. A Spaniard learning this, dressed up a pair of ecclesiastics, landed them, and whilst the function was proceeding, seized the whole congregation, and carried them triumphantly to market.

The following communication will show the value of Fernandian cotton. But, alas! labour is at 30s. per week :—

"COTTON SUPPLY ASSOCIATION.
"Offices: No. 1, Newall's Buildings,
"Manchester, February, 1864.
"Captain R. F. Burton, H. B. M. Consul,
" Fernando Po.
"Sir,—Your communication, with the two samples of cotton, had the due attention of our Committee, and I have now to hand you their report upon the latter.

island and I are now "fast friends." It is perhaps as
well to "begin with a little aversion." *

"1st. Fernando Po.—Dull in colour, clean, staple fine, and fair length;
value 28*d*. per lb.

"2nd. Congo.—Dull brown colour, staple coarse and weak; value
27*d*. per lb.

Middling Orleans Cotton being worth 28¼*d*. per lb.

"The Committee would be glad to learn that such cotton as your
samples, especially the first, could be sent from Fernando Po in large
quantities to this district, where trade is languishing, and our population so severely suffering for want of a supply of such cotton.

"We shall be glad to have any further particulars respecting the pro-
duction of your immediate neighbourhood, and the price at which such
as your sample No. 1 can be collected, and any other information you
may be kindly disposed to furnish.

"I am, Sir,

"Yours respectfully,

(Signed)   "ISAAC WATTS, Secretary."

* The following sick list is taken from official documents, compiled at
Fernando Po. Of thirty invalids, sent up from the lowlands in November, 1863, there suffered from—

	Dec.	Jan.	Feb.	March.
Fever (simple and intermittent) .	14	16	11	1
,, (remittent malignant) . .	3	2	2	0
,, (intermittent malignant) .	0	0	1	0
Dysentery	3	1	2	0
Various	2	3	2	0
Total . .	22	22	18	1

It must be observed that in all cases, except those of simple inter-
mittents, the disease was contracted in the lowlands; moreover, that of
sixty-three, the grand total, not a patient died.

CHAPTER II.

I DO NOT BECOME "FAST FRIENDS" WITH LAGOS.

ON Nov. 29, 1863, I embarked on board H. M. S. S. Antelope, Lieut.-Commander Allingham. A red ensign at the fore, manned yards, and a salute of 17 guns, banished from my brain all traces of Buena Vista and the Bubé. Our cruize was eventless. We of course fell in with a tornado off Cape Formoso, the gentle projection in the hypothenuse of the Nigerian Delta. The good old iron paddle-wheeler, however, though no "skimmer of the seas," advanced at ease through the impotent blast. On Dec. 2, we found ourselves rolling in the roads of pestilential Lagos, our lullaby the sullen distant roar, whilst a dusky white gleam smoking over the deadly bar in the darkening horizon threatened us with a disagreeable landing at the last, the youngest, and the most rachitic of Great Britain's large but now exceedingly neglected family of colonies.

H. M. S. S. Investigator was signalled for on the
next day; the Handy being as usual "unhandy"—
broken down. The acting commander of the former,
Mr. Adlam, kindly gave me an in-passage to ship
the presents sent by the Foreign Office for the King
of Dahome.

The town, however, and the townspeople as well,
wore a new and greatly improved appearance, the work
of the great benefactor of West African cities, "General
Conflagration." Three fires had followed one another
in regular succession through November, December, and
January, 1863; and the fire god will continue to "rule
the roast" till men adopt some more sensible style of
roofing than thatch and "Calabar mats." There was
also a distinct improvement in local morals since the
days when the charming English spinster landed here,
and was obliged by the excited and *nôn-culottées* natives
to be escorted back to her papa's ship by two gentle-
men with drawn swords.

Nudity has been made penal. Where impaled
corpses of men and dogs scandalized eye and nose, and
where a foul mass of hovel crowded down to the beach,
now runs a broad road, a Marine Parade, the work of
the first governor, Mr. Coskry, during his short but

useful reign. Finally, Sydney Smith's highest idea of civil government, a street constable, everywhere glad-dens the Britisher's sight. In France we should have seen the *piou-piou;* in England they prefer the " peeler ;" and the peeler-governed scoff and wag the head at the piou-piou-ruled, and *vice versâ.* I confess to holding that British Prætorian, the policeman, to be like the beefsteak, and Professor Holloway's pill—a bore, a world-wide nuisance : the "meteor flag of England " never seems to set upon him. Camoëns might have ad-dressed him as another Sebastian :—

> Thou being dread ! upon whose glorious sway
> The orient sun first pours his quick'ning beam,
> And views thee from the heaven's middle way,
> And lights thee smiling with his latest gleam.

et cætera.

On the other hand, nothing could be worse than the animus between white and black and white-black ; it was systematically aggravated by the bad prints of the coast, and by the extra-philanthropic portion of the fourth estate at home. The place is also, I have said, pestilential ; out of a grand total of seventy Europeans, not less than nine have lately died in thirteen days ; others are expected to follow, and no man is safe at Lagos for a week. Breathing such an air, with such an earth below them, with such a sun above them, and with such waters within them, it is hardly to be wondered at that the Lagoonist's temper is the reverse of mild.

Thus we arrived at an evil hour; all stood in armed peace, alert for war; and the hapless Investigator put the last strain on the back of Patience. Startled by the display of fight, I hastily collected the presents, whilst Mr. John Cruikshank, the Assistant-Surgeon, R.N., detailed on duty to Dahome, obliged me by laying in a few stores. On December 4th we hurried from the City of Wrath. The bar showed blinders only; we would have crossed it had the breakers risen mountains high.

On Saturday, December 5th, we anchored off notorious Whydah, a few hours too late to catch the last glimpse of the Rattlesnake's·top-gear. This was unlucky. Commodore Wilmot, commanding West Coast of Africa, who, taking the warmest interest in the mission, had adopted every possible measure to forward its success, after vainly awaiting my coming for nearly a fortnight, was compelled by circumstances to steam northward. Thus it was my fate to miss the only officer on the coast who knew anything about Dahome, and thus collation of opinion became impossible.

CHAPTER III.

WE ENTER WHYDAH IN STATE.

THE necessity of sending on a messenger to the King, who was preparing for his own Customs, and for my reception at Kana, detained H. M. S. Antelope till December 8th, when a special invitation returned to Whydah.

For some days the weather had been too dark to permit a fair view of a country so much extolled by old travellers, and which Captain Thomas Phillips[*] has described as the "pleasantest land in Guinea." But even under the clearest sky, with the present deadening influences, when the hand of the destroyer has passed over its towns and villages and fields, the traveller must not expect to find, like his brotherhood of the last

---

[*] Journal of a Voyage to Africa and Barbadoes. By Thos. Phillips, Commander of the "Hannibal," of London, 1693-94. It is a quaint old log-book, and supplies a good account of independent Whydah.

and even the present century, the "champaigns and small ascending hills beautified with always green shady groves of lime, wild orange, and other trees, and irrigated with divers broad fresh rivers." And of the multitude of little villages that belonged to Whydah in the days of her independence, it may be said that their ruins have perished.*

We landed as ceremoniously as I had embarked. The Commodore had dwelt long enough in Africa and amongst the Africans, properly to appreciate the efficacy of " apparatus " in the case of the first Government mission. Commander Ruxton, R.N., whose gun-vessel, the Pandora, still remained in the roads when H. M. S. Antelope, after firing her salute, departed, kindly accompanied us. After a rough and stormy night we landed, at 10 a.m., in a fine surf-boat belonging to Mr. Dawson, of Cape Coast Castle, ex-missionary and actual merchant at Whydah ; its strong knees and the rising cusps of the stem and stern acting as weatherboards, are required in these heavy seas that dash upon

* Mr. Duncan, Vol. I. p. 185, found fine farms, six to seven miles from Whydah, with clean and comfortable houses, chiefly the work of Foolah and Eya (Oyo ?) captives returned from the Brazils. " This "— says that traveller—" would seem to prove that to this country slavery is not without its good as well as bad effects."

the ill-famed Slave-coast. We remarked a little external bar, separated by a deep longitudinal line, the home of sharks, from the steep sandy beach ; it must act as a breakwater when the surf is not over-heavy. We landed amid song and shout, in the usual way ; shunning great waves, we watched a " smooth," paddled in violently upon the back of some curling breaker, till the boat's nose was thrown high and dry upon the beach ; were snatched out by men, so as not to be washed back by the receding water, and gained *terra firma* without suspicion of a wetting. Such, however, was not the case with our boxes ; indeed baggage rarely has such luck. On the beach we were met by the Rev. Peter W. Bernasko, native teacher, and principal of the Wesleyan Mission, Whydah, and taking refuge from the sun in a hut-shed belonging to Mr. Dawson, the party waited half an hour, till all had formed in marching order.

The Hu-ta,* *praya*, or sea-beach of the " Liverpool of

* Except when absolutely necessary for explanation, I shall not use, in writing native vocables, accents or diacritical marks : these serve only to puzzle the reader, without enabling him to reproduce the sound of foreign words.

In the future dictionaries, however, the words must be distinguished by accents, not as in English, by spelling, *e.g.*, " boy" and " buoy," " thy" and " thigh," and so forth. Amongst the kindred Egbas the native

Dahome," is a sand-bank rising some 20 feet above sea level, and bright with the usual salsolaceous plants. There are no dwelling-houses, nor do the white merchants of the upper town often sleep here. Seven several establishments of mat roofs and mud walls (the French being incomparably the best), serve for storing cargo, and for transacting business during the day. There are usually three to four ships rolling in the roads, and the more sanguine declare that the great slave port might, if she pleased, export 10,000 tons of palm oil (340,000*l.*) per annum.

The Whydah escort of twenty men having duly saluted us with muskets, began the march towards their town, shouting and firing, singing and dancing. Our party was headed by a Kruman from Commander Ruxton's ship, carrying the white and red-crossed flag of St. George, attached to a boarding pike ; followed five hammocks with an interpreter, and my crew of six Krumen, armed, and brilliantly clad in "bargees'" red nightcaps, and variegated pocket-handkerchiefs, scanty as the old *caleçon* at once happy Biarritz. We

etymology of English words has run wild, *e.g.*, "Tamahana" for Thompson, "Wiremu," as in New Zealand, for Williams, and "Piripi" for Philip.

were exhorted to take and to keep patience, the task before us being a foretaste of what would sorely try us at the capital.

A few yards of loose sand led out of the factory site to the Lagoon, a river-like but semi-stagnant stream, dotted with little green aits, running parallel with and close to the shore. Its breadth was 300 yards, and it wetted the hips, being deeper in December of the " dries," than I had seen it in June. For this reason some have suspected that it comes from the far north, where the rains which have now ended on the coast are still heavy. It is a boon to the people, who finding all their wants in its quiet waters, are not driven to tempt the ravenous sharks and the boisterous seas outside. The Lagoon fish is excellent ; there is a trout-like species with a very delicate flavour, and here, as on the Gold Coast, many prefer the lighter lenten diet to meat. Its oysters are good enough when cooked ; before being eaten raw, their insipidity should be corrected by keep-ing for some time in salt water,* and by feeding with

* The Lagoon is salt only when the sea flows into it at high water. The people then wait till the tide has ebbed, and find on the mud-surface an efflorescence of salt, like hoar-frost, the work of rapid evaporation. It is scraped together, and packed in log huts for im-portation inland: most people prefer it in its original dirty and muddy state, others clean and whiten it by boiling.

oatmeal. We saw piles of shells large enough for a
thousand " grottos," and were told that this is the only
lime and whitewash in the land.

From the Lagoon we issued upon the De-nun,* or
custom-house, also called Je-sin-nun,—"Salt water side."
The dirty clump of ragged mat-huts stands on a little
sandy oasis, garnished with full and empty barrels, with
whole and broken canoes and fishing nets, with porters at
work, and with a few women sitting for sale before their
little heaps of eatables, in fact, with all the parapher-
nalia of an African fishing village, including noise and
" Billingsgate."

The two direct miles of swamp and sand between the
De-nun and the town is a facsimile in miniature of the
fifty miles between Whydah and Agbome. It is a
" duver,"—a false coast : not a pebble the size of a pea

---

* "De-nun," which Mr. Duncan (Vol. I. p. 282) writes " Dtheno," and
evidently thinks to be a proper name, e.g., " the small kroom (a Gold
Coast word) of Dtheno," is the " Bode" of the Egbas or Akus.   The
word " De" means custom-house dues ; " nun," properly " mouth," or
" side," is a monosyllable of many significations. De-gan is the custom-
house " captain," who, as well as his guards, is locally called Decimero,
from the Portuguese. The reader will observe that the terminal *n* in
Dahoman words, is invariably a pure nasal, and sounds like the French
" raison." In " Je-sin-nun," the first word signifies " salt," the second
" water," and the nasal is so little defined, that an English ear would
distinguish only " see," or " si."

is to be found, which fact suffices to prove the land to
be the gift of the sea, not a sweep from the northern
rocky mountains by rivers, rain, or gradual degradation.
As in lower Yoruba generally, the sandy soil would be
very unproductive but for the violent rains. The surface
is a succession of "small downes," dorses and gentle
ridges running parallel with the shore from east to west,
not unlike the wrinkles or landwaves behind S. Paul de
Loanda. Each rise is bounded north and south by low
ground, almost on the Lagoon's level, with deep water
during the rains, rarely quite dry, and at all times a
fetid and malarious formation. These features in the
upper country are often of considerable size, and three
of them, as will be seen, were the natural frontiers of
independent principalities. After the last water, a
steady but almost imperceptible rise, like that from
Kana to Agbome, leads to the town of Whydah.
The road is detestable, and absolutely requires hammock men ; the slave-dealers have persuaded the authorities that whilst it is in this state, their town will be
less liable to unfriendly visits.

Passing up a *marigot* or branch channel, worn down
by porters' feet to a deep wet ditch, we soon reached
the half-way place, a second sandy oasis, the site of

the village of Zumgboji.* It is a poor place—an enlarged edition of the De-nun—containing a few thatched mat-huts, with " compounds," or bartons, of the same material, and outlying fields of grain and vegetables, where Fetish cords acted hedges. We all descended from our hammocks, despite the heat, to greet the head Fetish-man, a dignitary fat and cosy as ever was the *frate* or the parson of the good old times. He stood with dignity under a white " Kwe-ho," the tent-umbrella, which here marks the caboceer ; it was somewhat tattered, because these spiritual men care not to make a show of splendour. He snapped fingers with us, after " Country custom," palm never being applied to palm except by the Europeanised ; as throughout Yoruba the thumb and mid-index are sharply withdrawn on both sides after the mutual clasp, and this is repeated twice to four times, the former being the general number. After the greeting, he sat down upon what is called a Gold-Coast stool, cut out of a single block of

---

* The Ffon, or Dahoman, a dialect of the great Yoruba family, has, like the Egba, or Abeokutan, language a G and a Gb, the latter at first inaudible to our ears, and difficult to articulate without long practice. On the other hand, it has a P (*e.g.*, in Po-su), as well as a Kp (for instance, kpakpa, a duck), whereas the Egba possesses only the latter.

wood,* whilst two young if not pretty wives handed to us drinking water in small wine-glasses. This appears to be a thorough Dahoman peculiarity, which extends even to the Court. When pure † the element is considered a luxury, it serves to prepare the mouth for something more genial, and it is a sign that treachery is not intended. We were then regaled with rum— Brazilian Caxaça—too sour even for Ruxton's Kruman, who regarded the proceedings of the day with the *goguenard* air of a Parisian *diminutif* at a rustic *Maire's* ball. Three toasts are demanded by ceremony, and they must be drunk standing. You bow, you *choquez* the glasses in continental style, and you exclaim, " *Sin diyye!* "—" This is water!"—when it is not—and your compotator responds " *Sin ko* "‡— " (May the) Water (cool your) throat!" In former days the spirits used to be poured from one glass into

* When last in England, I saw sundry of these articles at the Turkish Bath in Jermyn Street, and very much out of place they looked.

† At Whydah the wells are about thirty feet deep, and the water is bad : they want a lining of lime and charcoal at the bottom. In the English fort, according to Mr. Duncan (Vol. I. p. 120), after digging twenty feet deep, the soil was the same as at the top: at twelve feet they came upon a family sepulchre, decomposed human bones, and rusty anklets and armlets.

‡ The o in this word, as in Po-su, is sounded much like aw in the English " yawn."

all the others, showing that they did not contain poison.
The custom is now obsolete. Happily it is unnecessary
to swallow all the trade stuff to which hospitality is
here reduced ; you touch it with the lips, and hand it
to a neighbour, who is certain to leave no heel-taps.
If he be a common fellow, and you wish to be peculiarly
countrified, you sign to him to kneel ; he opens his
gape like a fledgling to its parent, without touching
the cup or glass, and you toss the contents into his
mouth, taking care that half of it should deluge his
beard, if he has any.*

After again snapping fingers, which, barbarous as it
is, I infinitely prefer, near the Line, to hand-shaking,
we remounted hammocks, and crossed the 400 yards
of Zumgboji's sandy islet. At the further end we
again alighted to receive the compliments of the village
captain†—here all are captains—a thin, and almost
black old man, the type of a Dahoman Caboceer. He
presented us with kola nut (*Sterculia acuminata*) and
Malaguetta pepper (*Amomum granum paradisi*), which

* Some of the waggish kings have made their servants lie flat
on the ground, and swallow, in that position, a bottle of rum at a
draught.

† The Dahoman word is "gan:" our caboceer is a corruption of the
Lusitano-African "caboceiro," a head man.

eaten together greatly resemble the *Pan supari* or areca nut and betel leaf of the East Indians.* After a few minutes we were once more allowed to advance. Another brownish-yellow water, with a black miry sole which called loudly for quinine, formed the path ; then we issued upon a hot open sandy and grass-cleared road, 15 feet broad, and leading with gradual up-slope to the town. In the middle of it is a dwarf ficus, called the "Captain's Tree," because here the first reception ceremony of merchant skippers has been from days of old and is still performed. The place around is named Agonji—the "Gonnegee" of the History—where enemies have so often encamped when attacking Whydah. Under the friendly shade we saw a table spread with a bit of white calico cloth, and around it the Mission boys had ranged chairs. Whilst expecting the town caboceers we had an opportunity of glancing at Whydah land.

The country now wears an unwholesome aspect, and the smell reminds me of the Campagna di Roma, threatening fever and dysentery. The tall grass is not

* The Preface to the History of Dahome, written by some unknown hand, and unworthy of the rest of the book, confuses them, informing us that the kola grows on lofty trees, and seemed to Bosman to be a species of the " areka or beetle."—p. ix.

yet ripe for burning ; in two months it will disappear,
rendering an ambuscade impossible, and allowing a
pretty view of Whydah. Not a tenth of the land is
cultivated ; the fallow system is universal, and when a
man wants fresh ground he merely brings a little dash
to the caboceer. The cultivators will begin in February
to fire the stubbles, and the women will turn up the
earth with hoes, and let the charred stalks and roots
decay into manure. The seed is sown by two sowers ;
one precedes, and drills the ground with a bushman's
stick or a hoe handle ; the second puts in the grain and
covers it with the heel, an operation left to a third
person if there be more than two. The seeds are not
mixed. From three to four grains of maize, six to ten
of Guinea corn, and two of beans, are deposited, against
risk of loss, in the same hole. The first harvest takes
place in September. The people will then at once
burn, hoe, and sow again, getting in the second crop
about December. In the interior the winter yield often
does not ripen till January or February, and if the
light showers of the season are deficient, it is burned
by the sun. The produce, though not counted, is said to
be a hundredfold. This should satisfy the agriculturist,
however covetous. Truly it is said that whilst the poor

man in the North is the son of a pauper, the poor man in the Tropics is the son of a prince.

We were not kept waiting long ; at that time no great men lingered in Whydah. As usual the junior ranks preceded. Each party, distinct like our regiment, advanced under its own flag, closely followed by its band, composed of four kinds of instruments, which can hardly be called musical. The rattle is a bottle-shaped gourd covered with a netting of fine twine, to which are attached snake's vertebræ ; it is held in the right, with the neck downwards, and tapped against a thin strip of wood in the other hand. There are also decanter-shaped rattles of woven fibre, containing cowries, but these are not common. The drums are of many varieties, and all of unequal sizes, to vary the sounds : that which takes the lead is the hollowed log, described by all travellers from Jamaica to Zanzibar, and to African ears it is full of meaning as a telegram. The horn is a small scrivello with a large oblong hole near the point, so as to act as a speaking-trumpet, and pierced at the top, where the left thumb, by opening or closing it, converts it into a two-noted bugle. Mungo Park commends it for its resemblance to the human voice ; an older traveller describes it as "making a

grating bellowing noise, like a company of bulls or ass-
negros." The panigan,* or African cymbal, as it is
unaptly called, is generally a single unbrazed tongue-
less bell, about a foot long, including the handle, which
is either of solid iron or brass, and sometimes silver
knobbed, or of pierced metal-work ; a thin bit of bamboo,
some ten to eleven inches long, causes the tube to give
out a small dead sound. It is the Chingufu of the
South Coast, and my ears still tingle with its infliction
on the lake Tanganyika. Sometimes this " gong-gong "
is double, a shorter appendage being lashed or soldered
to the larger instrument at the apices by an angle of
45°, or a pair of similar-sized bells are connected by an
arched iron bar. The player strikes first the long then
the short tube, thus—ting ! tang ! or in double sets, one,
two ! one, two ! This renders the sound different
(similar to our public clocks in England when striking
the quarters), and two notes become evident. Nor is
the band complete without the voice accompaniment of
fierce shouting and singing which would almost drown
the organ of Haarlem.

After each band came a shabby white um-

* The performer is called Pani-gan (gong-gong), ho (beat or strike),
and to (he who does).

brella,* of which there were five, denoting the number of colonels or soldier chiefs. They were distinguished by a superior dress; one man wore a dwarf pair of polished silver horns fastened to a lanyard fillet, and projecting above the organ of " Causality."† They were followed each by a highlander's " tail," and the total may have amounted to 250 men. The greater number wore the uniform of the English or Blue Company, here called " Brú," indigo-dyed tunics or kilts extending to the knee and loosely closed over the breast, and cotton caps or white fillets, with sprawling crocodiles of azure hue sewn on to them, one on each side of the head. No two costumes were quite alike; some had bark strips in their hair, round their waists, and fastened to their billy-cock hats; others wore felts and straws; whilst all had their Fetishes or charms—birds' claws and small wooden dolls smeared red as though with blood. The " Ffon Chokoto," the Egban Shokoto, and the East Indian

* Throughout Africa, like Asia, it is a sign of dignity. Here it is figuratively used for the dignitary himself. " Seven umbrellas have fallen," means as many commanding officers have been killed.

† M. Wallon, Lieutenant de Vaisseau, who twice visited Agbonne in 1856 and 1858, says that these horns are a sign of eunuchry, but they are not so.—Le Royaume de Dahomey (Revue Maritime et Coloniale, Août, 1861 : a second part, containing that officer's journey to Agbonne, was promised, but has never, I believe, appeared).

Janghirs, *femoralia*, or short drawers, hardly reaching,
to the knee, must, by imperial order, be worn under the
war tunic by all the soldiery, male and female ; sometimes long calico tights, in Moslem fashion, are seen.
Their arms were tolerable muskets, kept in very good
order, but of course invariably flint ; useless horse pistols,
short swords, and African battle-axes with blades three
fingers broad and the tangs set in the hafts.   Their
ammunition was supposed to be contained in home-
made cartridge-boxes of European pattern or in bandoleers, which acted for waist-belts, and comprised
about a dozen wooden cylinders, like needle-cases, containing at least four times the amount of powder that
would be used by us.

The style of parade is one throughout the kingdom.
Each several party advanced at a *pas de charge*, bending low, and simulating an attack.   This is here, as in
Uganda, and amongst sundry tribes of Kafirs proper,
an acknowledgment of greatness.   Then the chief of
each *peloton* came forward, snapped fingers with us
as we sat on our chairs under the tree, our guards
ranged on the right, a mob of gazers—women scratching and boys pulling—on the left, and an open space
in front.   This personal greeting over, he at once

‚returned to his men. Afterwards forming a rude close column, the only known manœuvre, the several parties perambulated us three times from right to left, and ended by halting in front.* There, with a hideous outcry, hopeless to describe, captain and men, with outstretched right arms, raised their sticks, bill-hooks, or muskets to an angle of forty-five degrees, the muzzle in the air, like a band of conspirators on the English stage. This is the normal salute, the "present arms" of Dahome.

Right soon, fatigued with these serious manœuvres, our warriors fell to singing and dancing, a passion amongst these people; all are *fanatici per la musica* here. Ruxton, fresh from Canada, could not help remarking what a contrast a pow-wow of redskins would have presented. The chorus had a queer ballet appearance, and a civilised composer might have borrowed a motive or two from the recitative. It became even more theatrical when the largest corps advanced, singing, and upholding in their left hands leafy branches, palm boughs, and long grasses, which were

* In this circumambulation they showed us the left shoulder, and I afterwards observed that the right side is always presented to the king. So Mr. Duncan (Vol. I. p. 223) was told that on horseback he must not form circle to the right, that being a royal privilege.

afterwards thrown upon and trampled to the ground,
An *énergumène*, with a horse-tail, the symbol of a
professional singer or drummer, first shrieked extempore praises of the king and his guests, pointing the
compliment by shaking the forefinger, as is done to
naughty boys in England, and then the whole rout
joined in the response. At times a chief or a warrior
would plunge into the ring and perform a *pas seul.*
The principal dances were two. The bravery dance
consisted in grounding the musket, sword, or tomahawk, to show that the foe had fallen. The performer,
whose face must be blackened with gunpowder, like
a musical and itinerant Ethiopian, then took a billhook
with a broad blade ending in almost a circle, and with
the tang let into the wood, a weapon more for show than
for use ; or he preferred a crooked stick, like a short-cut
houlette, or the third of an East Indian " latti," garnished
with rows of square-headed nails, or strengthened with
a ring-like twist of iron. Thus armed, he went through
the process of decapitation. It was conventional
rather than an imitation of reality : the left hand was
held with the edge upwards, and parallel to the body,
moving in concert with the weaponed right, which
made a number of short drawing cuts, about two feet

from the ground, whilst the legs and feet performed *écarts* which are here indescribable.

The other was the regular Dahoman dance. It is a tremendous display of agility, Terpsichore becoming more terrible than Mars. One month of such performance would make the European look forward to a campaign as to a time of rest. The jig and the hornpipe are repose compared with it. It is grotesque as the Danse Chinoise, in which the French dancing-master of one's youth, of course an *ancien militaire*, used gravely to superintend the upturning of thumbs and toes. The arms are held in the position preferred by the professional runner, the hands paddle like a swimming dog's paws, the feet shuffle or stamp as if treading water, the elbows are jerked so as nearly to meet behind the back with a wonderful "*jeu des omoplates*," and the trunk joins in the play, the posteriors moving forwards and backwards to the pedal beat-time. The body is not, as in Asia, divided, as it were, into two, the upper half steady, and the lower taking violent exercise. Here, there is a general agitation of the frame, jerked in extreme movement to front and rear. As all these several actions, varied by wonderful shakings, joltings, grimaces, and contortions, must be performed rapidly, simultaneously, and in perfect measure to the music, it is not only a violent, it is also a very difficult performance, exceeding even the Hindoo Nautch, or the Egyptian Alimeh's feats. As a calisthenic exercise, it is invaluable. The children begin as soon as they can toddle. It is, perhaps, the most amusing thing in Dahome to see them apeing their elders.*

The dancing was relieved at times by a little firing. Ammunition did not seem to superabound, and I detected several warmen privily borrowing from their neighbours, which showed that the defaulters had been making away with government stores. The parade ended with the normal drinking, after which we were allowed to remount and to proceed.

A few yards from the "Captain's tree" led us to the southern extremity of the town. It is entered by a trivia; the path to the right leads to the Portuguese fort, to the left is the French factory; whilst we

---

* Mr. Duncan (Vol. I. p. 292) compares the shoulder motion with the gymnastic exercise used to expand the chest of the British soldier, but much quicker. The rest of the dance is a " rotatory movement of the hips, changing to a backward and forward motion of a most disgusting description." The Lifeguardsman was marvellous " nice" and " proper."

pursued our way straight in front, through the Ajudo Akhi-men, or Whydah market. Crowds were collected to see the king's "new strangers," who were bringing tribute to Dahome. The men bared their shoulders, doffing their caps and large umbrella hats, whilst the women waved a welcome, and cried "Oku," to which we replied "Oku de 'u"* and "Atyan," the norma salutations of the country. Followed by an ever-increasing train, we passed a long gaunt structure, called the Brazilian Fort. In the open space before it, on civilised chairs, clad in white turbans, in loose blue dresses, and in snowy chemisettes, allowed to expose at least half the walnut-coloured back, and emitting, with the jauntiest air, volumes of cigar smoke, sat a number of "yaller" ladies. Conspicuous amongst them by her chevelure, which looked like a closely-fitting cap of Astrachan wool, ceasing abruptly without diminishing

* In the Egba tongue, Oku,or Aiku (hence the trivial name, "Akoo people "), is a noun, "immortality," and an adjective, "not able to die, alive." Oku de 'u is the normal Dahoman salutation, Oku being understood to signify, "I compliment you," or "thanks"; whilst de 'u is explained by "still doing," or "still making." Various shortenings of the word are exchanged, e.g., oku de 'u, de 'u, 'ú, 'u, till both saluter and salutee have had enough. At an early hour they say, "Oku de 'u Afwan," good morning; or "Afwan dagbwe á?" is it a good morning? In the evening, "Oku de 'u baddan!" good evening! Atyan means "Are you well?"

towards the neck or temples,* was the Bride of Whydah, the fair Sabina, of whom many have had cause to sing,—

Nec fidum fœmina nomen
Ah, pereat! didicit fallere siqua virum.

Arrived at the English Fort, we dismounted at the place where the drawbridge has been, and, accompanied by the military chiefs, we repaired to a shady arbour in the middle of the enceinte, a normal feature in the European habitations of Whydah. There we found a table thickly covered with bottles of water, sherry, gin, rum, and other chief-like delicacies. We drank with the visitors, as the custom is, to the health of Her Majesty of England, to the King of Dahome, and to our own "bonally." Half stifled with heat and human atmosphere, we were allowed, by ceremony, to retire at three p.m., five mortal hours spent in accomplishing the work of forty-five minutes! The reception concluded with a salute. The chiefs fired in our honour forty muskets, powder-crammed to half way up the barrel, and we gave them

---

* In marking this as a characteristic difference between the hair growth of the negro and the white man, it must be remembered that in these regions, as in Asia, all manner of pile is removed either by the razor or the tweezers.

seventeen cannonades in return. The style of loading
great guns quite satisfied me why so many eyes and
hands are missing at Whydah. The Sikhs, under
Runjit Singh, used to astonish the weak mind of the
British artillerist by the rapidity of their fire, sponging
being dispensed with, and the powder baled into the
muzzle from an open tumbril near the carriage. But
Asiatic recklessness is not to be compared with that of
the negro.

The landing rites concluded on the next day.
About noon the troops marched up in loose column
to the cleared space before the English Fort, and
were formed, with abundant pushing, objurgation
and retort, into the half of a square. They
repeated the scene of yesterday : single braves
advancing crouched to the combat, making violent
improvisé speeches, pointing forefingers, tossing heads,
and spitting out their words, so that a stranger
would suppose he was being by them grossly in-
sulted. There was the usual decapitation, singing
and dancing, chorus and ballet; even the small boys
sprang into the arena, displaying admirable activity,
and stamping with the grace and vigour of young
bears.

The preliminary concluded, all flocked into the compound, and the civilian chiefs crowded the large room. The old Ka-wo,* whose jurisdiction extends to the Ahwan-gan or war captains of all the maritime regions, preferred, after salutation, to sit on his stool of state, in a white night-cap, under an umbrella in the court-yard. The viceroy and the Chacha, or commercial chief, being absent at the capital, their places were occupied by three dignitaries. The first mandarin was the Ainadu,† acting-viceroy for Gelele, the present king, a short, dark, pock-marked man, with very little clothing. The second magistrate, who, if white-washed, might pass muster for a very ugly European,‡ was Nyan-kpe (the

* The word must not be confounded with "Gau," the commander-in-chief of the Dahoman army. The "Ka-wo" is the "Caukaow or General of Whydah," mentioned in the History, and spoken of as the "Cakawo amongst the Dahomans." The tradition is, that it was an honourable name given, long before the days of Agaja, the conqueror of Whydah, to a brave chief, who pursued the enemy over the Wo (pronounced Waw) River, which divides Whydah from the Nago, or Agoni (i.e., Egbado, or lower Egba) country. Etymologically, the word is explained by Ká (for ká-ká, i.e., very much, or) long (i.e., following the foe till the) Wo (river). It has, since the conquest, been continued by the Dahoman kings.

† This is the title of office; the personal name in Dahome can hardly be said to exist; it changes with every rank of the holder. The dignities seem to be interminable; except amongst the slaves and the *canaille*, "handles" are the rule, not the exception, and most of them are hereditary

‡ I may as well state at once, that amongst the pure negroes I have never

Lesser), who represented the acting-viceroy, for Gezo, the last king. I must observe here, without entering into details, that Dahoman officials, male and female, high and low, are always in pairs,—a system, methinks, which might be adopted by more civilised nations settled in Western Africa. Duplicates are required by climate, and whilst the invalid is at home on sick leave the convalescent might act for him. Here, however, the objects of the double tenure are twofold ; the new king does not wish hastily to degrade his father's old and unfaithful servants ; knowing their misdeeds, he neutralises their influence by appointing as their aids younger men, of higher rank in the empire, and he ousts them when he reasonably can. Meanwhile, he supposes the aspirant to represent his own as distinguished from his sire's rule. The other motive is to keep the elder in check, and perhaps to give the younger, as candidate for the better appointment, an opportunity of mastering the really complicated details of office.

The third chief then and there present was the Atak-

seen the "purely Caucasian features" alluded to by young African travellers : amongst the negroids, or noble race, sometimes, but rarely

pa-loto, alias Podoji : * he is spy, or to use a more delicate term, "second in command" and assistant to Prince
Chyudaton, the sub-viceroy, of whom more presently.
He acts as assessor to the other dignitaries in super-
vising the custom-takers and the royal store-keepers,
and in settling small causes, such as petty debts and
the disobedience of wives and slaves.

The chiefs at once took high grounds, gruffly
declaring that they brought the King's word, that is to
say, a royal message, and directed us to stand up. I
refused so to do till the royal cane, the symbol of the
owner's presence, was brought into the assembly, and
was prostrated to by all in the room. They then
welcomed me, saying that the monarch had sent as
reception gift, a goat, a pig, a pair of fowls, and forty
yams. Of course the offering came from themselves,
and required a suitable return, that is to say, anything
between twice and twenty times its value. Having

---

* The words mean literally, Podo-ji (he who steps in), No-to (the
interior court of any royal house or palace-yard). The more common
expression is Légédé. It denotes a spy or reporter, with whom every
official in Dahome is provided. The "miching malecho" system is here
perfect : if a captain is sent to prison, he must be accompanied by his
Légédé, who prevents the wives sending food, and who is answerable
for the sentence being carried out in its strictness. Dr. M'Leod (p. 86)
quotes a native saying, "The *swish* walls can speak in this country."

despatched them, we descended into the court, and presented a case of gin (=five dollars) to the Ka-wo. After a long speech he perorated by offering to fight for me. My reply was, that as a commandant of Amazons, a dignity conferred upon me during my last visit, I could fight for myself. Under the cover of loud applause excited by this mildest of retorts, we made our escape and withdrew into the fort.

The same chiefs did not fail, after my return from Dahome, to call and beg another present. I refused them peremptorily, thinking it unadvisable to establish such a precedent. The African, like the Jew to whom you have paid only twice too much, is miserable if he fancies that you escape from him with a farthing.

The first night surprised me by the contrast of the din of voices inside the house, and the dead silence beyond its walls. The streets are empty at dusk, as in the days of the Norman curfew; few venture out after dark without a lantern, though the use is not, as in Cairo and most parts of Asia, imperative. The constabulary is admirable; two men squat in forms like hares, and startle the stranger by suddenly rising and by flashing their torches to scan his features: if he has lost his way they will escort him with all the politeness of a policeman. At times the Ka-wo, who is the local Sir R. Mayne, goes his rounds, and the stick falls heavily upon those caught napping. Hence, even in this head-quarters of the demoralising slave-trade, and where every man is a finished rascal,* crimes of violence are, among the natives, exceedingly rare. Murder at Whydah is unknown, except *en cachette;* housebreaking, save after a fire, is almost impossible; and a man will leave with impunity clothes hanging up in his courtyard,—he would not do it twice at Lagos. Mr. Bernasko, who has lived here eight years, never hesitates to walk out at night armed with nothing but a walking-stick. Theft is reduced to petty larceny, which, however, is universal; there is nothing that these people will not pilfer, and they well keep up the character given by all travellers to their forefathers. In out-stations, like Godome, there is of course much more of open crime, and the discipline of the subject is exceedingly lax. Whydah is a "white man's town," and under the direct supervision of the King, who rarely

* Mr. Duncan (Vol. I. p. 113) says, "The natives of Whydah are the most depraved and unprincipled villains in all Africa, or perhaps in the world. Were it not for M. de Suza and his friends, indeed, there would be no safety for white men."

interferes with the administration ; hence the frequent small abuses. If any evil report reaches the capital, a royal messenger comes down, and the authorities tremble.

CHAPTER IV.

A WALK ROUND WHYDAH.

THE three following days enabled us to study the topography of Whydah. The present town stands about 1·50—2 direct miles north of the sea; separated from the shore by a broad leek-green swamp, by a narrow lagoon, and by a high sandbank, whose tufted palms and palmyras, of a deep invisible green approaching black, form a hogsback, over which the masts of shipping only can be seen from the houses. The site wears the tricolor of S'a Leone,—light and milky-blue sky, verdigris grass, and bright red argillaceous soil, with a blending shade of grey. The "ferruginous-looking clay," which in India and China has been suspected of emitting a "pestiferous mineral gas," and of causing the "*cachexia loci*," seems here to lose part of its injurious power. The town is not exceedingly unhealthy, despite its extreme filth, and

although the deep holes from which the building
material has been extracted are as great a nuisance as
in Abeokuta and Sokoto. Indeed, as a rule, it is less
deadly than other places on the Slave Coast, especially
Lagos and Badagry. The nights are cool, and the day-
breeze is, if anything, somewhat too strong for safety.
At this season the people do not suffer from mos-
quitos, "much provoking the exercise of a man's
nails," as the old traveller has it.

Beneath the surface soil there is a substratum of
pure white sand overlying argil deeply tinctured with
iron oxide from the northern hills ; and another bed of
pure sand is supported by white clay to a depth of
thirty-five feet : it is supposed that below this figure
marine deposits would occur. The highest part of the
town, that is to say the west end, is not more than forty
feet above the sea, and this we may assume to be the
height of the first floor of the English Fort, which lies
about the centre. After a shower the land is as viscid
and muddy as that about Upper Norwood, and such
indeed is the condition of the whole country, especially at Kana and in the capital. The earth when
powdered, puddled, and exposed to the sun, becomes
hard like bricks, which could be made, but are not

wanted.   The old English fort has lasted upwards of a century.

The greatest length of the town, which extends from south-east to north-west, is about two miles by half a mile in depth.   There is no attempt at fortification, as there is in the capital; but every house could be held against musketry.   From the beach a few of the tallest habitations, backed by giant trees, meet the view, and prepare the visitor for something grandiose.   The squalor within, however, contrasts sharply with the picturesque aspect from without.   Whydah is a ruined place, everything showing decay, and during the last three years it has changed much for the worse. As in all Yoruba towns, the houses are scattered, and, except round the principal market-place, there is far more bush than building.   The environs are either marshes or fields, palm-orchards, or bosquets of great but savage beauty; the fine and highly-cultivated farms found near Whydah by Mr. Duncan* no longer exist.

The population of the town, which could accommodate 50,000 souls, is variously estimated.   Some have

---

* Travels in Western Africa in 1845-1846.   By John Duncan, late of First Life-guards.—Vol. I. p. 185.

raised it to 30,000. Dr. M'Leod (1803) calculates 20,000. M. Wallon (1858) proposes 20,000—25,000, but he is by no means a correct observer. The French Mission, which has perhaps the best chance of ascertaining the truth, lays down the number at 12,000; and during war this may be reduced to half. The Christians (Catholic) exceed 600; about 200 boys are known to the missionaries, and on an average during the year the latter baptize 110. The fathers are also of opinion that the population diminishes.

The word "Whydah" is a compound of blunders. It should be written Hwe-dah,* and be applied to the once prosperous and populous little kingdom whose capital was Savi. A "bush town" to the westward, supposed to have been founded and to be still held by the aboriginal Whydahs, who fled from the massacres of Dahome, still retains the name Hwe-dah. The celebrated slave-station which we have dubbed "Whydah," is known to the people as Gre-hwe or Gle-hwe,† "Plantation-house."

---

* Hwe, in the Ffon dialect, means a house and grounds, as in Gre-hwe, for which see the next note. No one, however, could explain to me the etymological meaning of Hwe-dah.

† Gre, or Gle—it is hard to know which to write—is a "plantation," not a "garden," as it is often translated; Gre-ta, or Gle-ta, is a bush or

A very brief *résumé* of its stirring past is here necessary. According to tradition, Whydah, as I shall still call it, was originally a den of water-thieves and pirates, who paid unwilling allegiance to the kings of Savi. About the middle of the seventeenth century it rose to the rank of a prosperous ivory mart and slave port. In 1725, it was first attacked by Agaja the Conqueror, fourth King of Dahome, the Guadja Trudo of the History, nominally for selling to him muskets without locks, really because, like all African monarchs, the height of his ambition was a point on the seaboard where he could trade direct with Europeans. The place after capture was called by him " Plantation-house," meaning that it must supply food to Agbome the capital. So the History informs us the King of Eyeo (Oyo) used to say that Ardrah (Allada) was ". Eyeo's Calabash," out of which nobody should be permitted to eat but the king himself.

The Europeans, ever greedy of change in these dull lands, seem at first to have favoured Dahome against

uncleared ground; and Gre-ta-nun, or Gle-ta-nun, is a bush man. Mr. Duncan (Vol. I. p. 141) says, "The former name of Whydah was Grih-wee, or Grighwee, but since its subjection to Dahomy it has become part of that territory, and received its present name"—the reverse being the case.

Whydah. For which reason, and because they are officially called " King's Houses," the Forts receive certain honours. Before the Viceroy can leave the town, and when he returns to it,* he must visit them officially in person, and he must pray at the Portuguese Fort, which is held to be the head-quarters of the white man's faith. He enters with his suite, and as the King's representative, he wears his sword, this, however, as well as the fetishes with which he is hung round, must, previous to the function, be removed. Before the present establishment was sent, the black priests at Whydah used to offer him holy water, now it is refused, and he walks to the font to *barbouiller* his face ; the missioners perform prayers, but without their sacramental robes, and he follows suit to the best of his ability. The King often sends a message requesting the orisons of the white men, which are not refused to him ; and Christianity being a recognised religion in Dahome, on the day of S. John—midsummer—he transmits by his Viceroy a pot of oil and a bottle of rum as his acknowledgment of faith. These viceregal visits

* The Viceroy never goes to war; he is supposed to look after Whydah. His deputy, the Sub-viceroy, is expected to be present at all campaigns.

have at times been dangerous : in 1745, the Eunuch Yevo-gan " Tanga," raising the standard of revolt, proposed to seize the English Fort, and was prevented only by the vigilance of the governor, Mr. Gregory. Offences committed in the " King's houses " are visited with a double penalty ; a native stealing from them will surely be put to death ; on the other hand, he may take sanctuary in and cannot be ejected from the Portuguese Fort without the consent of the missioners. The English Fort has the shameful distinction of being protected by two fetishes, Dohen and Ajaruma, the Defenders of White men.*

Whydah, like the capital, is a congeries of villages divided into five " salams " or quarters, each under its own caboceer, and governed by the Viceroy, who has dwarfed the minor officials to mere captains. These are

1. Ahwanjigo, or Salam Français, on the north-west and west, French Town, directly under the Viceroy.

2. Ajudo, Ajido Chacha, or Brazilian Town, under the captain, Nodofré.

---

* The History of Dahome mentions a third, now ignored, "Nab-bakou," the "titular god of the English Castle in Whydah." See Chap. XVII. of this book.

3. Sogbáji, or English Town : it has no governor ; the King urged me to take it, but I declined, without receiving orders from home.

4. Dukomen, Portuguese Town, on the east and west, under the Caboceer Bonyon. These four quarters have their forts :* the last is

5. Zóbeme, or Market Town, lately under the Caboceer Nyonun, whose successor will be presently appointed.

I now propose to conduct the reader through the town, and to describe its principal sites.

Beginning from the south-east, we remark the De-nun or toll-house which guards the entrance of every Dahoman town, and the multitude of little fetish huts, where the trader, after doing his devoir to the King, is expected to be not less dutiful to the gods. The streets are mere continuations of the bush-paths, but except in the wettest weather, they are not bad walking after Sandy Lagos. They are formed by the walls of the compounds and the backs of the houses, which are all built in a uniform manner. The material is the red *pisé*

---

* In the Dahoman tongue, " Zojage " is a Frenchman, " Aguda-yevo " a Portuguese or Brazilian, " Kan-kan-yevo " a Dutchman, " Payonun-yevo " a Spaniard, and "Glensi" an Englishman. The "English mother," an officeress at Court, is called " Glensi-no." In Mr. Duncan's time the Portuguese quarter was far superior to all the others ; it is not so now.

of Britanny and Sindh heaped up in three or four
courses, but by law never more ; each course is from
a foot and a half to two feet high : the material has
neither straw nor stone, but sometimes, as in Pópo,
oyster-shell is used to strengthen it.   Each layer is
covered during erection with a weather thatch, and is left
to dry, for three days in a harmattan, and for ten in the
wet seasons : it presently hardens to the consistency of
freestone, and is, in fact, the national *adobe*.   The rain
torrents wash away the softer parts, and cut cracks
down the sides if not protected from above : a certain
mixture of salt in the soil causes the base to crumble
the more readily, because here they do not, as on the
Gold Coast, support it by growing cactus.   A careful
man repairs his wall in the early " dries." The establishments are extensive, sometimes covering acres.   I saw
only one being built, whilst many allowed me to walk
over the broken-down walls, and almost all were
externally in ruins.   As in Asiatic Turkey, however,
the interior often belies the wretched exterior, and
behind the blown-off thatch, leaving bare ribs and poles
perilously protruding, there are snug inner rooms.   The
poorer classes have compounds of matting.   The roof,
not unlike that of an East Indian bungalow, is made of

palm, palmyra, and thick grass, mounted on a frame of lopped and cleaned branches, with girders of bamboo ; and often it is raised in the " flying " form, to secure coolness. There are no windows, except in the Forts. Their places are taken by doors opening under the projecting eaves, that rest upon stout posts and trunks, especially those of the valuable and abundant palmyra.

Striking into the main street, the tolerably straight road, which running from east to west bisects the town, we sight the Portuguese fort, the smallest but the best situated for quiet and coolness. Of these buildings there are now four at Whydah, in order of seniority, French, Brazilian, English, and Portuguese. The first-named people began the trade, and the second is probably erected upon the old Dutch factory, although the name is clean forgotten. The Brandenburgher (Prussian) African Company also built a strong factory at Whydah in 1684, but it long ago disappeared. With the exception of the Brazilian fort, all these buildings lie in a line from E. S. E. to W. N. W. : after the stone defences of the Gold Coast, these swish establishments are by no means imposing, and, except in the case of the Frenchman, for " Fort " we must read " Factory" or " School."

The Portuguese Fort is surrounded by a moat, whose depth is concealed by a mass of vegetation : the people of the country prefer for defence a ditch in this state.   The defences, a square compound bastioned at the angles, and the battery of rusty guns, are here purposely neglected.   The main building, a large double-storied house, with walls thick as an old Norman castle, fronts westward.   Lately repaired, it has a central saloon flanked by dormitories, and a long refectory on the ground-floor.   It is pierced with a deep hollow gateway, protected outside by two honeycombed guns.   Over it is the Lusitanian scutcheon, minus the wooden crown, which perished during a late fire.   Portuguese ordinances are still affixed to the door, and at the southern bastion the blue and white flag yet flies on high days and holidays.   In the compound are a detached chapel and belfry with two bells, date-less, but belonging to the former occupants : both are of swish work, and their mat roofs are distinguished from afar by two little wooden crosses.   On the north and fronting the chapel is a range of small ground-floor rooms and refectory : These the missionaries find less unhealthy, curious to say, than the double-storied building, where, they assert, the sea breeze gives them fever.   They have been careful, however, to dig under their *pian' terreno*, and to lay down a board flooring, whilst they look forward to raising houses on piles six feet high with a draught of air beneath. All is industry in this " Fort," a garden and a southern range of buildings are being made, quarters for the workmen and school-children are already available, and the church and belfry are considered to be merely temporary.

The " Vicariat Apostolique de Dahomé," was erected by the Holy Father in 1860, and its spiritual direction was entrusted to the new congregation of the African Missions, whose mother-house is at Lyons, 243, Rue de la Guillotière. In 1860 the congregation of the Propaganda named as superior of this mission the priest François Borghero, of Genoa, member of the congregation of African Missions, whose superior-general, residing at Lyons, is M. l'Abbé Augustin Planque, of Lille. The first despatch of missionaries left Toulon January 3rd, 1861, on board H. I. M. S. Amazone. It was composed of Messrs. les Abbés F. Borghero (Italian), François Fernandez, a Spaniard of the diocese of Lugo, in Galicia (died in 1863, at Whydah), and Louis Eddé, a Frenchman of the diocese of Chartres (he died *en route* at S'a Leone). The two first

named arrived at Whydah April 18th, 1861 ; on May
6th of the same year they took possession of their present " Fort," by permission of the Dahoman authorities,
and with the consent of the Portuguese resident at
Whydah. Since the departure of M. Iréné Lafitte, who
is intended for one of the European establishments, the
personnel is composed of six members.* There are ten
boarders ; the number of the other scholars greatly
varies, because the boys attend or stay away as they
please. Of adults, I do not believe that a single convert has been made ; and the reverend fathers would
do well to turn their attention towards Lagos and
Abeokuta.

This Vicariat is not obnoxious to the charge commonly brought against Catholic establishments, namely,
that though ardent, enduring, and self-sacrificing, they
are too accommodating to heathenism, and thus they
are unabiding ; whilst Protestant missions, like the constitution which hatches them, are respectable, comfortable, and feeble, offering salaries to married men, who,
in squabbles about outfit, passage, furlough, and convey-

---

* Namely, five priests, MM. Borghero, Emile Cordioux, Verdelot,
Nodiet, and Vermorel, all French except the first, and one minor,
François Cloud, who is about to proceed for ordination to France.

ance of children, manage to spend about 500,000l. per annum. Their uncompromising opposition of idolatry has more than once brought the members into trouble. In November, 1861, M. Borghero visited the King at Agbome, and the list of his demands may be found in the published account of his journey to the capital.* In March, 1863, the fort was struck by the lightning-god, Khevioso, the Shango of the Egbas; and they are not wanting who suppose that the fetishes, having been worsted in dispute by the Padres, took the oppor-tunity of a storm to commit the arson. As the inmates impiously extinguished the fire, they were heavily fined; and, on refusing to pay, the Father-superior was imprisoned. In June of the same year occurred another dispute, about a sacred snake that was unceremoniously ejected from the mission premises, and doubtless this anti-heathenism will bring them to further grief. They look upon things *en noir*, and naturally desire, but with little hope, to see Whydah in civilized hands. I found them intelligent, amiable, and devoted men, in whose society time sped pleasantly and profitably. To the excellent Superior especially I had reason to be grateful

* See Annales de la Propagation de la Foi (No. 206, January, 1863). Paris, 34, Rue Cassette.

for the loan of vocabularies and other papers. If I say too little, it is for fear of expressing too much.

Near the French Mission, and at the south-eastern end of the town, is the establishment of M. J. Domingo Martinez, the best house in " Whydah." The compound walls are, to obviate fire, tiled, not thatched, and a small grove of orange trees enlivens the interior. There is an old ground-floor tenement, by no means uncomfortable, with large, lofty, and cool rooms, furnished with musical boxes * and other knick-knacks, whilst portraits and oil-painting, rarities in unartistic Africa, depend from the walls ; and near it a large double-storied tenement, also tiled, is being built as a dwelling-place and a store for oil trading.

When I last called upon M. Martinez he had been unwell for some weeks : Mr. Cruikshank, who was consulted, did not think his case dangerous. He died January 25th, 1864, when we were at the capital, and the death was brought on by a fit of passion — not an uncommon occurrence in these hot-

---

* These articles are one of the curses of the West African coast. Your white friend can pay you no higher compliment than to wind up the abominations, and your black friend will start, if he has them, half-a-dozen at the same time.

tempered lands.*   He had long been virtually king of
Kutunun, a little post inland of Jackin, on the Denham
waters, and of late much coveted by the new "Pro-
tectors" of Porto Novo.   The latter managed their
dollars so well, that the King sent his cane to M. Martinez, and a polite message, to say that his friend would
presently be joined by a brother white man.   At first
the recipient stared aghast; soon understanding the
trick, he was seized with a trembling of passion; he
presently fainted, and he died the same night, I pre-
sume of apoplexy.

M. Martinez was a caboceer of Dahome, entitled to
the umbrella, the chair, and the other insignia of his
order.   During his later years he has often said—and
many a man has had, and will have, to say the same—
that he had learned these people too late.   The King
claiming *droit d'aubaine* over the property of all his
defunct subjects, the key of M. Martinez's house was at
once, after his death, appropriated by the Viceroy of
Whydah.   He has left a large family, all by native
women.   His eldest son, Domingo Rafael Martinez, is a

* So during the late fire at Whydah, the Chacha, M. Fr. de Souza,
when he saw his house destroyed, very nearly died of passion. The
same uncontrollable fits of rage have been observed amongst the Hotten-
tots and the South African bushmen.

youth about twenty; he is not uneducated, speaking English and French, although his father thought it best to keep him in irons for some years, and thus unteach him the use of the knife. It will be well for the heir if the deceased has left a "bag" at Bahia.

M. Martinez is a sore loss to the slaving interest. A dozen years ago there were at Whydah 200 Spaniards and Portuguese, including Brazilians and half-castes. By glancing his eye below, the reader will see how much the number of these "slave consumers" is reduced.* And the next decade will find all the sur-

* The following is a list of the Portuguese, Brazilians, mulattos, and civilized Africans now remaining at the great mart. Five Portuguese, viz.:—

1. Antonio Viera da Silva, established at Whydah, Grand-Popo, and Agwe.

2. Francisco de Souza Maciel.

3. Ignacio de Souza Magallaes; Whydah, Porto Novo, and Badagry.

4. Jacinto Joaquim Rodriguez; Whydah and Porto Novo.

5. J. Suares Pereira: Whydah and Agwe.

Fourteen Brazilians:—

1. Francisco Antonio Monteiro.

2. F. J. Medeiros, now at Agwe (some say he is a Portuguese, born in the United States).

3. Francisco Olimpio Silva, at Porto Seguro.

4. Marco Borges Ferras.

5. João Pinheiro de Souza, commonly called Taparica.

6. Gulielme Martins do Nascimento.

7. Marcelino dos Martins Silva.

8. Ricardo Augusto Amadie: he speaks French and English.

9. João Victor Angelo.

vivors engaged in cotton or in palm-oil—the "doulo-meter of the slave-trade"—or in nothing.

M. Martinez had his good points : he was always courteous and hospitable, even to his bitterest enemies, the English ; morever, to his praise be it spoken, he

10. Josè Francisco dos Santo, commonly called Alfaiate, *i.e.*, the Tailor.

11. Angelo Custodio das Chagas.

12. João Antonio Dias.

13. Francisco Giorge.

14. Domingo Rafael Martinez, son of J. Domingo Martinez.
And four Brazilian women, viz.:—

1. Maria Elena do Carmo.

2. Benvinde Teresa de Jesus.

3. Leopoldina Teresa de Jesus.

4. Maria da Piedade do Nascimento.

N.B. There are a few Brazilians of minor importance attached to the above houses.

The ten following are Africans or Brazil liberateds, who are mostly Nagos (Egbas) or Whydah men. None of them are at all important, and there are a few others whose names do not deserve mention.

1. João Antonio de Rego.

2. Elisbaõ Lino.

3. Thobias Barreto Brandao.

4. Joaquim das Neves.

5. Damiaõ de Oliviera, who is considered the best mason at Whydah.

6. Antonio d'Almeida.

7. Josè de Fonçeca Muniz, the son of the late J. C. Muniz.

8. Pedro Pinto da Silveira. This is the well-known slaver, Pedro Cogio, of Little Popo. He has a son residing at Whydah, and managing the affairs of Josè Alfaiate. His name is,

9. Domingo Francisco da Silveira.

10. Pedro Fellis d'Almeida.

All these are "God-men," which, in Anglo-African, is opposed to "devil-men," or heathenry.

invariably, like the first Chacha, de Souza, discounte-
nanced native cruelties and human sacrifice. He be-
friended the Church Mission in 1846, when hopelessly
stranded at Badagry, and being a slaver, he gained, as
might be expected, little gratitude. Peace to his
manes, and may he escape the Dahoman Deadland,
where I much doubt that he would be warmly welcomed!

Passing along the main street we now enter the
Zóbeme,* or Great Market, one of the Whydah "lions."
It is, or rather was, a long thoroughfare, covering at
least an acre, with offsets, cross streets, and here and
there a cleared space. The booths are low, square,
open thatch-sheds, raised upon *chabutaras*, or benches
of well-worked red clay, about one foot above the pas-

---

* No one could explain the meaning of this word. Zó means the later
rains, and must not be confounded with Zò, fire, which is pronounced
with a depression of the voice. The Yoruban languages, like the Chinese,
depend upon accents and intonations which are not ours. For instance,
So or Soh, slightly aspirated, is a stick. Sò, with a falling of the voice,
has the same signification as Khevio-sò, thunder. Só, with a rising of
the voice, means a horse; and with an almost imperceptible variation of
voice, means bring; e. g., Só zò wá, bring hither fire! Sô (pronounced
Saw), means yesterday or to-morrow, a fair specimen of linguistic
poverty, and leading to numerous mistakes. But these delicacies of
intonation are inherent in monosyllabic tongues. That childish form of
human language also delights in imitative words, as Koklo, a "cackler"
or fowl (in Prakrit Kukkur), Kra-kra, a watchman's rattle, and so on.

sages. They are either joined or in broken lines, and all are kept clean with *bois de vache*. A detached hut proclaims the gin palace ; the material,—bottles and decanters of Brazilian rum and cheap French liqueurs, with glasses of all sizes,—stands on white cloths,. and business seems to be brisk. Nor are the victualling arrangements less complete ; half the shops contain either raw or cooked provisions, and many a "working man" breakfasts and dines in the alley. This rude bazaar is fullest at 4 p.m., when swarms of people, especially women, meet to buy and sell, "swap" and barter all the requirements of semi-civilized life. For the articles most in vogue, I may refer the reader to a previous publication,* and almost any book of travels treating of the countries of the Upper Niger will show him how far the system is capable of being carried out. At Whydah, as at Bombay and Aden, the prices have increased, or rather have doubled, during the last ten years ; and despite the complaints of commercial depression, the value of coin still diminishes. It is a curious contrast, the placidity and impassiveness with which the seller, hardly taking the trouble to remove

* Wanderings in West Africa. Abeokuta, Chap. III. See also Mr. Duncan, Vol. I., p. 121.

her pipe, drawls out the price of her two-cowrie lots, and the noisy excitement of the buyers, who know that they must purchase and pay the demand. There is no lack of civility to us amongst the people, and the children cheer and jeer White Face without any awe. The two normal African complexions, red-yellow and brown-black, are very distinct at Whydah, and here and there we meet features which might belong to an ugly Sinaitic Bedawi. There are also palpable traces of Caucasian blood in what the Anglo-Indian lady called " European infantry," a parody upon the " European infamy " of the garrison chaplain.

The only picturesque part of the market-place is to the eastward, where there is a hutless space, lined with shady trees, especially the Hun-ti, or Bombax, under which the venders congregate in the glare of the day. Conspicuous for its beauty is the Lisé tree, which the Fantis of the Gold Coast call Akyen. The Portuguese have named it the " African cashew." Tall, thick, and with the darkest green foliage, it is set-off by studs of scarlet apples depending from long stalks. The fruit, which is eaten at Agbome, is insipid, as are almost all wild growths, and not a little like a raw turnip. The flower gives a delicious perfume, and the wood supplies good potash for soap. The other trees are mostly thick-leaved oranges and limes, whilst the hedges are of the malarious croton (*Croton tiglium*), which here, as in Yoruba generally, attains the rankest dimensions.

It is impossible at Whydah to mistake the religiousness of the Pagan, though we vainly look for any trace of human relics. Even in the bazaar, many a hut will be girt round with the Zo Vodun,* a country rope with dead leaves dangling to it at spaces of 20 ft. *After* a conflagration this Fetish fire-prophylactic becomes almost universal. Opposite the house gates again we find the Vo-sisa defending the inmates from harm. It is of many shapes, especially a stick or a pole, with an empty old calabash for a head, and a body composed of grass thatch, palm leaves, fowls' feathers, and achatinæ shells. These people must deem lightly of an evil influence that can mistake, even in the dark, such a scarecrow for a human being. Near almost every door stands the Legba-

* Vodun is Fetish in general. I hardly know whether to write it Vodun or Fodun, the sound of the two labials is so similar. New comers are apt to confound this Fetish with the Azan or fringe of dried palm-leaf, which, fastened about a tree, places it under the protection of the Bo-Fetish. When a man wears the latter round his throat, witchcraft can do him no harm; and if a war captive, he may not be killed.

'gban, or Legba-pot, by Europeans called the " Devil's Dish."* It is a common clay shard article, either whole or broken, and every morning and evening it is filled, generally by women, with cooked maize and palm-oil, for the benefit of the turkey-buzzard (*Percnopter niger*), like the Pinda offered to Hindu crows. " Akrasu,"† the vulture, is next to the snake, the happiest animal in Dahome. He has always an abundance of food, like storks, robins, swallows, crows, adjutant cranes, and other holy birds in different parts of the world. He may not be killed with impunity, and he rarely loses his life except on the most solemn occasions. The knowledge of his safety renders him so tame that he will refresh himself among the poultry ; and gorged with daily banquets, the " beast of a bird " will hardly deign to take wing before being trodden upon ; I have seen him eating amongst the crowd before the King's tent, and half ready to show fight if interrupted. When hungry, he seems always to consider you as if you were butcher's meat.

* The food which it contains is called Legba-nun-dudu, or "eating for Legba."

† There are two kinds, Akrasu, the common *Percnopter niger*, and a larger grey species, with a very hooked beak, called by the people Akkun.

Travellers abuse this "obscene fowl," forgetting that without it the towns of Yoruba would be uninhabitable. Moreover, except after a meal of carrion, it has by no means the "foul aspect" which Commander Forbes ascribes to it, nor is its "familiarity" at all "sickening." The fact is, that officer saw human sacrifice everywhere, although the rite never takes place at Whydah, the condemned being sent up to the capital for execution. The turkey-buzzard perched on the topmost stick of a blasted calabash tree, is to unromantic material Africa what the peafowl, weather-cocking the tall Mawri is to more engaging Asia. It always struck me as the most appropriate emblem and heraldic bearing for decayed Dahome.

The new comer must not confound the "Vulture's dish" with another display of earthenware. Places are consecrated by planting dwarf flags round a forked stick, or round a tree cut down to a reversed tripod, which supports a red clay pot or pot cover. Upon this the passers-by deposit a little food or palm-oil, and sometimes cabalistic messes, to bring luck or to ward off danger.

Legba himself is a horrid spectacle. A mass of red

clay is roughly moulded by the clumsy, barbarous artist into an imitation man, who is evidently, like Jupiter,

A devil of a god for following the girls.

The figure is at squat, crouched, as it were, before its own attributes, with arms longer than a gorilla's, huge feet, and no legs to speak of. The head is of mud or wood, rising conically to an almost pointed poll; a dab of clay represents the nose; the mouth is a gash from ear to ear, and the eyes and teeth are of cowries, or painted ghastly white. This deity almost fills a temple of dwarf thatch, open at the sides. In nine cases out of ten he has returned, human-like, to an undistinguishable heap of dust, but it would be sacrilege to remove the sacred rubbish. Legba is of either sex, but rarely feminine. Of the latter I have seen a few, which are even more horrid than the male; the breasts project like the halves of a German sausage, and the rest is to match. In this point Legba differs from the classical Pan and the Lampsacan god,* but

* How strong a superstition this worship is, may be gathered from the annals of the monotheistic Jews, amongst whom Maacah, the queen-mother of Asa, set up the "horror" in a grove.

the idea involved is the same. The Dahoman, like almost all semi-barbarians, considers a numerous family the highest blessing, and fatherlessness the greatest curse in mundane life, and what men think in these lands must be minded by women. The peculiar worship of Legba consists of propitiating his or her characteristics by unctions of palm-oil. The " Ana-tinkpo," or knotted clubs planted around the figure with their knobs in the air, are possibly derived from Oshé, the weapon of the Egba " Shango."*

Issuing from the bazar to westward, we pass on the right a large ruinous tenement, built by a quadroon merchant, Mr. Hutton, of Cape Coast Castle, whose " Gothic House" there has just been converted into Government quarters. After he was drowned on the Lagos bar (1857), this place was sold to a Spaniard, known only as D. Juan, who presently perished, of course by poison, at Badagry. As the last proprietor owed 200 dollars to the king, it then became royal demesne.

We are now at the English factory, which will re-quire description; it has played a conspicuous part

---

* There is also a great demon in Egba land, who uses a knob-stick, called Oggo, and who therefore is known as Agongo-Oggo.

in local politics, and it may perchance do so again. Williams Fort, as it is called in old writings, was built for the Royal African Company of England, by Captain Wiburne, brother to Sir John Wiburne ; its foundation is therefore nearly two centuries old. In Barbot's * day (1700) it was 100 yards square, with four large earthen flankers, mounting twenty-one good guns ; the trench, crossed by a drawbridge of boards spread on beams, was 20 ft. deep by 18 ft. wide, and its establishment consisted of twenty whites and one hundred gromettos, or slaves, attached to English Town, under the orders of a governor. The old traveller places it three miles from the water-side, between the Danish fort (now quite forgotten) on the west, and within half-a-mile of the French and Dutch forts. In its day it has sheltered, under Governor Tinker, the King of Whydah, when Savi, his capital, was taken by Dahome ; Governor Wilson gave protection to Ossue, the leader of the Whydahs and Popos ; rash Governor Testesole was, by orders of the Great King, murdered, and some say eaten ; Governor Gregory defended it

---

* A Description of the Coasts of North and South Guinea. By John Barbot, Agent-General of the Royal African Company and Islands of America, at Paris. This old book is a mine of information.

against Tanga, the rebel ; brave Governor Goodson, by
the fire of his fort won back Whydah for Dahome ;
Governor Abson here lived thirty-seven years, and left
behind him Sally, of tragical end ; stout Mr. Hamilton
procured the release of Dr. M'Leod, and Governor
James, the younger of that name, who succeeded the two
former, is still known as the King's friend.

The shape of the enceinte is a square or parallelogram, enclosing several acres, surrounded by a well-
grown moat, and formerly defended at the angles by
once round bastions, with their rusty guns, a total of
twenty-four carronades still lying there and about the
court.   Even in 1803, we are told that only three or
four of the cannon were sound enough to be used in
saluting, the others being so honeycombed and corroded
that those firing them would have been in more danger
than those fired at.   The compound is divided into
unequal parts by a wall running from east to west ; to
the north, where a garden should be, there is a foul
Fetish figure throned amidst a mass of filth,—yet the
people wonder that they suffer from small-pox and
measles !   The main building, fronting south, to catch
the sea breeze, is a huge half-whitewashed barn, red
and crumbling below, with a ragged, tattered pent-roof

thatch above ; the walls, pierced with irregular shuttered holes, are 4 ft. thick, and the " great hall " * and
five dwarf rooms inside suggest comparison with the
ab externo size of the edifice. The interior is as shabby
as the exterior, the floors yawn wide, and the ceiling
threatens to fall. As usual in these buildings, there
is but one entrance, a gloomy and cavernous gateway, like the Arab's " barzah," under the main building.
The barton between the house and Fetish-ground contains out-houses and offices for servants and followers;
a well, which at times fails ; instead of " steeple house "
a shingled chapel, which is also school-room ; a " cook-
house " (not a kitchen) ; a bathing-place, bachelor's
quarters, four rows of umbrella trees, under whose shade
is the usual trellised arbour, and the old " Hog-yard,"
which name, however, is now forgotten.

The Hog-yard is a square detached house in the
centre of the enceinte, near the old circular powder-
magazine; it derives its peculiar appellation from the
fact that white men were buried here. The founder of
the fort, Captain Wiburne, was the first tenant, and it
has been since used as a family vault for the servants of

---

* It was the mess-room of the governor and his officers, with whatever strangers might be staying in the place.

the "Company." Captain Thomas Phillips tells us a characteristic tale of this institution. A Mr. Smith, the chief factor, being sick, one of the kings of Whydah insisted upon sending a Fetish priest to his relief. The reverend man, carrying brandy, rum, rice, oil, and other creature comforts, entered the Hog-yard, and thus addressed the deaf and dumb inmates :

"O ye dead whites that live here! you have a mind to have with you this factor that is sick, but he is a friend to the King, who loves him, and who will not part with him as yet!"

Then, repairing to Captain Wiburne's grave, he cried out :

"O thou captain of all the dead whites that lie here! this is thy doing : thou wouldst have this man from us to bear thee company, because he is a good man, but our King will not part with him, and thou shalt not have him yet!"

Thus saying, the holy man made a hole over the grave, and poured in the various articles which he had brought with him, telling the ghostly tenant that if he wanted those things, they were all there for him, but the factor he must not expect, and should not have.

The historian goes on to say that the Englishmen

present, disgusted by this mummery, kicked the Fetisheer out of the fort, and that Mr. Smith incontinently died,—a proof stronger than any Holy Writ to the negro mind that black man's "medicine he be good."

In the Hog-yard also reposes Mr. James, called by the natives "Huze-huze." In December and January, when the Whydah Fetish fêtes take place, the native priests flock with drums to perform idolatrous rites at his grave.

I summoned the Caboceers, and protested against these proceedings in the capital of English Town.* They of course promised to report my objections to the King, and certainly thought no more about the matter. The English fort at Whydah is a scandal, morally and physically. Compared with the French Mission, it gives exactly the measure of difference between the white man and the mulatto,—even in these lands, where climate is so much against the former. The Wesleyan Mission should be ashamed of it.

---

* English Town is one of the most populous parts of Whydah, and lies behind its Fort. Like the other quarters, it is chiefly inhabited by the descendants of Fort slaves, and they are bound to do corvée for English visitors. They speak a little of our language, and they muster perhaps 300 families.

A few hundred pounds would make the place respectable, by the expulsion of the Fetish, and by the restoration of a building which has now passed out of
government's hands.   The sound of psalmody is certainly not wanting, indeed, the "holloaing of anthems,"
as Falstaff calls it, is *satis superque;* and besides the
school-children, there are nearly a score of he-fellows—
schoolmaster, cook, barber, tailor, interpreter, and
others—loafing and lounging about the court and
arbour.   They should be made at least to work their
cost in salt.   I only hope that an English Company
will, at some not distant day, take the restoration in
hand.

In 1842-43, the Wesleyan Mission was nominally
established at Whydah by Mr. T. B. Freeman, the
"Bishop of the Gold Coast," and Mr. Dawson, the companion of his travels.   Eleven years afterwards they
were followed by the Reverend Mr. Bernasko, the present principal and the sole occupant of the English
Fort, accompanied by a Mr. Laing, now doing duty at
Annamaboe.   They began by a *mélange* of commerce
and conversion, which was far from being favourably
received by King Gezo.   Perhaps for that reason they
have been taken *en amitié* by his royal son.   Gelele has

given over to them six youths, sons of the old Fort slaves
of the English town ; he will not, however, allow the
number to be increased.   The total of the congregation
is a dozen men, mostly Fantis, and all coloured.   The
school-muster greatly varies : when I was last there, it
numbered forty-six pupils, of whom twenty-three were
boarders, including the human presents given according
to custom by the King to his various visitors at Agbome.
Amongst others under the charge of Mrs. Bernasko, is
" Jane," popularly called the Commodore's Wife, a huge
porpoise, a female Daniel Lambert, and a fair match
for three men.   There also are the two girls, " one
about twelve, the other sixteen, very pretty and intelligent,"* dashed at Agbome to Captain Wilmot for
education in England.   Tastes in the matter of beauty
differ.   I found " Amelia," the younger, aged at least
sixteen, and an uncommonly plain and dingy specimen ;
whilst " Emma," the elder, had passed eighteen, and
wore an expression of intense stupidity, combined with
the external development of a female " Legba."   They
are thus too old to learn, and in these days it is not

* See Appendix III., Despatches from Commodore Wilmot, respecting his visit to the King of Dahomy, in December, 1862, and January,
1863.   Presented to the House of Commons by command of Her Majesty,
in pursuance of their address, June 16, 1863.

so easy as it was to become African "princesses."
Finally, neither of them can be termed Dahoman,—
the former is an Ishaggan, and the latter is a Makhi
captive.

For the English name in these parts, I am sorry to
see Mr. Bernasko so situated. He has small pay, a large
family, and many calls upon his purse. But it draws
down contempt upon a faith when its teachers are
compelled to trade for their livelihood, and to keep
within a few yards of their chapel a shop in which
cloth and pottery, rum and ammunition, are sold.

Passing out of the English fort, we see in front and
on the off side of "Main Street," two brick pillars
inclined like the leaning towers of Bologna, and showing where once was the factory garden. Here grew the
orange-grove alluded to by Dr. M'Leod, and the thin
tamarind under which Governor Abson was buried.
It has long been abandoned to the weeds, and a dozen
sheep and goats now pick a scanty meal. On the
right hand and to the south-west of William's Fort, is a
large ruined establishment that belonged to Ignacio de
Souza, a son of the original Chacha. He fell into disgrace four to five years ago, under the suspicion of
having reported to a British cruiser the intended

departure of a slaver, and he mysteriously disappeared.
His property was "broken" by the "Don-pwe people "* here, a sign of complete and irretrievable ruin.
It is a custom borrowed from the old kings of Whydah.
The house has lately been granted by the King to a
Mr. Craft, a mulatto, not a negro, as his semi-scientific
auditors at Newcastle firmly believed him to be. The
repairs will cost about £600, but this agent to the
new "Company of African Merchants" says that he
will easily make it pay. *Però veremos!*

Bending towards the north of the English fort, we
pass through a large empty space now being cleared of
grass for the Christmas "play." It shows a big tree-
grown hole whose earth has been excavated for
building, and a central shed erected by the present
King for his "Blue" guards to marshal, dance, drink,
and settle the palavers peculiar to their corps. The
"Blues" outside the palace, also called "English Company," correspond with the "Fanti company" of women
inside : they are held to be body-guards, but they are

---

* Don (young), and pwe (small or young, as in Pwe-vi). These are
a troop of *petits jeunes hommes*, who must do something to distinguish
themselves, organised by the King for his especial service, and to coun-
teract the lazy and crafty veterans. These *moutards* are under a head-
man, and each great Caboceer has at least one Don-pwe.

not regulars. For this reason it is called, after one of the royal houses at the capital, Jegbe.

Beyond this square is a dark circular clump of giant trees,—splendid figs, calabashes, and bombaxes rising from a dense bush which doubtless has witnessed many a deed of darkness. One would suppose that they were fetished to preserve them; but the Tree and the Ocean, as well as the Snake, formed of old the peculiar cùltus of Whydah. At its eastern end is the second lion of the town, and a very minute one, the Danh-hwe,* or Boa Temple. It is nothing but a small cylindrical mud hut—some fetish houses are square —with thick clay walls supporting a flying thatch roof in extinguisher shape. Two low narrow doorless entrances front each other, leading to a raised floor of tamped earth, upon which there is nothing but a broom and a basket. It is roughly whitewashed inside and out, and when I saw it last a very lubberly fresco of a

* Or Danhgbwe-hwe, or Vodun-hwe, *i.e.*, Fetish House *par excellence.* In all these words the *n* is highly nasal. A common snake is called Danh; the python, Danhgbwe, a purely Whydah word, which must not be confounded with Dagbwe, "good." Dr. M'Leod corrupts the word to Daboa. 'Gbwe means a bush, but according to my interpreters it is no component part of Danhgbwe. Hwe signifies, I have said, a house and grounds, in fact the whole establishment, as distinguished from Ho, a room (as in Zá-ho, a ceiling'd or store-room).

ship under full sail sprawled on the left of the doorway. A little distance from the entrance were three small pennons, red, white, and blue cottons tied to the top of tall poles.

The Danhgbwe is here worshipped, like the monkey near Accra and Wuru, the leopard of Agbome, the iguana of Bonny, and the crocodile at Savi, Porto Seguro, and Badagry. The reptile is a brown yellow-and-white-streaked python of moderate dimensions ; and none appear to exceed five feet. The narrow neck and head tapering like the slow-worm's, show it to be harmless ; the negro indeed says that its bite is good as a defence against the venomous species, and it is tame with constant handling. M. Wallon saw 100 in the temple, some 10 feet long, and he tells his readers that they are never known to bite, whereas they use their sharp teeth like rats. Of these " nice gods " I counted seven, including one which was casting its slough ; all were reposing upon the thickness of the clay wall where it met the inner thatch. They often wander at night, and whilst I was sketching the place a negro brought an estray in his arms ; before raising it, he rubbed his right hand on the ground and duly dusted his forehead, as if grovelling before the king. The ugly brute coiled harmlessly round his neck, like a "doctored" cobra in India or Algeria. Other snakes may be killed and carried dead through the town, but strangers who meddle with the Danhgbwe must look out for "palavers," which, however, will probably now resolve themselves into a fine. In olden times death has been the consequence of killing one of these reptiles, and if the snake be abused, "serious people" still stop their ears and run away.

When under former reigns a native killed a Danhgbwe, even accidentally, he was put to death ; now, the murderer is placed somewhat like the Salamanders of old Vauxhall, in a hole under a hut of dry faggots thatched with grass which has been well greased with palm-oil. This is fired, and he must rush to the nearest running water, mercilessly belaboured with sticks and pelted with clods the whole way by the Danhgbwe-no,* or fetish-priests. Many of course die under the gauntlet. Thus there is a *baptême de feu* as well as a *baptéme d'eau ;* fire and water, to say nothing of the gauntlet, must combine to efface the god-killing

---

* No, at the end of a compound word, means primarily mother (*e.g.*, Danhgbwe-no, snake-mother): tropically, master of, or in the Arabic sense, father of (*c.g.*, Abu Hanash, father of snake). Its general use shows the superior dignity of the lower sex in Dahome.

crime.* The elder de Souza saved many a victim by stationing a number of his slaves round the deicide, with orders to hustle and beat him in semblance not in reality. This was truly the act of a " Good Samaritan."

Ophiolatry in our part of Africa is mostly confined to the coast regions; the Popos and Windward races worship a black snake of larger size; and in the Bight of Biafra the Nimbi or Brass River people† are as bigoted in boa-religion as are the Whydahs. The system is of old date : Bosman, at the beginning of the last century, described it almost as it is at present. It well suits the gross materialism of these races, and yet here men ought to be tired of it. As will afterwards appear, the snakes lost their kingdom; yet we are told that when the Dahomans permitted serpent-worship to continue, the Whydahs, abundantly thankful, became almost reconciled to the new stern rule.

Snake worship is both old and widely spread; ‡ we

* Mr. Duncan witnessed this " absurd and savage custom," and detailed it in vol. i., p. 195.

† There the python has exceeded, I am told, nineteen feet in length. Dr. M'Leod says that in Dahome many have been found from thirty to thirty-six feet long, and of proportional girth, but he does not say that he saw them.

‡ Man's natural sense of personal fear probably originated the many fanciful ideas concerning the sævissima vipera :—it is truly said, *Timor*

recognise it among the Psylli of the ancients, and in
the Roman Ophiolatreia of which Livy wrote *anguem*
in quo ipsum numen fuisse constabat. In the Christian
Church the animal was adored by the Ophites, perhaps
on the same principle that the Sheytan Parast pro-
pitiates H. S. M., or that certain ignorant Roman
Catholics have burned the candle at both ends in
honour of the Powers of Light and Darkness. The
Ophites were thus opposed to the orthodox, who held
the unfortunate animal to be the " fatal destroyer of the
human race," the " type of the devil and deluder of
mankind." Barbot quotes upon this subject the
Golden Serpent of the first Israelites, the Brazen
Snake of Moses, the Dragon of Babylon, and the
Thermutis or Asp of Egypt, where it was accounted
one of the most valuable symbols of religion." Eras-
mus Stella informs us, in his Antiquities of Borussia,
that people began worship by ophiolatry. Sigismund,
baron of Huberstein, in his account of Moscovy, says,
" that snakes were adored in Samogitia and Lithuania."

fecit deos. The surpassing subtlety of the brute, the female supposed
to devour the male, and the young their parent, with the monstrous
imaginative offshoots—dragons, fiery snakes, the great sea-serpent,—all
such romantic zoology seems to have originated from one and the same
source.

The Naga of India was the Couch of Vishnu and the type of eternity; it is still revered by the snake-charmer.* Herodotus (2. 74) mentions the sacred serpent at Thebes. The Romans during a plague brought Æsculapius, son of Apollo, from Epidaurus, in the form of a huge serpent, and with great sacrifices and ceremonies lodged him in an island of the Tiber. Finally, I may observe that from the Slave-Coast "Vodun" or Fetish we may derive the "Vaudoux" or small green snake of the Haytian negros, so well-known by the abominable orgies enacted before the "Vaudoux King and Queen,"† and the "King Snake" is still revered at S'a Leone.

On the other side of the road the devotees of the snake are generally lolling upon the tree roots in pretended apathy, but carefully watching over their gods. Here too are the fetish schools, where any child touched by the holy reptile must be taken for a year from its parents—who "pay the piper"—and must

---

* In bygone days at Baroda of Guzerat I studied snake-charming under a native professor, when some of my brother officers—after filling the house with the hugest ranæ, to testify their abhorrence of frog-eaters—killed in waggishness a fine cobra. The terrified Hindu would never again "darken" those doors.

† The orgies are derived from the old fetish practices, which may be found in Bosman and Barbot.

be taught the various arts of singing and dancing
necessary to the worship. This part of the system
has however lost much of the excesses that prevailed
in the last century, when, at the pleasure of the strong-
backed fetish men, even the king's daughters were not
excused from incarceration and from its presumable
object. The temple is still annually visited by the
Viceroy, during the interval after the Customs and
before the campaigning season. He takes one bullock,
with goats, fowls, cloth, rum, meal, and water to the
priest, who, holding a bit of kola nut, prays aloud for
the King, the country, and the crops.

Close to the Boa Temple is the palace of the Yevo-
gan,* or Viceroy of Whydah. This is an important

* It is an old Whydah title, dating before the conquest. In the old
days, the "Coke" was the head Caboceer in the absence of the Yevo-
gan (Dr. M'Leod, p. 68). I cannot find the title now. The word is
spelt with a complexity of error. The History gives Yavoughah; Mr.
Duncan, Avogaw and Avoga; Captain Wilmot, Yavogah; and others,
Yavogar, showing how easily the H, the R, and the highly nasal N, may
be confounded by unpractised ears. The French prefer Jevoghan.
Commander Forbes, who realised the fact that Ffon is a monosyllabic
tongue, but who did not take the trouble to ascertain the only important
part of his discovery, namely, what the syllables are, produced the
curious etymology Ee-a-boo-gan.

The word is Yevo-gan, "White man's captain,"—Whydah being held
to be a white man's town. Yevo means a white man, the oibo or oyibo of
the Egbas. Ye is a shadow, and vo signifies ripe or red. Gan has been explained as a captain or chief, and must not be confounded with gàn, metal.

post, and the holder is the third dignitary of the
kingdom. He is proposed by the Meu or second
minister, his after patron, and he is installed by the
King, under whose indirect protection he is. The
Viceroy is surrounded by the cleverest spies and
councillors ; on his own ground he is strong, but once
in the capital he falls into the hands of his protector.
He is ever liable to be summoned to Agbome, and
etiquette compels him to ride a wretched garron, upon
which he is supported by his slaves. His soldiers may
amount, not to 2000, as some say, but to 200. He is
at once council, jury, and judge ; he cannot, however,
put a Dahoman to death even for crime without sending him for examination to the King. He has un-
limited powers of imprisonment and bastinado ; indeed,
the local system seems to be that which kept the old
British man-of-war in such grand discipline ; all are in
ranks, and the superior "sticks" every one below him.
He is great at embezzlement, and woe betide the

Again, Commander Forbes and M. Wallon tell us that the P. N. of the
Yevogan is Dagbah, Dagbwa, and Dagba. The phrase Da-gba implies
"he holds a large gourd or calabash"—Whydah being, as it were, the king's
cornucopia—it was a title which the present man took for himself. Mr.
Duncan, vol. i., p. 117, erroneously explains the word to signify that the
King would drink water with him—the strongest mark of friendship.

litigious wight whose cause falls into his hands.   Both
he and his lieutenant must be propitiated before he
will forward a visitor's message to the King ; and both,
though they can do little to assist, are powerful in
impeding progress.*   However, a piece of silk, and a
few bottles of French "'tafia," suffice for each, and
both vouchsafe a return in provisions.   I reserve a
personal description of the Yevo-gan till we meet him
at Kana.

The Yevo-gan's palace is a large enceinte to the
north of the town, with four principal entrances.   That
on the north-east is the "Bwendemen." †   It opens upon
a square or space full of fetish huts, one of which
covers the skull of the African wild buffalo, now extinct
in these parts, and under the straggling trees deputa-
tions are received.   To the north is "Ganhori ;" the
western entrance is known as "Ohongaji ; " and the
southern, leading to the Snake House, is "Agoli."   The
interior is the normal labyrinth of courts and tents,
each with two doorways ; you reach the audience

* The present sub-viceroy being a cousin and a particular friend of
the King, has unusual powers of persuasion; but such is by no means
always the case.   The "Prince," of whom more hereafter, is considered
a firm friend to the English nation.

† The first gate made when building the house is always so named.

chamber after some twenty turnings, though perhaps
it was a few yards from the entrance passage, and it is
concealed, like the owner's " wifery," by mud walls.
The great man, after the usual formality of canes and
compliments, causes visitors, if they allow it, to *fare
anticamera*, till his toilette is satisfactory, in a palm-
nut paved outhouse near his pony's stable. Dignity
makes this demand ; the negro grandee must not
appear curious or anxious to see his visitor, who will
ensure a better reception next time by making the
loudest demonstrations of indignation. The dignitary
receives in a small clean verandah, where, as chairs
may not be used by the lieges of Dahome, he is
found reclining upon the uncarpeted floor. He escorts
the visitor beyond his walls, and he never fails to
beg that a decent horse may be sent out to him from
Europe, Asia, or the other quarters of the " inhabited quarter."

Crossing Main Street from north to south, we proceed
to the south-west of the town, where stands the Brazilian fort, the residence of the de Souza family. The
huge mud pile occupies the base of a rude triangle,
called a square, under whose shady trees, in the
mornings and evenings, black cattle muster strong.

Smaller tenements, in the south of Europe style, have been added to both sides. The old man, however, would not inhabit the house on the proper right of the fort, from a superstitious fancy that it would be fatal to him. The western turret or gable of the huge central building, which faces southwards, may be seen from the sea, affording an excellent mark to the aspiring gunner. The peculiar feature of the Uhon-nukon,* or Praça, is a circular wattling, six feet in diameter, planted round with the tall thunder-fetish shrub.† No one sees the interior, and even after fires that have calcined the live hedge, it is carefully covered with leaves. It is said to contain a round shot fired from the roads, probably out of an old long carronade (32-pounder, 9 ft. 6 in. in length, and 56 cwt.), by Commander Hill, R.N., who, in 1844, succeeded Mr. Maclean as Governor of the Gold Coast. The missile fell opposite the house of M. Martinez, and was removed to this place, where it has ever since been held fetish.

* Uhon (gate), and Nukon (before), *i.e.*, the space before the gate.

† By the natives it is called Ayyan or Soyyan; held in the hand, a leaf prevents the gun from bursting, and the sticks are used in thunder-worship, hence the name in the text. It is a tall shrub, with broad ensiform leaves, like a Pandanus, but of a darker green, and it grows all about the coast, extending as far as Agbome. Sometimes it is pollarded, and in this state it is set round other sacred trees.

The founder of the family, M. Francisco Fellis de Sousa or Souza, left Rio Janeiro in 1810, not, as Commander Forbes * says, a fugitive for political crime, nor as Captain Canot† asserts, "a deserter from the arms of his imperial master," but simply as a peasant who wished to see the world. He first settled at a place which he called Ajudo,‡ near Little Popo, and presently he became Governor of the Portuguese fort here. About 1843 he was raised to the Chachaship, the principal agency in commercial matters between the King and all strangers; he thus became captain of the merchants, and the second dignitary at Whydah. As he could command refusal of all articles offered for sale, and he had the regulation of the " De "—alcavála,

* Vol. i. p. 196. Commander Forbes was also misinformed when he states " when Da (de) Souza died a boy and a girl were decapitated and buried with him, besides three men who were sacrificed on the beach at Whydah (vol. i. p. 33). All denominations at Whydah deny this; nor is it probable after the deceased's life-long opposition to this particular enormity.

† Captain Canot; or, Twenty Years of an African Slaver. Entertaining, but superficial; the author manifestly does not know that "Chacha" is a title, not a name.

‡ There are some four "Ajudo" hereabouts, all so called by the old De Souza, meaning "Deos me ajudò"—God helped me. Some wrongly write Ajido. Others prefer Ajuda, help, aid; the full phrase being "Com ajuda de Deos;" hence the Ajuda Palace, in Portugal. From directions of letters, I believe Ajuda and Ayuda to be the popular Portuguese and Brazilian names for Whydah.

octroi, or excise—he became very wealthy. He was ever hospitable and generous to Mr. Duncan* and other Englishmen, although he owed to us the loss of a score of ships. He won the esteem of honest men, despite his slave-trading propensities, by discouraging torture and death; whilst, unlike too many other whites, he systematically refused to be present at human sacrifice. When far advanced in life, he had the honour to entertain the Prince de Joinville, and he died in May, 1849.

On the elder De Souza's demise, the Chachaship was contested by three of his one hundred children. Isidore, the King's favourite, succeeded; but, like all the juniors and African born of the family, he departed life young. Followed Antonio, commonly called Kwaku, or Wednesday,† a debauched man, rich, prodigal, and bigoted; he had thousands of armed and trained slaves; he built a swish-house with rum instead of water, wishing to imitate the King, who for such purpose uses blood;

* "A more generous or benevolent man perhaps never existed," says that traveller (vol. i. p. 194. See also vol. ii. p. 295).

† So called from the day of his birth, a Gold-Coast custom. The word is here corrupted to Cocò. Kwabna (Tuesday) and Wednesday are "strong days" of birth; children that appear on Fridays, Saturdays, and Mondays are "weak as water." Mr. Duncan (vol. i. p. 193) remarks, "On no account will a native sleep with his head towards the sea, nor enter a new house to take possession as a dwelling on a Tuesday or Friday, both those days being reckoned unlucky."

and he threatened to compel Gezo perforce to become a Christian. His career was short, and he was succeeded by his uterine brother,* Ignacio, whose mysterious fate has been mentioned. The present Chacha, popularly called S'or Chico, is "Francisco," also a son of the old De Souza, aged about forty, tinted between a mulatto and a quadroon, with features European in the upper half, and African below, a scant beard, and a not unpleasant expression of countenance. He has little power, and thus the whole authority of the place has been centered, much to the detriment of commerce, in the hands of the wicked old Yevo-gan.

The family is charged with exercising a pernicious influence over the minds of the King and the people of Dahome. It is still numerous.† The daughters of the

* The mother was a large woman from Agwe, dashed to the old Chacha. Her name was Akho-'si, *i.e.*, King's Wife, but she had· no connection with royalty.

† The following is a list of the present heads of the De Souza family, all being "Hijos de Whydah":—

1. Francisco Fellis de Souza.
2. Manoel   ,,   ,,
3. Antonio   ,,   ,,
4. Juliaŏ   ,,   ,,
5. Januario   ,,   ,,
6. Candido   ,,   ,,
7. Antonio   ,,   ,,   vulgarly called Pito.
8. Andrea   ,,   ,,

house being too high to marry, temporarily honour the man who has the fortune to please them, and are said to reproduce in the Brazilian factory the state of morals that prevailed in the palaces of the old Persian kings and the Incas of Peru.

Passing up the Ajudo Akhi 'men, or Ajudo Market, by which we entered the town, we turn to the north-west, and once more pass into Main Street. Here we find the third bazar, Zo mai 'khi men, " Curfew market."* It was so called by the old Chacha, who would not allow the grass to be burned hereabouts, having a large store of gunpowder in Zomai House, a big swish building, now in ruins. There is nothing remarkable in this market.

```
 9. Julio Fellis de Souza.
10. Lino      ,,        ,,
11. Josè      ,,        ,,
12. Pedro     ,,        ,,
13. Ignacio   ,,        ,,
```
The names of the sisters who are at all distinguished, are—
```
1. Maria Amalia Fellis de Souza.
2. Sabina        ,,        ,,
3. Francisca     ,,        ,,
4. Antonia       ,,        ,,
```
There are many young children; about a hundred are known. The only grandson of any importance is Antonio Francisco de Souza, son of " Kwaku," and aged about twenty-eight. The late Isidore left two boys, Leandro Sancho and Sicinio Agripo, and two girls, Maria das Doses and Joanna Isidora, who are looked upon as Africans.

* Zo (fire), Ma (not), I (come), 'Khi (from akhi, market), Men (in).

Bending northwards, we find the French fort, as usual—in these days, at least—the finest building in the place, with all the military air proper to the Grande Nation : it is, indeed, the only tenement that does not cry for repair. Still, it is a peaceful establishment, belonging to M. Régis (Ainé), of Marseille, the well-known emigrationist now reduced to palm-oil. It occupies the site of the old French fort, whose governor, in the days of Louis XVI., had such influence over the country, and which in its career was twice destroyed by the Dahomans, whilst several governors lost their lives. Barbot* gives a detailed history of its original foundation in 1669—1671, by MM. Du Bourg and Caralof, with the consent of the King of Whydah, for the French West Indian Company. The old traveller places the factory at " Pilleau or Pelleau "—names now unknown—" a little beyond the swamp, and two miles from the sea." It is badly situated ; the air hereabouts is malarious, and hotter than at the other three forts. Behind, or northwards, is Salam Français, or French Town, peopled, like the rest, by the descendants of the

* Book 4, chap. i.   Where also may be found a long account of the squabbles of the two founders, and the disputes with their seniors, the Dutch Company.

Fort grumettos. They are now reduced from 1500 to a very small number, and they are considered a treacherous runaway race, the worst hammock-bearers at Whydah.*

A marble tablet over the drawbridged gateway of the French fort informs us that it was restored by M. Régis, in 1842, and it is said that the repairs cost as much as though it had been re-made with stone. The main building fronting the sea southwards is tiled, not thatched, a necessary precaution, as will be seen, against the fires here frequent, and it has a tall central belvedere. The two bastions to the north-east and south-west have been whitewashed and repaired; the former, being nearer the town, mounts six guns, not including four fixed in the swish; and the latter had a telegraph for signalling to the ships in the roads. Besides which, a battery without *affûts* lies on the ground opposite the entrance. The ditch is uncleaned and efficient, whilst the three remaining walls of the

---

* The French factory is composed as follows:—
1. M. Marius Daumas, agent *en chef* of the factories of M. Régis, since 1863 French consul for Whydah and Porto Novo (where he mostly resides), and chief of the Whydah factory.
2. M. Béraud.
3. M. Ardisson.
4. M. Pellegrin.

enceinte are of coarse red clay, and by no means in good order, suggesting the idea of a " dicky," which is also characteristic. The immense compound contains a well, a cooperage, a smithy, a trellised arbour, and other necessaries. Outside the gateway it was proposed to found an establishment for the French missioners, who sensibly went eastwards, and found a site one to three degrees (F.) cooler. Here one of the agents attempted to plant cotton, and necessarily failed for want of regular labour.

It is not unamusing to compare with fact M. Wallon's account of this factory. Its disinterestedness in supplying rival *barraconniers* with Zanzibar cowries, its high sense of honour, provoking the hostility of the Yevo-gan, and its grand prospects as a civilizing and Christianizing agent, are dreams—not of the wise. The connection of France with Whydah has not been, and is not, a credit to our rivals ; nor is he their friend who tells them the contrary. The Maison Régis is a barracoon, a slave-yard, where, with detestable hypocrisy, " emigrants "* and " free labourers " were lodged in jail till they could be transported *à loisir*. Such is the

* Most people know that with the *profession*, " emigrant," like " captive," means a purchased slave.

establishment which a French naval officer pretends to
praise. But M. Wallon himself, when in the "Dialmat,"
had proceeded to the capital in order to procure 40,000
hands. If the house has become a centre of licit commerce, it has not to thank its proprietor, his agents, or
the officers that aided and abetted him. Finally, after
the death of King Gezo, who mightily affected Frenchmen, it has fallen into utter contempt; the present ruler
treats its *gérant en chef* as a servant. M. Daumas,
although calling himself French consul, was, after his
last visit to Kana, in 1863, ordered not to quit
Whydah, and he was compelled to fly on board a
French man-of-war.

We now resume our route westwards, passing sundry
fine houses, especially those of M. Nobre, a friend of
Gezo, who during the same year followed his royal
patron to the dark world, and of M. J. C. Muniz, whose
African son has just come into possession of his property. Issuing from the habitations, we visit the western-
most point of Whydah Town, the Zo Mai 'Khimen
Kpota, or "Fire Come not in Market Hillock."* It is a
swell in the open ground, which commands a full view

* Kpota means a gentle rise of ground, opposed to Sò, a hill, and to
Sò dáho (literally big hill), a mountain.

of the shipping.   Here we may see the coffee-like shrub
which produces the fruit known on the Gold Coast as
the "miraculous berry."*   A little to the N.W. are two
huge cotton trees ; that nearer the town is called Foli
Hun, or Foli's Bombax, with the following legend
attached to it.

The Whydahs, assisted by the Popos, had made
many a stout-hearted but vain attempt to recover their
city, especially under their brave leader Shampo, a
refugee Dahoman.   This general growing old, was succeeded in the command by his son Foli or Fori (the
"Affurey" of the History), and, in 1763, when Tegbwesun (Bossa Ahadi) was on the throne, the fugitives
once more attacked his garrison.

At first the Whydahs were successful ; they marched

* The Fantis call it Sabla or Sambalá (which the Preface to the History, p. viii., and Introduction, p. 5, turn into Assabah, and opine to be
an oxyglycus) and the Ffon terms it Sisnah.   It is the Ossessossa of the
Bonny R., and grows everywhere on the Gold Coast and in the Bights.
The fruit is a brab-like berry, cherry red and yellow, with a thin white
pulp and a large black stone.   It is hardly capable of making " a lime
taste like a very ripe china orange, or vinegar like sweet wine" (loc. cit.),
but it sweetens water with a cloying taste, and remains long upon the
palate.   Perhaps it might be useful in sugar making.   Dr. M'Leod
exaggerates still further its peculiarities—" Whoever eats this berry in
the morning, must be content, at least for that day, to forego the
natural flavour of every kind of food, whether animal or vegetable"
(pp. 21, 22).

in without opposition ; and when old "Honnou,"* the viceroy, attempted to defend his town, they wounded him and repulsed his troops. "Baddely," the second in command, fought bravely, till, pressed by a superior force, he was compelled to shelter himself under the guns of the French fort, and the latter, although the enemy had begun to burn down the suburbs, ungratefully politic, fired nothing but blank cartridge to defend their friends.

The Whydahs and Popos, inspirited by this treacherous proceeding, advanced through the town ; after another action to the S.E. of, and just outside, the suburbs, where the Godome entrance now is, they drove the enemy into the bush. When passing the English factory, one of the savage soldiery espied a white woman, Governor Goodson's "wife," combing her long hair, and protruding her head from the window, to see, I suppose, the "fun." Exclaiming, "What animal can that be?" the man pierced her throat with a musket-ball ; upon which the Englishman let fly a storm of grape-shot and

* These names are from the History, which ignores the Governor's "wife," merely saying that Mr. Goodson had prepared to give the rebels a very warm reception, and fired into them accordingly. On the other hand, King Gezo has often told the tradition as above narrated. The "wife" might have been, and ten to one was, some fair mulattress.

musket-bullets, which made a prodigious havoc amongst the friendly Whydahs. The Portuguese fort, suspecting some treachery, took up the fire, and all the others followed suit, thus completing the discomfiture of the townspeople. The Dahomans, who, under "Baddely," were lurking near, and collecting their men from the plantations, resumed the offensive with such fury, that they killed thirty out of thirty-two hostile umbrellas, or general officers. Foli, overwhelmed with grief and shame, sat down under that Bombax and shot himself. In memory of his deeds, the fourth market-day at Whydah is called Foli-'hun-glo.*

This was the second occasion upon which the English gave Whydah to the Dahomans. Tegbwesun acknowledged that his good son had the sole merit of the victory, and the memory of "Ajangan" is still green in the land. To the present day the King always remarks officially to Englishmen who do not understand him, that from the first the British were the greatest friends of his family.†

* Commander Forbes (vol. i. p. 114) says, "This was market-day at the four-day market at Forree." The *l* in Foli is sounded somewhat like the peculiar Sanskrit *l* (ಳ).

† See in Commodore Wilmot's Despatch the usual garbled account of this affair; such as it is, however, people believed it in Whydah till I

There is now no society in Whydah ; * the quondam millionaires retain their hospitality, but not the means of gratifying it. The old days of sporting, picnics, and processions, of dancing, loving, drinking, and playing, are gone, probably never to return. The place is temporarily ruined, and dull as dull can be, except when the occasional breaking of the blockade gives it a kind of galvanic life. Such was the case in October, 1863 ; the roads were stopped on the 7th, and three days afterwards a fine steamer, carrying 900 souls, got off between Godome and Jackin.† All the principal venturers gave a banquet, ending in a *tripotage*, which began at 4 P.M., and ended ten hours afterwards ; none but the members of the Lyons Mission were exempted from attendance ; even the non-slaving traders and others were there drinking pro-slavery toasts which would have given a philanthropist " fits."

collected the true details. Some, indeed, and they were not few, referred it to the first capture of Whydah by the Dahomans.

* Dr. M'Leod (A Voyage to Africa), in 1803, considers Whydah the " Circassia of Africa, not from the fairness, but from the glossy blackness of the ladies' skins, and the docility of their dispositions." Commander Forbes (1849) seems to have suffered from the "meretricious gaze of the females," which he attributes to the "personal depravity of the slave merchants." I saw no signs of this debauchery ; the people were civil and respectful—the one thing needful in the African.

† According to some, in the preceding month a brig had cleared from Grand Popo, carrying 300 head.

All here is now in transition state. Slave exporting is like gambling, a form of intense excitement which becomes a passion ; it is said that after once shipping a man, one must try to ship another. And the natives of Whydah give the licit dealer scanty encouragement. Having lived so long without severer toil than kidnapping, they are too old to learn labour, they allow their houses to fall, their plantations to re-become bush, their streets to be half-grown with rank grass, and their swamps to reek undrained.

Let us hope that a step in advance is now being taken. Much might be expected from the soldier-like discipline of Dahoman despotism, if compulsorily applied to honest labour.

CHAPTER V.

COMM. RUXTON left Whydah December 10, and our departure appeared imminent. Unfortunately, certain Wen-san-gun,* or royal messengers, announced their arrival; they had walked from the capital in three days, and though fire would not have made them own it, they required rest.

The King had despatched two of his Akho 'si,† or

---

* The French have dubbed these officers *Racadère*, for what reason I know not. The English of old times called them "Half-heads," from their shaving off a moiety of their wool; in those days they wore a demi-dozen strings of human teeth over the shoulder to the knee. Now few can display such decoration. Dr. M'Leod appropriately termed them the *mortal messengers*, in contradistinction to the *immortals*, sent, as will presently be explained, to the Shades.

† Akho 'si properly means king's wife; it is applied to the eunuchs, who, as customary throughout Yoruba, form part of the royal establishment. Mr. Duncan (vol. i. p. 275) signally mistakes the meaning of "king's wife." The operation is performed in the palace, at the age of eighteen to twenty, by evulsion, others say by scission and extraction, and the victims remain anorchides. Of course many die; sometimes, it is said, five out of six. There is great difficulty in Dahome about gaining

eunuchs, and the senior, Mr. "De-adan-de," was a person of some dignity : had he been his master he could not have displayed it more haughtily ; but when we saw him at Agbome, his deportment became all servility. The junior, Ya-mo-ji 'a, was remarkable only for the sable blackness of his skin, and for a compound prognathism, supernal and infernal, which, in the profile of his muzzle, suggested porcinity. These *castrati* spoke with manly organs, probably because they had been neutered at a late age ; moreover, in tropical latitudes, the painful change called the breaking of the voice, is by no means the infliction of which the temperate climates complain.

This *par nobile* of officials was accompanied by the Kakopwe,* one of the King's head servants, sent "to the outside " when great officers are to be summoned on " King's palaver " to the capital. The next in rank was fat So-kun,† the English guide, a nephew of the

information touching these matters : the boldest speak in whispers when a stranger begins to question concerning what takes place " within." The names of our eunuch envoys were as follow : De (here), adan (brave) ; De (here) means " He is valiant in Dahome." Ya-mo-ji 'a is supposed to signify, " Cannot-get-such-a-son-to-be-born."

* Kakopwe (in Forbes, Koao-peh) must not be confounded with the Kan-gbo-de (in Forbes, Camboodee), the King's body attendant, whose lieutenant he is.

† So-kun is an unintelligible name in the " Bo-fetish."

Meu, or second minister ; his "father," or patron, is the Buko-no, the English "landlord." So-kun was duly provided with Bu-ko, his spy, from the "landlord's" household, a sharp and obliging lad, and this pair would keep the royal servants in check. As all caboceers hold their places *ad placitum regis*, our bevy of officials, amounting to ten in number, soon arranged about porters, hammock-men, and similar small fry.

There is little to notice in the palaver which the messengers' arrival necessitated. We passed the usual compliments, and we drank the normal toasts. Deadan-de, before "giving King's word," produced his credentials, in the shape of a "shark stick," * a tomahawk about two feet long, ending in a knob carved into a conventional Squalus, a bit of iron like a broken axe-edge protruding below the jaw ; an equally grotesque effigy of the "tiger of the deep," beaten out of a dollar, being tacked on to the upper part of the handle. " Cannot-get-such-a-son-to-be-born " had a carved "lion stick," † whose shape is not easily distinguished from the aquatic animal. These emblems of valour are preferred by the present ruler to the "crocodile

* Wa (shark), and kpo (a stick).
† Kini-kini (lion), and kpo (a stick).

stick," * or the nail-armed crook,† with which the late Gezo used to present his captains.

The royal messengers sent every day to inquire after our healths, and the slave that bore the cane expected for such suit and service a glass of trade rum. This, at the capital, will be done by all the great officers, and most regularly from the palace. It is hardly probable that the King knows anything about it; and if the process becomes troublesome, it may readily be arrested, by telling the storekeeper to stop the liquor. As a rule, the Wen-san-gun delay the stranger for at least a week by the most specious pretences. They draw from him "subsistence money,"—the old local word,—at about the rate of fourpence a day each; and when the journey ends they expect a piece of cloth, at the employer's discretion. Such are the paltry considerations which here waste the visitor's precious time.

I gave the messengers to understand that if they were not ready in three days, they must remain behind, and afterwards overtake us. This put them on their mettle. Already our heavy luggage, carried by twenty-two porters, had been sent forward to the

* Logun (crocodile), and kpo (a stick).

† Má (knob), and kpo (a stick). Mr. Duncan (vol. i. p. 226) gives sketches of these weapons.

first stage, followed by a second gang of thirty-seven. Four sets, or thirty hammock-men, completed the equipage, making a total of ninety-nine mouths, including the messengers and guides, and not including interpreters and body servants.*

On December 13th, all was ready. Before setting out, however, I must briefly sketch the party. Mr. Bernasko was accompanied by his son Tom, a small boy of eleven, who already spoke half-a-dozen of the coast dialects ; and Tom had his 'kla,† in the shape of "Dick," *alias* Richard Dosu, an imp ten years old, and looking five, whose devilries were a comedy. There were two interpreters, on the Dahoman principle. The first was John Mark, popularly called Máriki, or Mádiki,‡ the Hun-to,§ or nominal head of the English Town,

* In Appendix II. the reader will find a list of presents, supplies, and expenses required and incurred during six weeks' to two months' stay with the King of Dahome.

†On the Gold Coast a confidential slave, who is killed when his master dies.

‡ The Dahoman cannot articulate any terminal consonant, except the highly nasalized n ; he says "Tomú" for Tom, " Gunái 'tú " (goo'nait-'oo), for good night, and so forth.

§ Literally "canoe father," a title given to merchant captains, governors of petty places, head singers, and drummers. Uhun or Hun is the generic name for a vessel: thus yevo-hun is a white man's ship ; ajo-hun, a trading vessel; ahwan-hun, a man-of-war, and zo-hun, a fire-ship, or steamer.

Whydah. He is the son of Mark Lemon, whom Commander Forbes describes as a "perfect Dahoman, too big
a fool to be a rogue," and in whom Mr. Vice-Consul
Fraser found a very fair average of rascality. John is
great-grandson of an English corporal who commanded
the fort under the second Governor James. After
the fashion of the country, the founder of the family is
buried in an inner room of his own home, and a table
is annually "spread" for his old ghost to come and
feed. I found John good-natured, obliging, and more
than usually intelligent ; indeed, after a little drilling
and scolding, he became a tolerable language master
and interpreter. He has, however, no weight with the
King, and—he is confessedly though partly an Englishman—it made my blood boil to see the contempt with
which he was treated by the negro officers, and the
patience opposed by him to their injuriousness.

The second interpreter was a very different man.
Mr. Beccham was a Makhi slave "dashed" to the
Wesleyan Mission, and sent to Cape Coast Castle for
education. With the ready cunning of the servile, he
at once introduced himself there as " Prince Bah;" and,
such was his power of " brass," it was long before
his base origin was found out. Returning to Agbome

after many years, he made an impudent attempt to assist in rescuing from the palace two Dahoman girls, who, having also been brought up on the Gold Coast, could not endure a return home.   The "prince" was seized, and handed over to the Meu or second minister, who in these lands is governor of Horse-monger Lane.   It was a treat to see the face with which he described the horrors of his three days' incarceration—the heavy chains, the handful of grain, the cup of dirty water once per diem, and the nights on the hard floor, bitten by the Iwe worm,* which, in dread of a terrible bastinado, he did not dare to kill. The imprisonment, however, had completely cowed him ; he used to weep with fear if ordered to go anywhere, or to say anything, from which his vivid fancy could distil danger, and nothing but the strongest drink, constantly adhibited, carried him through his trials.

The others were of less importance.   Mr. Hilton, coloured tailor and barber, from the Gold Coast, called himself the ensign, and carried the flag of St. George. Having served on board an American ship, he had

---

* The Iwe is probably the Italle of the Egbas, a grub bred in or issuing from mud floors, and celebrated for attacking those who lie down.

preserved the twang. He was also idle, useless, impudent, and, of course, a drunkard. On one occasion
his cups led him to break into the King's harem, and
but for the respect paid to his missionary master, he
would have lost his head. John Valentine, formerly of
the Mission, and the son of a white soldier, was the
spy upon all our movements. Joseph was a Popo
rascal, who had once before deserted and left me in
the lurch at Agwe. And Menza Cook was, like most
of the Gold Coast people, able in his art. The rest
were the usual "tail," coming up, as the natives say, "to
eat." These were, a youth from Danish Accra, called
Hansen, because he had no other name; Josè Pinto,
a Portuguese orphan, who was already no mean
linguist; and various catechumens, the slave boys of
English Town, dashed by the King to Mr. Bernasko,
and named Philip, Isaac Nahum, Laja (Elijah) Hoole,
Sosu, and so forth. They were hideous to behold,
as the African "hobbledehoy" always is; and their
gigantic joints and extremities, of which the head only
was dwindled, seemed connected with their limbs by
loose wires. Their other qualities were hunger, naked-
ness, filth, and idleness. They spent nearly two months
eating and drinking, sleeping and dozing, talking and

laughing, quarrelling and gambling, before they put up for themselves a shed. It was one day's work. They never finished it. The first thing an African convert does is to claim, like the modern English convict, a life of utter sloth.

The sun was already warming when our *cortège* wound, in the misty morning air, through the town entrance on the north.* It is sentinelled by an enormous Bombax, useless, but of a beauty and a grandeur well meriting the golden chains with which the nature-loving Persian hung his favourite plane. Its every branch is a tree, and its buttressing base measures 150 feet in circumference : under its ample shade the ground is kept cleared for fetish meetings.† The natives call it Atin-daho, the Big Tree, or Atin Li-'hun, the " Cotton Tree (of the place) Li," the latter being a local name. Our six hammocks, including those of John, Mark, and the sharp boy Tom, were preceded by the youth Bu-ko, who, bearing the King's cane and a hide-

* For the distances, altitudes, and other purely geographical features of the march, the reader is referred to Appendix I.

† The characteristic feature of the East African " park-land " is the vivid ring of luscious verdure invariably sheltered under the shade of each large tree. Here, as in England, vegetation in such places is generally deficient.

whip, easily cleared the path by driving all the carriers into the bush, and by dispersing even the juveniles, whose modesty was a phenomenon in African puerology. We traversed the town in a few minutes. The last house belongs to one Sogro, a caboceer or captain, called, like all others, " King's cousin :" here travellers returning from the interior halt for a few minutes, enabling their canes and party to precede them. Like most establishments of some pretensions in Dahome, the house has a tall entrance with a weather-thatch, and a few matted roofs project a little above the mud walls of the enceinte.

The hammock in Dahome is not an unpleasant conveyance, especially when the warmed back is at times cooled by walking. These barbarians, however, have not, like the Hindoos, invented a regular four-in-hand ; two men are easily tired, especially by standing still, which is wearisome to them as to loaded camels. When they reach a rough place, another pair, diving in between the usual number, roughly clutch the cloth at the rider's shoulders and heels, bumping, if possible, his pate against the pole. This explains the old traveller's complaint about being " trussed in a bag and tossed on negroes' heads." They do not carry on the shoulder, but on their skulls: the notably short and sturdy African negro neck * dictates the choice, and a thin coil of rags or dry leaves amply suffices for the defence of craniums formed rather for butting than for beauty. Our hammocks are of modest cottons, whereas the old factors used silks and broadcloths : before appearing in state, however, we shall find something gaudy with red and blue. The cloths are nine feet long by four to five in breadth, and at both ends small lashings draw 'the conveyance together like the old net purse. A noose passes through these lashings, and the clews are then rove tight to pegs inserted into the frond of a bamboo tree (*Raphia vinifera*). This pole is objectionable ; the brittle material often gives way, when a bad fall on the occiput is the result : it is better to send for a good Maderan article, which is strengthened with iron hooks instead of being weakened by peg-holes. The pole is nine feet long : over it is shipped a fringed or valanced awning, fortified by three cross laths, and provided with a running line to tilt it down on the side next the sun. The noisier the hammock-men are, and the more they

* The shortness of the pure negro's neck is one of his most character-istic features: hence he and his female in European attire always appear high-shouldered.

abuse their employer—in their mother tongues—the better for him.

Beyond Sogro's place, with its maize-fields, and the scattered line of lofty Bombax and umbrella-trees which backs the town, we issued upon a rolling plain, open and fair to view. The tall thick Guinea grass, which is being burned down before the dry-season sowing, rises from old ridges that evidence no remote clearing in a land ever liable to be overflowed with bush like the waves of the sea. The bright leek-green vegetation of the young herbage stands out gaudily from the black charred stems and the red loam of the ground. The road is excellent, ten to twelve feet wide, sandy, and lately cleared of grass : it is thronged with carriers in Indian file, mostly women, bearing huge loads lashed to the usual Yoruba basket. The monotony of the surface is relieved by clumps and groves of palm-tree, which are stunted in the open, and which tower in the bush to exceeding height, seeking goodly light, air, and sun. In other places the palmyra (*P. nobilis* or *Borassus flabelliformis*), and the oil-palm (*Elæis Guineensis*), are scattered like the trees of an English orchard, all the latter being numbered, with a view to revenue.[*]

---

[*] This variety everywhere yields the best palm wine, which is supe-

The palmyra (locally called cocoa, and by Mr. Duncan " cabbage palm") is a noble tree, useful as ornamental. The hard wood makes excellent cabinet-work, and is so durable that after 200 years rafters remain as sound as when first cut. Of course it is barbarously wasted. The fruit, which hangs in picturesque corymbs about the rounded neck, resembles a bunch of red and rusty oranges, but four times the size ; hard and stringy, it is still edible, with a slight flavour of gingerbread, and after bush fires it strews the ground with a faint per-

rior to the finest cider ; but as the people fell the trees like Krumen, they are forbidden by a paternal government, which encourages the growth for exporting oil, to make it, except " in the bush." When rumless, they must content themselves with bamboo-wine, which tastes like soapsuds laced with vinegar. Although one might hardly expect it, the yield of the cocoa-nut tree is by no means well-flavoured.

The palm, after being felled, is allowed to lie for a couple of days, the cabbage is removed for food, and in its place a pipe, generally a bit of papaw-stalk, conducts the sap into the calabash below. At times, to make the juice flow more freely, a lighted stick is thrust into the hole, which is afterwards scraped clear of charred wood. This "toddy" is the drink of the maritime regions, where it is most impudently watered, and we shall not taste it beyond the Agrime swamp.

The oil-palm extends from the sea to the north of Agbome, at least fifty-two direct miles, but how much further I cannot say. It usually bears fruit twice per annum, in six to eight bunches at a time, especially during a wet year. The nut is best here when gathered during the rains ; whereas in the Bight of Biafra, at that time it becomes watery, and the yield is trodden out by both sexes, in canoe-shaped troughs.

The palm oil of Dahome is of excellent quality, and a Mohamed Ali would soon make the land too rich for slave exporting. But these are negroes.

fume of the mango.   Here the people, unlike those of
the Congo River, do not draw wine from the palmyra.
When young the head of the bulging stem is often twice
as thick as at the foot, giving to the tree an inverted
appearance.   When full grown, the central and sym-
metrical wave adds, as in the Grecian column, greatly
to its beauty and solidity.   In old age, it often loses its
head-tuft, and appears from afar like a huge flag-staff.
There is music also in the fan-palm ; its flabelliform
leaves rustle in the sea-breeze like the rushing of waters
or the pattering of rain upon thick foliage—delicious
sounds in a thirsty land.

   After a quarter-of-an-hour we had crossed a bulge
of grassy ground whose inland counterslope leads down
to a narrow but a dense transverse line of bush, Bombax,
and broad-leaved figs.   Here the smell of the hardly
eatable wild mango mingles with many a baser savour.
The jungle-strip through which our path winds may
be 200 yards in breadth, and is the result of the superior humidity diffused by the Agbana water.   This
marigot runs from east to west.   In May, I found it
thigh deep with brown horsepond lying upon a fetid
black bed of vegetable decay : in December, it wets the
calf ; in February, it will show only caked mud, and

during the rains it will be troublesome to travellers. The reader will remember that I have already shown him * a miniature facsimile of this country.

The foul marigot was easily crossed; we then ascended another wave of ground, and found on its flat surface the little village of Yonu-Pakhon, half buried in the plantain-bush to our right. Another descent led into a thick copse, where, during the inundations, water must run strongly in a hollow parallel with the road. Again a gentle ascent to clear and level ground, placed us amongst the small plantations outlying the grey thatches and the mat huts of Savi. Mixed with a large proportion of bush, were poor maize and wilted cassava, which, in the form of the insipid and unnutritious farinha,† is the staff of life at Whydah, and in Southern Dahome. There are also mangos, plantains, a

* Chapter III.

† The full phrase is Farinha de paõ (wood-meal), being exceedingly like saw-dust. The History (Introd. p. 4) sensibly remarks, "It is the cheapest and least nutritious of all the substitutes for bread in the tropical climates; although it has lately been introduced into this country (England), and is now sold by the grocers and apothecaries at a high price, as a pretended remedy for consumption, under the name of *tapioca*." The same words, nearly a century afterwards, will apply to the Revalenta Arabica, the flour of "Adas," or lentils, which no Egyptian Fellah will eat if he can help it. And yet "this nutritious and delicious food," &c.

few cocoa-nuts, oranges, the African apple growing almost wild, and orchards of well-trimmed oil-palms.

The sound of drumming now halted us to form up for a ceremonious entrance ; at two hours before noon the sun made me regret the comfortable obscurity of my former march. But " it had to be done." Our stools—the traveller must not forget these articles when visiting Dahome—were ranged under shady trees, and presently the envoys of Akponi, the caboceer, who is under the Yevo-gan of Whydah, came out dancing and taboring a welcome. We remounted, and entering Savi took post under a tall but thin-leaved ficus. In the most public part of the town, we could see nothing but " compounds," huts, and hovels of weather-browned palm-thatch, with here and there a white calico flag emerging from the bush or the fruit trees.* This, however, is a characteristic of all Dahoman towns, which are made to look meanest from the road. The grandees, like the sub-regulus Chyudaton, who are ever liable to be summoned north, here have " palaces "

---

* Commander Forbes writes of Savi—" It has one peculiarity : in Whydah all the houses are of clay ; in Savee, of palm-branches, and very low." Had he wandered through the town, he would have found many tenements of the same description as, and some even better than, those of Whydah.

for inns. I was shown a fine house of red swish, banded with red and blue pigments, in an enceinte containing all sorts of conveniences for white travellers, with a detached kitchen, feeding rooms, and sleeping huts for servants. The aneroid proved that Savi is 44 feet higher than Whydah town ; and we tasted, the last for a time, the vivifying sea breeze.

" Savi " is written " Savee " by Commander Forbes ; Sabi, or Sabec (the latter is probably a misprint, copied into the Ethiopic Directory), by others ; and Xavier, by Mr. Norris.* It was the ancient capital of the kingdom of Hwe-dah, Fidah, or Whydah, a royaume not exceeding the principality of Lichtenstein, but provided with an army of 200,000, not of seventy, soldiers.† Bosman, Barbot, and Phillips, at the end of the last century, dwelt lengthily upon its wealth, its fertility, and its wonderful populousness, the rascality of its people, and the villany of its royal animalculæ. In 1722 the despot of Whydah, upon whose court that of modern Dahome seems to have been modelled, could afford

* See Preface. It is not a little curious that the map and the orthography of 1772 are still copied into our best charts of 1864.

† In quoting these apparently impossible forces, it must ever be remembered that the African army consists of the whole of the male population between 18 and 50. Thus it would be easy to raise 200,000 men from a total of 2,000,000 souls—in Negroland, not in Europe.

to " dash " a half-hundredweight of gold-dust to Captain, afterwards Sir Challoner Ogle, for capturing off Cape Lopez, and duly hanging, the pirate Roberts, in his ship, aptly named the " Royal Fortune." Savi was separated from its northern neighbour, Allada (Ardrah), by a dangerous swamp, which we shall presently cross. In these lands, where there are neither streets nor public buildings, and where the best houses are of swish, we must not expect an approach to architectural antiquities ; nothing now remains of the ancient glories of Savi ; even in A.D. 1772, we are told, only the moats of the many European forts could be traced. A long trench, with a tall growth of trees, was the sole remnant of the palace occupied by the Whydah kings, whose descendants, even in their exile, held their ancient capital sacred. Savi is now a fine large village, a market, and a halting-place for travellers ; its population has been rated at 4,000, which I would reduce by one cypher.*

Our reception at Savi must be described ; it will save the trouble of repetition. At every village, even where only two dancers could be mustered, upon us was the ceremony inflicted. Advancing in our hammocks, which

* Mr. Duncan rates the population of " Savay " at 150 souls.

were preceded by men capering, firing, and shouting
songs of welcome, we saw the Caboceer Akponi prepared to receive us in state under the ragged ficus on
the west of the town. Shaded by a tattered and bat-
tered old white calico umbrella, he sat upon a tall Gold-
Coast stool, with a smaller edition cut out of the same
block supporting his naked feet. He was a quiet-
looking senior, in a striped waist-cloth ; a single blue
Popo bead,* strung with a human incisor to a thread
—a chiefly decoration,—represented the rest of his
toilette. Our seats were ranged opposite the caboceer,
—mine in the centre, Mr. Cruikshank's on the right
the Yewe-no† on my left, the interpreters behind, and
the rest anywhere. After greetings and compliments,
ensued a ceremony never afterwards neglected—the
" King's wife" was whispered by the chief, and frequently she returned with a large calabash, covered by a
drinking cup of the same material, full of pure water.‡

* A semi-mineral bead of many kinds, dug up in this part of the
world, and a subject of some discussion. Every West African book
alludes to it, and I have no new information that would justify a detailed
description.

† Yewe-no, or God-mother, *i.e.*, God man, is the name taken by
Protestant missionaries, to distinguish themselves from Vodun-no, Fetish-
mother, or Fetish man. The French seem to prefer Mau-no, which is,
as will be found, equally objectionable.

‡ The water on this road is generally white as milk, and sometimes

De-Adan-de explained to the interpreter, who reported to us, that this luxury was sent to wash our mouths and to cool our hearts after the march. The officer first tasted it, and we all followed his example. The xenium, or guest-gift, was then placed before us. It varied with the wealth of the place. In a thriving town it consisted of a huge pot of water, a calabash of poor palm-oil, and a bowl of purer stuff, baskets of oranges and papaws, boiled maize, beans, and yams, cooked manioc, " akansan" wrapped in leaves, " cankey," " agidi," " fufu," and a very tasty pudding, called " wo." *

bitter to boot. The price, during the dry season, varies from 40 cowries or one string, to four times that sum, per gallon, in a country where a man can feed himself for 120 shells a day.

* Akansan is corn (maize), finely levigated by means of cankey stones, which resemble the " rubstones" of Ireland. Here, as in Europe, the instrument precedes the " quern ;" it is the rudest and the most laborious way of grinding, but the best. The nether stone is a smooth granite slab, convex behind, and above hollowed into a concavity by use: it is disposed at an angle, sloping from the grinder, so as to allow the ground material to fall off. Some 30 to 40 grains of well-soaked maize are placed upon it, to be bruised and pounded with a circular stone rubber or pestle, tapering, for a handle, at both ends. The housewives work like painters grinding colours, often stopping to wet the corn with water, and they are unpleasant to behold. The material is then placed in wallets like cowrie-bags, and during one day is allowed to ferment in the sun. It is afterwards mixed with water boiled in country pots, and laboured till the sediment, which is good for fattening sheep, goats, and pigs, subsides. The clearer portion is again strained, and boiled to the consistency of gruel. It hardens like blancmange when it cools; and lastly, it is packed in leaves.

A chicken, a fowl, or a goat denote a rich man.   Where
the King has palaces the wives forward dishes of palaver
sauce, stews of pork and poultry, rich with the Occro,*
and similar savoury dishes.   The return was rum or gin.
Owing, however, to the carelessness of So-kun, our boxes
were hurried forwards, and we were obliged to borrow
liquor on the road.   The guides expect a glass every
morning and evening when they come to salute, and
the hammock-men also have a ration of rum.   So So-
kun's hours were duly made bitter.

This African succedaneum for bread is wholesome, nutritious, cooling,
and slightly acidulated—the sour and the bitter are instinctively preferred in hot, damp, and bile-exciting climates.   It is almost always
procurable in Yoruba, a few cowries per diem support a man, and if
well made, as by the women of Hausa and the parts adjoining, it will
be relished by the traveller after a week's practice.   Mixed with water
and drunk, it forms a cool subacid drink, suitable for hot weather.

I cannot but suspect that the "Akassa Creek," which connects the
Brass and Nun rivers, derives its name from this "staff of life."

Agidi and cankey are coarser stuffs; lió is stronger than akansan:
kâji is the smallest and highest-flavoured, and there are other varieties,
as numerous as our breads.   Fufu is mashed yam.   "Wo," pronounced
Waw, and by some travellers written Dab-a-dab, or Dabb-adab, is a
kind of hasty pudding, eaten cold; a thick pancake of maize or Guinea
corn-flour, mixed with boiling water, and stirred about with sticks till
thickened to the consistency of batter; it is then picked out with bits
of gourd, and moulded till cold in a shallow calabash.   We found it by
no means unpalatable, especially when it came from "the palace."   The
Dahomans, it will be seen, are anti-Banting, and fond of azymous
food.

* Hibiscus esculentus, in Whydah called Nye 'un; in Agbome, Nenun.

After the offering was given and acknowledged, the dance began. As at Whydah, most of the fighting men had gone to the capital for the annual " Customs," and the largest number found in any village on the route was sixteen. Dressed in war tunics and armed with muskets, they were aligned by the master of cere-monies, horse-tail in hand, opposite the band, which consisted of the usual Chingufu or cymbals, horns, rattles, and drums. The latter, in a full band, com-prises the " grande caisse," supported between the performer's legs, and beaten with two clubs a foot and a half long : the treble to this bass is a tom-tom or tabor, suspended to the musician's neck, and tapped with the hand palm. There is also a connecting link between the two, a drum four to five feet long by one in diameter, open behind, and supported on bamboo trestles. The head is smeared with " awon," the gum of a tree, and it is operated upon by means of a stick in the right hand, and in the other a dwarf rattan bow with a leathern thong, the part applied. At the King's levees we shall meet with other drums.

Amongst the two hundred spectators were seven of the chief's elder wives, mostly fat, one white with leper spots, and all clad in simple blue baft. They passed to our right, and, presenting their backs, danced opposite a branch band of four rattles and otabals, seated upon the ground. They performed mincingly, threatened to raise their clothes by slightly lifting the corners, and they were presently joined by the youngest children, whose diminutive limbs tottered over the loose dusty ground.

Meanwhile, the twelve warriors carried us back to the days of the Curetes. They began with the "agility dance," all advancing in line. Then one would spring to the fore, paddling, stamping, agitating the lower part of his person; above jerking his elbows as if he wished to make the bones dash together; and pirouetting with legs far apart, one raised, and after the turning, brought down to the ground not on toe-tip, but on the whole length and breadth of the vasty sole, he would call forth the general applause of the lookers-on, who clapped with their palms time for the band and humoured the whims of the performer.

When perspiration made every coat shine like a sea-lion's hide, the men stood and the women sat to sing the chorus, which was,

" The flesh liveth not without the bone."

This part was worthy of the Italian opera. There
was the same time-honoured action, the same meaningless head-shaking of the artists when addressing one
another about nothing, the identical extending and
waving the right arm to no purpose, and the verit-
able Shakspeare-old stride and stand,—as if human
being out of Bedlam ever progressed in that way.
All was professional as a chorus of peasants in Son-
nambula.

Akponi then paraded stridingly before his men,
boasting of his devotion to the King, and his readiness
to serve the Akhosu-Jono, the " King's strangers."
Coming forward, he interpellated me. I was safe
within my slave's lands. If I ordered him to jump
(suiting the action to the word), jump he must ; if told
to fly (fluttering his arms), he must become a bird ; and
if sent beneath the earth (smoothing the dust with his
hand), he must go there. Dahomans delight in these
ridiculous displays, which are those of the Court, and
such is the true African's innate vanity, the King takes
equal pleasure in hearing the absurdest vaunts, whilst
the most Hibernian " blarney " is most prodigally
spouted at him by his lieges.

The speeches were delivered with immense vehe-

mence of voice and gesture : at times a screaming
question was addressed to the bystanders, who replied
with a loud long-drawn groan of general assent and
applause.   At times the normal Dahoman " present
arms" varied the proceedings. It was acknowledged by
removing the hat and thrice waving the arm.   As the
" decapitation dance " began, we excused ourselves on
account of the sun, and retired to breakfast.   If the
performance take place at a late hour, it is better to
give the chief a rendezvous at one's quarters in the
evening ; for the chorus will be followed by a dance,
and the dance by another chorus, and so on till the
village can no more.

When the sun began to slope, we took ceremonious
leave of Akponi, the caboceer, who preceded us with
umbrella and band, whilst the musketeers followed our
hammocks.   A few paces over descending ground led
us through the rude market, where a knot of women
sat before their baskets of edibles.   Then we struck into
the beginning of the bush (or forest) land, which, with
a few clearings, extends from Savi to Allada : it is so
thick that axes would be required by those wishing to
leave the path.   We halted at the De-nun, or octroi-
house, ever the entrance and exit of Dahoman, and,

indeed, of all Yoruba towns. The place of profit was denoted by a Jo-susu, or wind-luck,* which commonly appears at gates and entrances. It is a gallery of three thin poles, under which the road passes. From the horizontal limb depends a mat four feet square, painted with a St. Andrew's cross in red, in black, or in both mixed, and where the four arms meet a cock is crucified, like St. Peter, head downwards. As will appear, tricks are played with crucifixes in Dahome, and it is impossible to judge whether the Jo-susu is an aboriginal or an imported idea distorted. The unoffending " bird that warnèd Peter of his fall," appears in public always gagged by a thong passed between the mandibles and tied behind the head : a rooster may crow in the house, but if he give tongue on the highway or in the market-place, he is confiscated to the "market master," or to the fetish man. I could find no reason for the custom, but " we custom :" it is probably only an item of the whimsical perquisites which form part of the plundering system

---

* Jo or Jo-hun means the wind; Susu, luck or good fortune. It is a charm to prevent a bad wind (in the Kisawahili tongue, P'hepo, wind and demon or bad ghost, are synonymous) entering the house, and the fowl is crucified as a scapegoat. One was placed by the landlord over the gate of our house at Agbome, but I " abolished " it.

of all semi-barbarous hierarchical communities. The turnpike is universal throughout these lands. A rope is stretched by the collector across the road, and is not let down till all have paid their cowries.* The octroi is not unreasonable,† but most of the market folk being women, there is always a tremendous clatter. Fetish and tax-paying, I have said, go together. We were greeted by Ahopanu, the head publican, and the priest, who presented us with water and two fowls. They apologized for there being no food, and declared that, expecting us, they had cooked five days ago,—which was probably true.

After leaving the De-nun, we came to a wall of stiff grass, and a short descent leading to the Nyin-

---

* Cowries, it must be remembered, are merchandise, and the price varies accordingly : at present they are abundant, and therefore cheap. The dollar (4s. 6d.) now buys 2½ heads at Whydah and Agbome, 3 heads and 20 strings at Lagos and Abeokuta. The head, therefore, once worth a dollar, whence its name, now represents in Dahome 1s. 9½d., and the string, 1½d. and a fraction ; whilst 8 cowries are equal to a cent. There are a number of names for this shell-coin amongst the natives, beginning with a unit and ending with tens of thousands. Indeed high numbers can be counted by the natives only with cowrie nomenclature.

† The bullock pays 1 head of Zanzibar "blues," or large cheap cowries ; the goat or sheep 10-15 strings ; a basket of a dozen fowls 5-10 strings ; a small pot of palm-oil (5 gallons), or a basket of grain (30 lbs.), 5 strings ; whilst wood and water are not taxed. The port-dues of Whydah and Godome are of course different ; moreover, they vary with every reign.

sin * Swamp.   It is now about 150 feet broad, and
waist deep ; during the rains it is much worse.   The
banks are a forest of fern, of light green pandanus,
and of dull herbaceous shrubs : the water is dark as
coffee-grounds, reposing upon foul and feculent black
mud, into which the porters sink to mid-calf.   To the
right is a corduroy road, rudely made with rugged tree
trunks, of which men avail themselves when arrived at
the deepest part.   During my last visit it was almost impracticable ; it is now a little better, and somewhat like
the old " railway " of the western states of the Union ;
in February we shall find it repaired.   The swamp
flows, after rains, out of and again into the Whydah
Lagoon, thus converting at that time the site of the
modern Whydah town into a "continental island."
This was known to the old mappers, who, however,
have either made the northern arm of the lake stream
too considerable, or that feature has in the lapse of
time greatly shrunk.   Mr. Norris (1772) speaks of it
as a pretty deep and rapid river, with shelter for
numerous elephants, and in old times it was bridged
over with wooden piles, covered with faggots and
hurdles, and annually repaired.

* This is in the old Whydah language, at present not intelligible.

The Nyin-sin swamp, which separates the old kingdom of Whydah from its northern neighbours, Toli and
Allada, is a historical feature. The last king of Savi
was Kufon, the Boabdil of his country; he had ascended
the throne at the age of eighteen, and he had speedily
sunk into an effeminate and bloated debauchee. In
1708, when the old king died, there had been a great
civil war for the succession, many had fled, and others,
especially the chiefs, had been killed; for years the race,
demoralised by coast life, had shunned arms, and only
plebeians would consent to be generals over slave-
soldiers : Whydah was thus ripe for the gathering.

The warrior King, Agaja Dosu of Agbome, after
taking Allada with dreadful slaughter in 1724,* deter-

* The earliest sketch of Dahome is a letter dated Abomey, November
27, 1724, from Mr. Bulfinch Lambe (not Lamb), agent at Allada for
the English African Company, addressed to Mr. Tinker (not Tucker) the
commandant of the English fort, Whydah. The capture of Allada is
graphically, and in the main faithfully, described; and Commander Forbes
found it so curious and truthful that he reprinted it in his Appendix,
No. 1, from the end of "Smith's New Voyage to Guinea" (1745).

Mr. Lambe quitted Agbome about April, 1726. According to Captain
Snelgrave, he took with him, by the King's order, a Jackin negro, named
Tom, who had been made prisoner at Allada, and who, speaking English,
was sent to see England, and to bring back a report for the King's ears.
Instead of this he sold Tom to a gentleman in Maryland. Then hearing
in Antigua, in 1728, that the King had promised to him a shipload of
slaves if he came back in time, he persuaded Tom's master to give him
up, and returned with him to England in 1731.

mined to subjugate Whydah. Kufon contented himself with declaring that he would turn his enemy into a menial slave. Whereupon Agaja attacked the northern provinces of Whydah, which were under the hereditary government of a great caboceer called "Appragah."* The latter applied for assistance to head-quarters, and enemies at court caused him to be ignored : after a weak defence he submitted to Dahome, who received him kindly and presently restored him to his possessions.

Agaja then encamped upon the northern edge of this Nyin-sin swamp. He had no boats, his army could pass the river only by fording, and even this was impracticable except at the present path, where 500 resolute men could have repulsed a host. The infatuated Whydahs, however, instead of defending their frontier line, were contented to place with great ceremony Danh, the fetish snake, Dan-like, in the path.

Finding it was too late to revisit Africa after five years, Lambe forged a letter from the King of Dahome to George II., and made Tom Dahoman ambassador, under the name of Prince Adomo Oroonoko Tomo. "Prince Tom" was a great success till Captain Snelgrave ridiculed English credulity, the King's letter was declared supposititious by the Lords of Trade, and the slave-ambassador was sent back to his own country, "where, no doubt, he made an advantageous report of the sagacity and penetration of our countrymen."

′ I can learn nothing of this word, which occurs in the History.

Agaja had retired upon Allada to levy his whole force, leaving the field army under his general. The latter seeing only a snake to oppose progress, ordered 200 resolute fellows to try the ford. They not only crossed it unimpeded, but were able to penetrate into the capital.

The outguards of the town were asleep, it being 3 p.m., and when they were awakened by the shouting and sounds of martial music, all fled, crying that the Dahoman army had passed the river. The massacre rivalled that of Allada, the altars of the gods and the ancestral tombs were deluged with the blood of 4000 men. Kofun, however, and many of his train, escaped to the English fort, Whydah, after which they found their way to the islands near Popo.

Thus Savi and Whydah, in the beginning of March, 1727, became part of the empire of Dahome.

Crossing the Nyin-sin swamp, which requires five to fifteen minutes, according to the state of the bridge, we found ourselves once more on a solid path of red sand, rising regularly to a country of bush, of clearings, and of thin palmyra forest. The sun began to burn, and we looked in vain for shade, which the broad road rendered impossible. The *termites arborum* showed us their large nests hanging like huge black wens from the white throats of the trunks and boughs. After crossing another serration of thick strong bush, tall grass walls, and wild trees, we fell into a densely wooded descent, whose sole is occupied by the Adangwin * or Toli Water : it was approached by fetish huts and charred trees. We found it almost dry ; so will it be in February : in last May and June, however, it was a mixture of peat-bog and of horsepond, almost as black and filthy as its neighbour. Then began a regular ascent of steps in the land upon whose summit a loud drumming and singing informed us that we were approaching the terminus of the stage—Toli. The aneroid denoted a decided rise (140 feet) from Savi. The best and thickest part of the town lies to the east of the road : we were, however, led round the western suburbs, where we found the " corrobory " in full force, and not a few of the performers " unco' fou."

There were two umbrellas under a shady tree. The blue belonged to a silver-armletted † caboceer, Ahwan-

* This is also in the old Whydah tongue.

† These are made of dollars beaten out thin, hollow cylinders, half a foot long, fastened with hooks and holes, with plain surfaces or with grotesque figures. Most of them are made at Agbome ; some show, by the human heads upon them, that they are of European origin.

ho, or "war belly," a blear-eyed senior hard to deal with, as are all King Gezo's ancient officials.   The white was of Wubikha, junior governor, and reputed to be our friend : a dark, fat, smiling, "jolly" individual, with a loose pig-tail of white cotton threads, each rove on to one of his many necklaces of beads and coral, and hanging half way down his spine.   As we took our seats before the band and snapped fingers with the chiefs, the circle lengthened into an oval, broken where women were singing at the opposite end.   There was some peculiarity in the dance, which was opened in the usual way by the two governors.   Came the black-smith * bringing his anvil, and holding with pincers the hot iron which he had been hammering : he showed us the bullets with which his master was preparing for war, and capered with his craft-instruments held high above his head.   The missiles were badly-fitting bits of cut bar, subcircular, and all facets ; they must fly wide, and they cannot hit hard.   Then rushed up the

* The blacksmith in these lands is not an object of superstition; the highest craftsman is the King's Huntoji or silversmith.   The instruments are rude in the extreme; the anvil is a half-buried rock, the bellows are of common African type, the hammer is a cone of iron held in the hand, and the grindstone is a bit of fine close granite, shaped like the article with which the English mower whets his scythe.

carpenter, saw and plane in hand, made an address, and danced with his tools *en l'air*. Followed the elephant hunters, braves, with blackened frontispieces; the bards, who are also captains; and the women, who performed rather prettily—compared with Savi. Lastly, the chorus gave us a taste of its quality. After half-an-hour we bowed to the caboceers, and escorted by Wubikha, who promised the rest of the ballet in the evening, we retired from the sun.

Toli, also written Tollee, Toree, and by Barbot Torry,[*] was in old times an independent state measuring about four leagues in circumference. Kingdoms in this part of Africa were not unlike those of England when she numbered 16 of E. Saxons, 14 of E. Angles, and 17 in Kent; and kings are like those of Ireland in the days of St. Patrick, when 200 were killed in one battle. It is now impossible to find the site of "Foulan or Foulaen, the seaport or principal town of the Torry country, seated on the Torry river, which runs almost east and west to Great Popo." The latter feature, however, can be nothing but the Adangwin swamp, which, after nearly two centuries of filling up, is now

[*] Barbot (Book 4) gives a fair account of this little place in the days of its independence.

stagnant.   Possibly, also, there may be upheaval in
the land.   Dahome has lately felt an earthquake, and
already during my short stay on the West African
coast, the shore about Accra is hardly to be recognised.

Toli is now a large market : the interior is fully
equal to Savi, which it a little excels in population.
The position, at the head of a plateau, with its fine view
of the terminal fall to the south, is beautiful, and at
dawn the thermometer showed 70 deg. (F.)   The air
is said to be unusually healthy.

We found lodgings at the house of Antonio Dosu,
known as Dosu Yevo, or the " after-twin white man :"*
he was lying ill with Guinea worm at Whydah, and his
establishment was not in a flourishing condition.   The
flibbertygibbet, Richard Dosu, his son, soon brought us
the necessaries for dinner, and being in no want of
time, we resolved to pass the night at Toli.

After the event of the day, we were conducted by
Wubikha, the good-tempered, to see the end of the
dance.   It was the merriest evening spent on the
march—perhaps during the whole of our stay in Dahome.

* Dosu is the general name of a boy born after twins : he is called
Yevo, or white man, from having been educated in a civilised manner
at Bahia.

Dr. M'Leod would have compared it to the "revelry of
devils and witches as witnessed by poor Tam O' Shanter
in Halloway Kirk." I confess to have enjoyed the
"demoniac scene." All the best-looking girls were
habited in men's straw hats, with breast-cloths girt
crosswise to imitate the soldieresses of the capital, and
a little attention to them took wonderful effect. The
airs were simple but harmonious, and could re-
form any recitative save that of the Gran' Maestro
Verdi, on whom all Europe delights beyond the
minimâ contentos nocte Britannos. And when we
clapped palms to the measure, the buoyant gaiety of
the caboceers knew no bounds ; it became a *manifesta
phrenesis.* The chiefs placed their weapons in our
hands as a call to dance, but explaining that the King
must first see the novelty, we passed on, as is the
custom, the knives to our servants, who performed
vicariously. The crisis was when double flasks of gin
were presented to the *danseurs* and the *danseuses :* we
retired deafened by the din. The tough nerve and the
hard brain of the negro find excitement only in the
loudest and shrillest sounds ; he is like the children in
England, who, at all times delighted with blowing off
powder, will grease the gun's muzzle to increase the

report. What causes headache and cerebral fatigue to the white man, only titillates the callous African sensoria.

After sunrise we set out down a path ten feet wide, *en route* to Azohwe, our resting-place. Beyond Toli, around which there are great fires before planting for the rainy season, grass disappeared except in the clearings. There were traces of cardamoms in the dense bush ; * the shrubs and tall trees formed deep lanes which promised a cool march. Hardly had we left the town, when we were stopped by four fetish men, drumming, singing, and capering in the raw clammy morning air ; the exercise appeared as inappropriate to the hour as that "dawn-wine" of which the Persian poets sing so lovingly. There was a pretty maize plantation on our left, with a tall fence of matted palm-leaves, and a door of the same material. The road narrowed from ten feet to three, and assumed the semblance of the noble natural avenues that beautify the lower parts of Fernando Po. Nothing could be softer and more picturesque than the contrast of the tall white spars with the twisted spiral creepers ; nothing

* On the Toffo road we afterwards found them in flower and fruit; the latter is eaten at Dahome, and, as will be seen, forms part of the King's diet on campaigns.

could be more delicate than the transparent lacery and filigree of the upper foliage picked out from the milky blue background of the heavenly vault that lent to the verdure a portion of its own azure. The shadow of the smallest shrub purpled the earth with a lovely distinctness, and the play of light and shade in the forest made a study fit for Claude Lorraine. After the normal stage, which never exceeded six miles, we reached a little market-place called Azohwe; it was approached by a decided fall, although the aneroid showed but a trifling descent.

Azohwe, the half-way house between Toli and Allada, derives its name from a man who ruled there in the days of Agaja the Conqueror. It lies on the left of the way showing a few thatches above a wall of red clay, and it is everywhere girt by a noble forest. The market is held outside the settlement under the ficus and fetish trees that form its approach; at that hour it was poorly attended. We were kindly received by the people, and an old woman from English Town, Whydah, made us exceedingly comfortable. After breakfasting in a cool hut, and enduring the necessary amount of dancing and drumming, drinking and wasting powder, we bade adieu to Azohwe.

The road became a lane of shrubbery with the brightest flowers, red and blue, pink and yellow, governed here and there by a queenly white lily. We saw none of the "blossoms of the air," the gorgeous butterflies, which I had admired before the rains; all were modest white and yellow. The animal which typifies the human animula, acquires strange bad habits in these lands; no one would sing "I'd be a butterfly," after disturbing one of its repasts.*

Ensued sundry long flats and well-wooded ascents, terminating in a large grass clearing, which, here and there patched with palms, bush, and forest, showed that we were entering an extensive place. At noon we cried Do-ddo!† at a cleanly swept De-nun, where fetish sheds swarmed. We were welcomed with water and provisions by the well-meaning old publican So-kun Do-gan, who brought in person a *carafon* of muscadel wine for ourselves, and a bottle of gin for those thirsty souls, our attendants.

---

* About the bad habits of these "butterfly schools," see Mr. Duncan, Vol. I. p. 209. He clapped his hat upon the heap, and secured fifty to sixty of all sorts and colours.

† Let down (the hammock), opposed to Zeiji, raise it up! But Dedde! Dedde! means softly! like the Fanti "Bleo." The monosyllabic verb in Dahoman when repeated, seems to reduplicate the middle consonant, *e.g.*, Do! Do! becomes Doddo!

After *force complimens* we resumed hammocks and traversed the maize plantations ; on our left were detached houses and long palaver sheds, dark verandahs formed by the thatched eaves. A few minutes took us to the great square, a copy *in parvo* of the *grande place* at Agbome. The parallelogram had scatters of trees and fetish huts, and on the south-west was a Singbo* or double-storied tenement of red clay, with five shuttered windows over the royal gateway. This, out of Whydah, is a royal style of abode, and is not permitted to strangers or to subjects. The palace compound appears to be a mass of bush and palm ; as usual, it cannot be entered, because the King's women and female slaves occupy it, and every gap is sedulously closed. At the north-west end, under the normal shed projecting from the palace wall, were three umbrellas, light blue, dark blue, and white, denoting the several dignities of the owners.

In compliment to the royal abode we were carried three times round the square, a large and noisy band following my hammock. Then dismounting, we ex-

* Singbo, Singbo-men or Singbo-eji, are terms applied to all double-storied buildings, as, *e.g.*, the forts at Whydah. Hence the "Simbome" of Commandant Forbes.

changed greetings with the acting chief caboceer, the Menjo-ten.* He was a fine middle-aged man with silver bracelets, his colleagues wearing brass. These, like the Tunisian decorations, show the differences of rank. He is said to be friendly to the English, and he certainly proved himself so on that occasion. Remarking the extreme solar heat, he led us at once to the house of the old Meu, four bare walls apparently converted into a *caravanserai*. Here we definitively learned, to the general sorrow, that all our boxes had been, by the stupidity or rascality of the English guide, carried on to the capital.

* Menjo (man born), Ten (in the place). His principal is the Akpulogan.

In Dahoman names and titles the following terminations mostly occur:—

Men (with peculiarly nasal N, sounding like "me") "in," as Danh-homen, and Agbo-men. In many local names it appears almost pleonastic, and thus corresponds with the Ni (in) of the Kisawahili and East African dialects, e.g., Kilima-ni, Mfu 'u-ni.

-*nò*, mother, carrier, master of, etc.

-*nun*, mouth, side, man.

'*Si*, from *Asi*, a wife.

-*ten*, prefix or affix, in the place, *e.g.*, ten-che-men, in my place. Also -*gon*, *e.g.*, *Atto-gon*, monkey's place.

-*to* (*taw*), father, or "he who does," *e.g.*, *wu-to*, he who kills.

-*ton* (with nasal n), belonging to, *e.g.*, *Beecham-ton-e*, it is Beecham's property.

-*vi*, a child, the son of.

Allada is called by older authors Ardrah,* another
instance of lambdacism, confusing the L and the
R.† The Ethiopic Directory gives Essaam ‡ and
Aratakassu or Alatakassu. It is the ancient capital

* In the oldest authors, Bosman and Barbot, it is called Great
Ardrah, and is placed at the distance of sixteen leagues from its port,
Little Ardrah, or Offra, with which it was connected by a good and
spacious road. The latter is clearly our modern " Porto Novo "—New
Haven—which the Yorubas call "Ijashe," and the Popos "Hwebonu."
Hence some writers, as Mr. Norris (1772), make Ardrah, or Assem, on
the Lagoon, and Ardrah, or Alladah, in the interior. So Commander
Forbes (Vol. I. p. 12) speaks of " Ardrah, whose capital Allahdah still
remains."

" Porto Novo " proper is the old " beach " or port of Hwebonu, and
is mentioned in the History. It lies four to five miles from its main
town, and was rebuilt by M. J. D. Martinez. We have blunderingly
transferred its name to the chief settlement on the Lagoon. Unless read
by this light, the History will in places—for instance, the troubles between Allada (Porto Novo) and Dahome, in 1786—be unintelligible.

† The Popos and Dahomans have the same lallation as the Chinese,
who call rum " lum." So the Genoese confuse the sounds in the word
" gloria," and the Neapolitans transpose the letters, as Galibardi for
Garibaldi.

‡ A long account of Allada, and description of the state and dignity of
the king, are given by Barbot, Book 4, Chap. II. But he derived his
description from hearsay. We can hardly accept the spacious and well-
built houses, the fine gardens, the cavalry, and other such details. The
kings, however, appear to have been comparatively civilised. Alkeny,
or Tezy, was educated at S. Thomè, with a tincture of Christianity,
and at the age of seventy he sent one D. Matteo Lopez as his ambassador
extraordinary to the Court of France. From Barbot we also learn that
about 1700 the Moslems were so powerful at Allada, that their great
" Marabou " had the privilege of seeing the king night and day. This
enables us to explain Essaam or Assem by the Arab, i.e., Aazem or the
Greater (town).

of a kingdom somewhat larger than Whydah, bounded
on the north by the Agrime swamp, and southwards
by Toli. The Dahomans look upon it with reverence
as the cradle of their race. The king does not build
his own palace of swish till he has sat on the sacred
stool of his ancestors in Allada House, and has been
invested with a fine silk coat, which completes his inau-
guration.*

The tradition touching Allada, which is not found in
books, but is known to every boy in the kingdom,
is this, and it explains how the error of making
two Ardrahs arose. About A.D. 1620, an old and
wealthy king of Allada proper died, and left his
property to his three sons. These agreed that the
eldest should reign in his father's stead, which he did,
in peace and prosperity, under the name of Allada
'Khosu, or King of Allada.† "Dé," the youngest, or
some say the second, rounded the Upper Nohwe or
Denham Waters of our charts, and founded Hwebonu,
which we have since known as Little Ardrah and Porto
Novo. Hence the Dahoman king still calls him of

* The History mentions this ceremony (p. 227). As will be seen, the
present King is not yet duly " crowned."

† This explains the Alatakassu of the Directory, a confusion between
the King's title and the name of the place.

Hwebonu " brother." The cadet Dako (the " Tacoo-doonou of our histories) went north, crossed the Agrime swamp, settled at a place called "Uhwawe," and less correctly, Hawowi,* between Kana and Agbome, where the Adan-we palace was afterwards built. Hence the History tells us that "the original capital of Dahome was "Dawhee,"† between the towns of Calmina (Kana) and Abomey, at about ninety miles from the sea coast."

Uhwawe belonged to a chief named Awesu, who allowed the ambitious stranger to settle there. Dako, by degrees becoming powerful, encroached upon a neighbouring kinglet, named Danh, the Snake or Rainbow. As his followers greatly increased in number, and he was ever asking more ground from Danh, the latter exclaimed, in wrath, "Soon thou wilt build in my belly!" Dako bided his time, slew the king, and erected over his corpse the old palace of Dahome,‡

* It lies on both sides of the road, and the people are still a distinct race from the Ffons proper or Dahomans.

† Which some writers, *e.g.*, the author of the Preface to the History, have determined, much against its grain, to be the Dauma of Leo Africanus, corrupted in Plancius' map to "Dauina," and misprinted by Commander Forbes "Dauna."

‡ The legend may arise from the name; one suspiciously like it (and these things can hardly happen in pairs) will presently be found in the

" in Danh's (or the Snake's) belly." Hereupon the Ffons * changed their name to Dahomans ; † and thus, about 1625, arose the once great military empire familiar to the ears of Europe.

The kingdoms of Dahome and Allada were friendly,

word Agri-go-men. The "History of Dahomy" explains the word by "The house in Da's belly," remarking in a note, "The belly, in the Dahoman tongue, is homy." But the nasal *n* and the terminal aspirate in Danh are sensible. Moreover the English slur at the end of Homy is here inadmissible.

The word Ho, "*venter*" is articulated with the guttural Arabic Ha (ح) sometimes, though erroneously, confounded with the Spanish Jota, which is the Semitic Kha (خ). Ho-men (stomach in) means the ilia. Thus the full compound word would be Danh-*ho*-me*n* (meaning either "Danh's intestines," or "In Danh's belly"). The people prefer the latter. This nasal *n* being unmanageable, both to reader and printer, I discard for "Dahome." The public, however, is requested to pronounce Dah-ome like Ashan-ti instead of Dahómy and Ashantí. The Portuguese, who are weak at gutturals, get over the Semitic Ha by changing it into a g,—" Dagomé."

* The History informs us that the Dahomans were formerly called Foys, and other authors have changed the word to Fohi, Fay, and Fonin. It is clearly derived from Ffon, which some write Ffun and Efun, the old national name for the Dahoman and his language. I am unable to state whether it has a common derivation with the so-called Efong people of Kakanda, living between Yoruba Proper and the Niger and Kwara rivers. What makes me suspect a mysterious and forgotten connection is the prevalence of the Afa practice (see Chap. XII.) in Dahome, which arose in Ife of Kakanda (Wanderings in West Africa. Abeokuta. Chap. V.). Ffon must not be confounded with Efŭtŭ, the language of a single tribe, Winnebah, on the Gold Coast. Those writers are in error who call the Dahoman tongue " Ewe."

‡ In their vernacular, Danh-*ho*-me*n*-nu*n* is a Dahome man, a Dahoman. The word Dahome is applied first and primarily to the old palace : secondly, to the capital, Agbome : thirdly, to the whole empire.

as became brethren, till 1724, when Agaja, the Scourge of God in these regions, resolved to open a road from the interior to the sea. Mr. Bulfinch Lambe, to whom allusion has been made, described, in his short account of that war ("that resulted in the capture of Ardrah, of which he was an unwilling witness"), the savage power and state of the conquering northerner. Being "shut up in a house by the king and old Blanco, as soon as the cry of war came," the white man narrowly escaped the death which hundreds found in the flames. A fellow hauled him over the wall, and he was carried through the town to the king's quarters, where the general was, and though that officer was in a great hurry, and flushed with victory, he took the stranger kindly by the hand, and gave him a dram, "which was some comfort to him." When Mr. Lambe went out, "there was no stirring for bodies without heads, and had it rained blood, it could not have lain thicker on the ground," whilst the slaves were being counted by giving a "bouge"* to each. After this he was led

---

* A corruption of the Portuguese "buso," cowrie. The names used by Mr. Lambe and his contemporaries for measures of shells, are:—

40 Bouges   = 1 Toky (or Toki), *i.e.*, a string.
5 Toky   = 1 Gallinha (because it was the price of a fowl), corresponding with our "bunch."

by the conqueror to the capital. He appears to have been a poor-spirited thing; he whines, curlike, about his confinement, and he is not ashamed to write to the English governor at Whydah,—" If there is any cast-off woman, either white or mulatto, that can be persuaded to come to this country, either to be the king's wife or else practise her old trade, I should gain His Majesty's heart entirely by it, and he would believe anything I say about my going and returning again with more white men from the Company." *

One of Agaja's "strong names" or titles is Allada Kho, or Lord of Allada. The town, however, once said to be nine miles round, never recovered after the dreadful slaughter of its inhabitants, and, unlike Why-dah, quietly submitted to incorporation with Dahome. It is now a large market, and a village more important than Toli, but nothing more.

Allada is well situated on a platform, and its climate is comparatively salubrious. Drinking water is said to

5 Gallinhas = 1 Ackey, then worth 2s. 6d.
4 Ackeys = 1 Grand Cabess (i.e., Cabeça or head), worth 10s.

It is a pleasant money, requiring a man to carry 2l.

* Even in West Africa the new American doctrine of miscegenation, in which the white woman must succumb to the "splendours of imperial (negro) manhood," though at times practised by the vilest of slavers, has been ever generally despised.

M 2

be procurable, after half-an-hour's walk, from a deep hollow to the east and south-east; it is not only plentiful, but sweeter and clearer than any found between Whydah and Agbome. The stranger, however, must obtain royal permission to visit the place, and will probably fail. There may be a stream flowing to the Nohwe or Denham Waters, but the mysterious fetish town, buried in the bush, and hidden from white eyes, is, I think, a fiction of the English fort, Whydah.

Allada is the Tours or the Sienna of Dahome, where the purest Ffon is spoken. At Agbome the aspirates and gutturals are exaggerated, the effect, perhaps, of a colder climate and a more rugged land. Whydah, on the contrary, unduly softens the articulation; as in Egypt, this may be attributed to the damp heat and consequent languor of the seaboard. At the port town, as may be imagined, there is a debased European *patois*. A Whydah man will say to you, " Naó tem cowries pour choppy choppy."

The evening concluded with the usual presents, and dancing on a very small scale. The caboceers joined their slaves, hence the polish of these barbarians, compared with our poor churlish clowns. The small boys, armed with *sabre de bois*,—the ξύλιναν μάχαιραν

— mingled amongst their elders, *sans* shyness or *mauvaise honte*, the Britannic curse. As usual, the dance was all antics, very excellent fooling. Few people, and no warriors, appeared. Six weeks afterwards, we learned that a large body of male and female soldiery, marching to attack Jabatan, a frontier town, were lurking behind the palace walls.

The night was calm, clear, and cool, with an exceedingly heavy dew. During the day, the trees had been blackened and the sky speckled by flights of reddish bats,* swarming like gnats or flies. The queer chirp of these modern pterodactyles, and the melodious *gazouillement* † of birds in the brake, awoke us at the earliest dawn.

* Captain Phillips notices bats the size of a blackbird at Savi. They abound between Whydah and Agbome; at the latter place they always flew from north to south over our heads about an hour before sunset. The Egbas have a distinct word for fruit eaten by bats, showing that the animal extends through Southern Yoruba. It is a fine large species, two feet across the wings, and is very lengthily described by Mr. Duncan, Vol. I. pp. 129—131.

† This is a French word, but I cannot help it—let reviewers say what they will. The sound of z in the song of West African birds is salient; our insipid "warbling" is tolerable and not to be endured. I distinctly deny that English or any other language contains all the desirable shades of expression; and I cannot see why, in these days, when French is familiar to us as in the times of William the Conqueror, we should be condemned for borrowing from it. "Rot your Italianos; I loves a simple English ballad," appears to underlie the feeling.

were obliged by civility to descend from our hammocks,
and to receive from the chief Atakpa the customary
gifts.

After another mile we entered Hen-vi—" Hold the
child "—so called because, like Sienna in Tuscany, it is
supposed to open its heart wider than its gates. It is
also known as Henvi Dò-vo (vaw), or Henvi the Red-
walled, and our " blind travellers ". have corrupted it to
Hawee or Havee. Like all those towns between Allada·
and the capital, it has its tattered " palace," and a
fetish-house in somewhat better preservation. A
tolerable-sized village, and surrounded by giant trees,
it looked pleasant and cool, though the sky was bathed
in the burning light of the tropical sun. There is a
market, but the water is bad and dear, and provisions
are so scarce that the price of the leanest chicken is
two shillings. There is, however, tolerable palm-wine
brought from the bush. At Henvi sets off the north-
western road, which, when the Agrime swamp is bad,
leads to the capital : it is, as will be seen, longer, but
easier.

We placed our stools next a tree opposite the large
gateway of the royal abode, and were entertained with
the usual dance. Here, however, there was something

of novelty,—the first of the "Amazons" made their appearance. The four soldieresses were armed with muskets, and habited in tunics and white calottes, with two blue patches, meant for crocodiles. They were commanded by an old woman in a man's straw hat, a green waistcoat, a white shirt, put on like the breeches of the good King Dagobert—*à l'envers*—a blue waistcloth, and a sash of white calico. The virago directed the dance and song with an ironed ferule, and her head was shaded, by way of umbrella, with a peculiar shrub, called on the Gold Coast "God's Tree."* The few men showed us some attempts at tumbling and walking upon their hands. Two of the women dancers were of abnormal size, nearly six feet tall, and of proportional breadth, whilst generally the men were smooth, full-breasted, round-limbed, and effeminate-looking. Such, on the other hand, was the size of the female skeleton, and the muscular development of the frame, that in many cases femineity could be detected only by the bosom. I have no doubt that this physical superiority of the "working sex," led in the Popo and Dahoman

* Yammi Dueh. Its prickly stem throws off at the summit three leafy shoots; the old Portuguese utilized this vegetable *bizarrerie* as St. Patrick is said to have done with the shamrock.

race to the employment of women as fighters.*   They
are the domestic servants, the ploughboys, and the
porters, and Gallegos, the field hands, and market cattle
of the nation,—why should they not also be soldiers?
In other matters they are by no means companions
meet for men : the latter show a dawn of the intel-
lectual, whilst the former is purely animal—bestial.
Hence, according to some, the inordinate polygamy of
the race.

After breakfasting in the house of a good old man,
one of the local Buko-no, or Diviners, we bade adieu
to Henvi of the Red walls.   In places the path was
girt with an impenetrable herbaceous growth, in others
there rose on either hand noble hedges of forest trees :
here the wintry leaves still strewed the ground, there
the jungle waxed thinner, suggesting the possibility of
passage.   Amongst the long white llianas, some thick as
a man's leg, and bracing down Cotton-woods eighty feet
high, I thought to recognise the gum-elastic creeper :
the Europeans, however, speak only of a ficus which
supplies a kind of caoutchouc.

A short hour placed us at Whe-gbo, a small place
on the right of the road.   My interpreters explained

* In the Bonny River the women appear to me larger than the men.

the name thus. On this spot the three royal brothers
of Allada disputed long and fierily about each one's
chance of being the greatest. As the question could
not be settled, a councillor cried out, "No one can
decide (*whe*) a palaver so great (*gbo*)." Upon that
ground the present hamlet is built.

When we had disposed ourselves under the fig and
fetish trees abounding at Whe-gbo, the war-chief Suza-
kon danced at the head of his half-a-dozen fellows, and
waxed inordinately fierce. It is not a little startling to
see how suddenly, the war-dress doffed, these ruffling
heroes subside into the servile and timid "nigger."
Though the little knot of Falstaff's recruits knew not
how decently to cut off an imaginary head, their great
captain boasted that the next month would see him in
Abeokuta. An exceedingly fat old woman joined her
confrère in the *improvisé* song, and professed her readiness to do or die by his side : we shook our heads
gravely, and the bystanders roared with laughter.
When the Ajablaku or civilian-chief had made his present, we urged on the hammock-men, who were becoming
frantic for *Ahan*, their rum.

Noon had sped before we left Whe-gbo. The trees
became even more gigantic than before, and presently

we fell into a long descent; it is the second step, Azohwe being the first. After two hours we reached Akpwe, at the southern extremity of the Great Swamp.

Its name is explained to be the fetish or supernatural part of the Loko or "Sauce-wood" tree. In old times it belonged to a people called Aizoh, who, until conquered by Dahome, extended from near Agrime to Toli, and from this place westwards to Toffo,* where they are mixed with the Ffons. It contains a royal palace, or rather precincts of a guttered tumble-down wall, with a barn-like shed built over the gate, where travellers may rest. We went to the house of the chief, who, not expecting us, had refused admission to our men. The poorest market on the road was found at Akpwe. As we near the capital the population becomes thinner, and the display less, whilst a dozen women and children are seen for every one man. The principal performers in the dance were our own porters.

On December 17th, almost before the birds had begun their matins, we arose and sent forward our fellows : this morning we were to cross *the* Marsh, the terror of travellers during the wet season. The people term it "Ko," the Swamp, which appears to be a proper

* For a short account of Toffo, see Chap. XXIV.

name, as a common bog is called "Agbábá." The Europeans know it by the Portuguese word, "Lama"—mire
or mud. For better distinction I propose to name it the
"Agrime Swamp." This northern limit separated the
old kingdom, Allada, from the original Dahome. To
the latter it is still an important strategical point
moating it to the south : at certain seasons it would be
almost impossible for the lightest of field artillery to
cross it.* The marshy forest forms a zone said to cut
through Dahome from the lagoon of Hwebonu (Porto
Novo) eastward, to that of Porto Seguro on the west.
Travellers differ about its course, and many declare
it to be stagnant. On the western road, however, I
found it distinctly draining to the west, and I therefore
conclude that it feeds the Haho, Avon, or Porto Seguro
Water. From December till June it may be crossed in
two to three hours, and thus its breadth may be six to
seven miles. Between July and November it is a
severe task : visitors to the King have spent two days
of continuous toil with ten hammock-men who were up
to their armpits in water, to their calves in mire, and
subject to perpetual tripping by the network of tree-

* North of Agrime the heaviest battering train would find no difficulty till it reaches the Makhi mountains.

roots catching their feet. The present has been an unusually dry year : we shall traverse the greater part without knowing it.

Whilst all was *en grisaille*, we struck, staff in hand, through the " dismal forest," as old writers call it. The hammock became useless, the mud, hard-caked like that frozen by a German winter, wounds the feet of the bearers ; they march at the rate of one mile an hour, and the frequent irregularities of the surface make them sidle into the bush, where tree stubs abound, and where falls are imminent. The path was tortuous, but easy to a walker, and hardly anywhere impassable to an American light waggon. The sixth King Sinmen-kpen (our Adahoonzou II., 1774—1789) was the Macadam of Dahome. Resolving to make the " Ko " passable to his strangers, he handed over a string, ten yards long, to each caboceer,—a significant hint. This passage, we are told, cost incredible labour and fatigue before the hurdle bridges over the swamps were widened and the gullies were filled up. There were two depressions of black mud, decayed vegetation, and beyond those points the surface, though caked and cracked, was of lighter hue ; its general unevenness told its difficulty during the rains. The only fetor in the bush was that of the large black ant, which suggests that a corpse is hidden behind every tree.[*]

The road was crowded with porters, hastening up to the Customs. After every 100 or 200 yards were dwarf thatches containing travellers' bedsteads, rough branches laid on cross-bars supported by forked uprights, and all in ruinous state. These were the remnants of huts used by the soldiery when firing to Whydah.[†] At the half-way house, Wondonun,[‡] we found by the aneroid that we had descended from 417 to within 134 feet of sea-level, explaining *the* Swamp's stagnancy. The little village is in a kind of island, which never floods ; it has, however, a temporary and a miserable look. Around it is a wild and wiry grass showing old husbandry, and extensive plantations of plantain.

We ranged our chairs under an open shed in the market-place of Wondonun, and were not excused the usual infliction. The single white umbrella there

[*] The experiments made by Mr. Duncan tend to show that the smell emitted by this species of ant is a poison to other insects.

[†] See, for a description of this ceremony, Chap. XXII.

[‡] Interpreted to mean a place where some monstrous prodigy was produced from *won* ("portent" or "bad thing," as, for instance, a child born with teeth, or speaking prematurely) and *Do-nun* (s.s. as *do kho, i.e.,* speak palaver).

present mustered his *corps de ballet* with two separate rings of different sexes. And we had the politeness to look on for half-an-hour.

Whilst the sun was still young, we left Wondonun, and struck once more into the bush ; the ground, though hard and flakey, was level, and presently tall black ant-hills showed that we had reached the northern edge of the swamp, where water does not regularly extend. A long hour placed us at Aiveji,* where drink and another dance awaited us. The soil from black mud had become white sand, and presently it assumed the normal red tinge. The surface was grass, burned in places : high and lush, it showed that the land had long lain fallow ; the later cultivation was denoted by finer and thinner wild growths. Aiveji is a little village of thatch, almost buried in dense verdure, and near the road was a scatter of tattered hovels, the " khambi" or grass camp of the East African interior.

Excusing ourselves from halting in the heat of the sun, we passed on to Agrime, the end of this stage. The level differs little from that of Wondonun : we are

* 'Ai' (ground), V6 (red thing), and Ji (on) : it is so called because built on red soil.

still but 232 feet above the sea. Here, however, we strike the " true Coast " of Africa ; the alternate dunes and morasses disappear for a regular and northerly inclination, whilst pebbles are now mixed with grass, shells, and broken palm-nuts, to temper the house-swish. The stones, all rounded and water-washed, contained a large proportion of iron, and a smaller quantity of copper. Some Europeans declare that they have found traces of gold,* especially in the pottery : I saw nothing but an abundance of mica.† Others have gone so far as to say that the King, like his father, is aware of the precious metal existing in that portion of the " Kong Mountains " which subtends the north of Dahome, and that this is his reason for

* Barbot, Book IV. Chap. I., speaks of the " country of Tafou, in which are said to be mines of gold ; " but he clearly did not know its whereabouts. According to Mr. Duncan (Vol. II. p. 307), gold is as plentiful in Dahome as in Ashanti ; but it is quite superseded by the slave-trade. No one believes him.

It is not a little curious that these people, like the Mandengas, the Fanti of the Gold Coast, and the natives of the Gaboon River, call gold " Sika." Mr. R. Bruce Walker, now of Lagos, informs me that, " At R. Frisco, near C. Lahou, which is the most westerly point on the West African coast, when gold is found, the people call it Asika." All these dialects being totally different, the word must have been borrowed by one tribe from the other, suggesting that all do not produce the metal. Can it be connected with the Asiatic " Sikkeh ? "

† The pottery made at Agbome glitters with mica, and these " paillettes " have probably imposed upon the credulous.

barring the road to travellers.*   Others more reasonably opine that such a secret could not possibly be
kept, especially when so many Gold Coast men are in
the country ; and, moreover, that the Dahomans are
not such fools as to leave gold undug.

Agrimen—"In the wall"—derives its name from an
old legend.   When Jemeken was the chief, it was
predicted to him that his wall must shake unless he
daily "ate" (*i.e.*, exacted as a tax upon goods passing
the place) a "kene" and a "tene" (160 and 9) of cowries.   When the King is in country quarters at Kana,
strangers halt here, send forward their message-canes,
and request permission to advance.   We were received
with the usual ceremony, a single soldier being the
performer in a circle of some twenty unarmed squatters.
Presently a messenger informed us that we were not
wanted till the morrow.   We spread the table under a
thick orange-tree, and strewed it with wild mangoes,

* According to the apocryphal M. Wallon, King Gezo used to say
that the mountains north of his kingdom produced gold, but that he
preferred the cowrie currency, as with it there could be no forgery;
moreover, no man could be secretly rich.   At present, when doubloons
are paid for slaves, the monarch monopolises all the gold in the country.
The last haul of doubloons was made by H. M. S. Prometheus, who
found 8000*l.* stowed away in soap bars.   Since that time, specie is
brought out in the mail steamers, and bills are drawn on Messrs. L——i
and Co., L'pool.

smelling like apples, and with cocoas, which extend
as far as Agbome; the pineapple here, as at the
capital, was found in a savage state, and without
fruit.   Our beds were hung in a new mud-house,
lately built inside the royal precincts for the use
of white travellers.   The place is one of dignity;
we were soon informed that it is not "etiquette"
to follow any walk where we could be sighted by
"King's wives."   A large cynocephalus, a ground-
pig, and divers interesting muscicapæ were to be
seen in the maize, but could not be shot, being in the
King's palace.   These ridiculous pretensions are doubtless invented by petty captains *pour se faire valoir*.
Unfortunately white visitors, from Frenchmen to Brazilians, have ever endured this bullying without a
murmur, and now the stain is hardly delible from the
black mind.*

This chapter may conclude with a few remarks
touching the route travelled over.

The aspect of the country confirms the general
impression that the Dahomans were, for negroes, an
industrious race, till demoralised by slave hunts and by

* The caboceer of Allada objected to Mr. Duncan measuring a
cotton tree without the King's leave.

long predatory wars. The land has at no distant
period been well cleared, and it is still easy to reclaim,
though in time the fallows will be again afforested.
Others opine that it has of late been the royal policy
to gird the capital with a desert, as the surest defence
against invaders.

However that may be, Africa, as far as I know her,
shows few such ruined regions as that viewed during
the last four days. The scantiness of the population,
and the disproportion of women and children to adult
males, strike every eye. The hackneyed excuse is that
there is a general muster for war or ceremony at the
capital : the fact is that, beyond a few towns in which
there is centralization, the country is a luxuriant
wilderness.

On the Gold Coast, and about the Gaboon River and
the South Coast, even a peasant will have his chair,
table, cot, and perhaps boxes for goods. Here he
never dreams of such ownership. The cause is, of
course, the ruler, who by spiritual advice acts upon the
principle that iron-handed tyranny is necessary to
curb his unruly subjects, and to spare him the painful
necessity of inflicting upon them death or the "middle
passage"—the Hamitic form of transportation. More

to make them feel his power than to ameliorate their condition, he will not allow them to cultivate around Whydah coffee and sugar-cane, rice and tobacco, which at times have been planted and have been found to succeed.* Similarly King Gezo stringently prohibited the growth of ground-nuts, except for purely domestic purposes. A caboceer may not alter his house, wear European shoes,† employ a spittoon-holder, carry an umbrella without leave, spread over his bed a counter-pane, which comfort is confined to princes, mount a hammock, or use a chair in his own home ; and if he sits at meat with a white, he must not touch knife or fork.‡ Only a " man of puncto " may whitewash the interior of his house at Agbome, and the vulgar must refrain from this, as well as from the sister-luxury of plank or board doors. And so in everything.

* * * *

It was a lovely evening at Agrimé, ushering in a cool clear night ; the atmosphere told us that we had

* Mr. James, thinking the tea-plant indigenous to Dahome, endea-voured to cultivate it, and of course failed.

† The only shoes permitted are the kind of leather bags called, Imá-len fo-kpá, or Moslem slippers, and these cannot be assumed without royal permission.

‡ Formerly caboceers were not allowed to drink out of a glass in the royal presence; now the King will even offer it.

changed the false for the true tropical Africa,—the
swampy outskirt for the hard hem of the rich garment.
The moon shone brightly, exciting the hyæna, and
inducing from the frogs many a βρεκεκεκεξ, κοαξ, κοαξ.
Unusually distinct was that dark mysterious oval which
sailoring men call the "coalsack," and our "jungle
clock," of which Dante sang,—

> "Io mi volsi a man destra e posi mente
> Al altro polo, e vidi quattro stelle
> Non criste mai fuorch' alla prima gente."

It may savour of heresy to say so, but I confess
never to have discovered the charms of this useful
but homely constellation. When the major axis of the
Southern Cross is perpendicular, the form resembles
that of a boy's lob-sided kite; horizontal, it is like
a badly-made four-legged stool.

CHAPTER VII.

SMALL RECEPTION AT AGRIME, AND ARRIVAL AT KANA,
THE KING'S COUNTRY QUARTERS.

On Friday, the 18th, about mid-afternoon, we were warned that the royal messenger or escort was approaching. A table was forthwith disposed outside the palace, opposite some elephant skulls and bones * heaped up under an ayyan, or thunder fetish shrub; and we ranged ourselves behind the board. After a few minutes a loudening hum of voices heralded a rush of warriors into the Uhon-nukon, or cleared space, with its central tree, fronting the royal abode. Dahomans much affect these sudden and impetuous movements, which impose upon the eye, making the few appear many. The flag-bearer was the first, waving, at the

---

* The animal, in 1803, was common throughout the country; now it is a "curio," having been well-nigh killed out. About three months before our arrival at Whydah, Mr. Dawson had bought a pair of tusks, and spoke of the occurrence as rare.

end of the thinnest of staves, a long calico rag with a preposterous blue anchor. Then, habited in the war uniform of the "Blue Company," dashed a tumultuous column of war-men, four deep and about eighty in number ; followed by two neat kettle-drums, and all singing the loudest chants. They saluted us by circumambulating the central tree, defiling before us from the left with right shoulders forward, jumping, springing, pretending to fire their weapons, and imitating all the action of an attack.

During this wild " pass round," sundry calabashes of food, carried on slaves' heads, appeared from our left, and were displayed in order before us. Meanwhile, behind the soldiery, in distinct procession, walked the civilians, seven married men preceded by a white calico-covered object which, conspicuously borne aloft on a carrier's head, announced itself as an old friend, the venerable liqueur-case of former days. Its damaged front and broken legs would disgrace an English pot-house ; but it has been the pride and ornament of the Dahoman Court for the last half century. Behind it, with much solemnity, marched Aiseku, a medicine boy of the Meu, or Second Minister ; and after him, habited in a shabby paletôt of brown-black alpaca, tomahawk in hand, stalked, with even greater dignity, Sosu Bleo, politely called Podoji-noto—less courteously, "state-spy" upon the old Buko-no.

The Blues, after grovelling in the dust before the Sublime Porte, cried out the royal " strong names,"* presented arms to it after their fashion, and formed up in line before our table. Then the king's canes were, according to custom, produced from their *étuis*, and all admired their novelty. Instead of King Gezo's *rococo* old lions, sharks, and crocodiles, we now found out, after some study, chameleons, parrots, and monkeys half-swallowed by snakes, the whole ornamented with thin plates of beaten dollars.† I handled them standing and bare-headed, whilst the messengers prostrated ; and in this position the usual questions, answers, and greetings were exchanged.

The old liqueur-case was uncovered, and, besides the invariable aqua pura, three case-bottles made their appearance, with muscadel wine, trade gin, and bad

---

* This old Africo-English term is a literal translation of the Ffon "nyi siyen-siyen."

† The wood is light, canary-coloured, and pretty much like what I have seen at Fernando Po. The stick-making industry seems here to pay : the cheapest specimens cost half a dollar. Before an axe edge of iron or silver can be added, the King's permission must be obtained.

Portuguese rum.   The Dahoman etiquette is to drink thrice of different liquors : foreseeing much of this kind of thing, I resolved at once to show preference to the muscadel, and, despite all protestations, to decline the rum.

Whilst we imbibed to the King's health and to my own, the escort fired salutes ; they then grounded arms, and began the usual "Gillie Callum," their "decapitation dance."   Amongst the knives and toma-hawks I remarked a jambiyah, or Arab side-dagger. The line moved from side to side, capering and raising the near leg, and at times all rushed like madmen round the tree.   Ensued solos of three chiefs, and the usual frantic singing and valour-boasting.   After empty-ing the gin and rum into the principals, civil and military, I retired.   The small reception ended with the King's dole of provaunt—five calabashes of stews and vegetables, with one pot of good water.   It sufficed for fifty, whereas we had a hundred mouths to fill ; ensued the usual scene of disgusting selfish-ness, the missionary youths, with "Elijah" at their head, greatly distinguishing themselves.

Nothing could be meaner than the whole display, which every year grows worse ; Gezo attempted to

keep up state ; his son is either unable or unwilling to
do so.

When all was over we set out in hammocks, preceded
by the guard firing at spurts carbines and muskets loud
as little mortars, and capering all the way. I have
heard an Englishman doubt the possibility of " polking "
from Dan to Beersheba—let him visit Dahome. A
delicate French grey, touched with the lightest pink in
the western sky, told us that the day was dying fast.
The soil, before whitish, again appeared deeply tinged
with oxide of iron, and the vegetation displayed
cactus, as well as the acacia which had characterised
the scenery between Agrime and its swamp. In
places it perfumed the atmosphere like that of the
Ezbekiyah Gardens at Cairo, where the native per-
fumers extract from the " locust " a faint and peculiarly
oriental perfume appropriately called Fitneh. The land,
semingly a dead level, had everywhere been burned, and
the lively young grass was sprouting out of death.
After about an hour we halted at a Danh-hwe, or
" Rainbow house,"* a little wall-less thatch-slope, like the

---

* For an account of the rainbow worship, see Chap. XVII. Danh, as
has been seen, also means a snake ; but the seaboard god has few
honours here.

Australian " breakwind," in the centre of a dwarf mud wall, circled with the thunder fetish plant. The head " religious " attached to the establishment came forth with the usual ceremonies, presented water to us, begged and received alms.

The next halt was at Zogbodomen, so called from its chief, who was slain by Dako,* the first Dahoman king. The few miserable thatch huts are shaded by the fleshy-leaved figs, called on the Gold Coast " Market trees," and are almost buried during the rains by densest grass, from which rise the stateliest palmyras. Presently crossing level ground, with vegetation here tall, there dwarfed ; now green, then brown ; we sighted from afar a deep depression stretching from east to west.

On the farther side of this valley, which during wet weather must roll in a considerable stream, stands Kana. I could not but feel, during my former visit, a thrill of pleasure at the first sight of the " country capital." It is distinctly Dahome ; and here the traveller expects to look upon the scenes of barbaric splendour

---

* Zogbodo also means a woman's top-knot of hair, the Shusheh of the Arabs. Mr. Duncan (vol. i. p. 205) writes Togbado ; not a misprint, but probably an error of his notes.

of which all the world has read. And it has its own
beauty : a French traveller has compared it with the
loveliest villages of fair Provence ; while to Mr. Duncan
it suggested " a vast pleasure-ground, not unlike some
part of the Great Park at Windsor."   After impervious
but sombre forest, grass - barrens, and the dismal
swamps of the path, the eye revels in these open
plateaux : their seducing aspect is enhanced by scattered plantations of a leek green studding the slopes,
by a background of gigantic forest dwarfing the
nearer palm files, by homesteads buried in cultivation,
and by calabashes and cotton-trees vast as the view,
tempering the fiery summer sun to their subject
growths, and in winter collecting the rains, which
would otherwise bare the newly buried seed. Nor is
animal life wanting.   The turkey-buzzard, the kite, and
the kestrel soar in the upper heights ; the brightest
fly-catchers flit through the lower strata ; the little grey
squirrel nimbly climbs his lofty home, and a fine large
spur-fowl cries from the plantations of maize and cassava.

   After two hours of slow travelling we passed the site
of a village now level with the ground : it is called
Logozokpota,* or the Tortoise's Rise. Here is a de-

   * An iron figure of the Logozo, the land tortoise, or terrapin, is much

tached thatch which the king visits before beginning his
compaigns ; and when passing it we were saluted with
five muskets—an honour always punctually reported.
Descending into the depression, we could see the town
—a city no longer—straggling beyond the northern
bank. A nearer glance at the habitations showed us
that they are those of Whydah and Savi, heaps of
haycock huts or penthouse thatches enclosed in " compounds " of mud wall or palm-leaf, and jealously
detatched. There is palpably more field than habitation, and far more fallow than field.

At this point we reached a trivia. Two paths
setting to the N.N.W. lead to the town ; the south-
eastern is in the direction of the king's drinking water,
called Hanan. I afterwards visited it. A well-cleared
road leads over several waves of ground, alternately
maize-field and palm-orchard, towards a serpentine line
of tall dark trees—a formation ever denoting water in
those lands. About half a mile from the outskirts of
Kana places the visitor at the rivulet ; it is a deep
ditch, sunk canal-like 10 to 12 feet below the ground-

used in the Bo-Fetish. The Egbas believe mirage to be caused by an
underground fire with which the tortoise fells the trees. I could not
find the idea in Dahome.

surface; the bed is black with vegetable humus, and the water after being puddled is white with clay. The direction is easterly towards the Denham Lake.

This streamlet is said to supply during the dry season all Kana. It is visited throughout the night by the humbler classes. At the earliest dawn the women slaves of the palace,* who are shut up during the hours of darkness, wend their way in long lines, carrying huge pots on their heads. They claim the road, which is consequently provided with a number of foot-made offsets. At the words, "Gan ja!"†—"The bell comes!"—even if it is tinkled by a slave girl-child four years old, the native must throw himself "into the bush," that is to say, out of the road, and await with

* They are not Amazons, as Commodore Wilmot (Appendix iii.) thinks, but the slaves of the fighting women, who each hold from one to fifty. When any of the king's wives appear they are preceded by such attendants, and are accompanied by Amazons, who, however, carry only their muskets. It is the same with the royal Fetish women when going to fetch water for the great Nesu; they are known by their white raiment and long strings of cowries. On these occasions the male lieges must run off afar and turn their backs. Women only clear the way.

† Gan is any metal; gan-wi (lit., black metal) specifies iron. The bell in question is a rude unbrazed affair not unlike that appropriated to our sheep, and it is carried suspended to a cord round the neck of the file leader. At the sight of a man it is vigorously shaken up and down with one hand.

averted face till the long train has passed. If a palace water-pot be broken, the nearest male would be accused and get into trouble.* When out shooting in the morning, we were often called to by these slaves, telling us not to startle them. The Dahoman officials show their loyalty by " clearing out" as far and as fast as possible. If a stranger does only what is strictly neces- sary, one woman will say, " He is a white, and knows no better !" and the other will reply, " And has he no law in his own land ?" The lower, the older, and the uglier the slave girls are, the louder and longer they tinkle— which is natural—and almost all of them seemed to enjoy the ignoble scamper of our interpreters and ham- mock men, whom the old women order to look the other way. At times, men and boy water-carriers for the palace, known by their switches, arrogate to them- selves the same right. This is one of the greatest nuisances in Dahome : it continues throughout the day ; in some parts, as around the palace, half a mile

* The same is the custom amongst the Dembos of the old Congo empire. A man who refused to quit the path when a chief's wife approached, or who stood talking with her, would be sold with his family into slavery : on the other hand, the woman, under pain of her lord's displeasure, yielded the way to a white man or a black-white—one authorised to wear shoes and other articles of European toilette.

an hour would be full speed; and to make way for these animals of burthen, bought perhaps for a few pence, is, to say the least of it, by no means decorous.

Continuing our way to the N.W., the next feature observed was the Gau Nehori, explained to be " Fetish place, when the Gau or commander-in-chief opens the campaign" by performing certain ceremonies. It is nothing but a long shed with a shady verandah, and a few huts under a splendid Ficus. A little beyond it, on the left of the road, is a white clay depression in the grass—a pool during the rains, and in the dries a surface pitted with empty holes 2 feet deep—this is the Gau-te.* Then came the Kana-'gbo-nun,† or town gate, consisting of a pole or two, but warning men that their heads are within the lion's jaws. The space is open; there are two ragged trees on the left; to the right lie a few small huts, and a gigantic Bombax denotes from afar the entrance to Kana.

When the party with much singing and dancing had been formed up, we were once more allowed to advance. This time, however, the circuitous official road was pre-

* I could not obtain a reliable translation of this name. Mr. Beecham rendered it " commander-in-chief's pool."

† Agbo (with the peculiar " gb " pronounced simultaneously, a gate), and nun (mouth, or side).

ferred.   The large open spaces were crowded with
spectators, whom the bright moonlight enabled to
satisfy their curiosity. On our left lay the blacksmiths'
quarter, dotted with round thatched huts, open at the
sides, and presenting all the appearance of the Central African smithy.   Another half hour being duly
wasted, we turned to the S.W., passed a couple of
dwarf temples, when the *impudique* Logba looked more
priapus-like than any priapus, and were carried into
the " English house," whence the crippled old landlord
Degen-no* came out to receive us.

This was a disappointment: although ex-officio guests
of Buko-no, the English landlord, we had looked forward to the comfortable hall and superior establishment
of the Akho-vi,† or Prince Chyudaton, the Lieutenant-
Governor of Whydah.   Of course we remonstrated
loudly about the narrowness of our quarters, and we
sent a message to the head doctor, without other result
than the usual " put off."   Let no reader of African
travel, however, suppose that anything so noble as

* A name always given to children that have been sent from Deadland by their great-grandmothers.

† Akho, or Akhosu (a king), and Vi (a child, son, or young one). So
" Tom " was known amongst the people as Yewe-no-vi (literally, god-
mother-son), young missionary.

jealousy influences these negro worthies. Their object in securing the guest is purely and simply for dirty pelf. I have heard and read much of African hospitality; but I have never seen a trace of it in the true Hamite.* He will take you into his hut, and will even quarrel with you if you pass him unvisited: he will supply you with food, and will assure you that you are monarch of all you survey. But it is all a sham : he expects a recompense in double and treble, and if he does not obtain it, his rudeness will be that of the savage *gratté*. The self-called " civilised " negro, like the *emancipados* of S'a Leone and Fernando Po, admit you into their houses, and keep you there as at an inn : they would be equally hurt and offended by your calling for the bill and by your forgetting to pay exorbitantly, but indirectly. The fact is, they would combine the praise of hospitality with more solid advantages ; and they do so with the transparent cunning of children. Such has been my experience in Africa—may others have fared better !

Kana is less correctly written Canna, Cannah, and

* " The people, I have said already, are void either of sympathy or gratitude, even in their own families ; and the poor horse is not held in half so much esteem as the swine, because they cannot eat it." This is a true remark by Mr. Duncan.

even Carnah : the old travellers prefer Calmina, or
Canamina, a corruption of Kana-mina, from a palace
once built there, according to "country custom," by
one of the Dahoman kings.* The History declares it
to have been the first place of importance which (about
1620) fell into the hands of the Foys (Ffons), or
early Dahomans, by the assassination of its chief. That
authority, however, uses the word " Calmina," which
should evidently be Kana, the " Mina " being an addition
of a later date. According to Commander Forbes,
" Cannah, formerly capital of Foy, then called Dawee,
conquering Agbome, has retained a peace of upwards
of 200 years." This sentence contains a treble in-
accuracy : " Dawee," as has been seen, should be
" Uhwawi ;" secondly, Agbome conquered Kana ; and
thirdly, they have hardly ever been at peace till the
present century.

As the History proves, Kana was a settlement

* "Mina" must not be confounded with Dutch Elmina, on the Gold
Coast ; it refers to Elmina Chica, on the Slave Coast. Locally all the
peoples between Little Popo and Accra are called " Mina."

When Dahoman kings fail to capture an attacked place, they erect at
one of the capitals a palace which is dubbed after the victor, and
this satisfies the vanquished. Hence, because Dahome was defeated by
Ashanti, the Kumasi palace at Agbome was added to the older establishments. Mr. Duncan errs (vol. ii., p. 274) when stating of the latter,

claimed of old by the independent "Oyos," or Eyeos,*
the northern and equestrian Yombas.   The Dahomans,
since the days of Agaja (A.D. 1708—1730), agreed to
pay to them an annual tribute in November, and the
failure of this subsidy invariably brought on a war.
When Tegbwesun (the Bossa Ahadee, of our writers),
about 1738, refused his contribution, Kana was plun-

"This palace was built and named about the time when the present king
(Gezo) threw off his allegiance to the kingdom of Ashantee, the king of
which formerly boasted that he could hold Dahomey in vassalage."

   * The word "Eyeo" has greatly vexed West African writers before the
days of Clapperton and Lander. D'Anville uses Gogo ; Rennell, Gugoo ;
Adams (1823) writes it "Hio." The "History of Dahomey" (1793)
gives us Yahoo (from Snelgrave) ; Oyeo and Okyou (Barbot) ; Eyeo
(Dalzel) ; and, in conclusion, they confound it with Anago, or the Egba
country. "Probably this may be the kingdom of Gago (Kuku, or
Gugoo !), which lies to the northward of Dahomey eight or ten days'
journey. The Moorish aspirated sound of G being nearly like a hard
H, as in the word George, spelt jorje by the Spaniards, and pronounced
Horké, or Horché ; whence Gago may have been sounded Haho, Haiho,
or Haiko." Admirable reasoning ! Mr. Norris's map places the Ayoes
or Eyeos north of Lagos, which is not far wrong. Bosman speaks of an
invasion of Ardra, in 1698, by a powerful inland people, which some
conjecture to be the "Eyeos." Oyo (pronounced Awyaw), *alias*
Katanga, was the capital of Yoruba Proper on the northern region,
destroyed in 1835 by the Moslem Fulas, and still, I believe, a heap of
ruins. When the falling structure crumbled, the maritime provinces
asserted their independence, and have ever since preserved it. The History gives wonderful accounts of Oyo's former power. It frequently sent
forth 100,000 horsemen. The general, it is said, used to spread a thick
buffalo-hide before his tent and make the soldiery pass between two
spears till a hole had been worn in it. When greater undertakings
were in prospect, two hides used thus to be treated.

dered ; in 1747 the foe retired after being duly
satisfied. The Oyos must have been troublesome
neighbours to Dahome, ever demanding increase of
supplies, interfering in domestic policy, harassing
them by constant wars, and assuring the Southrons
that " Dahome belonged to Eyeo." Mr. Norris, writing in 1772, shows that the town was in Dahoman
hands, but it has doubtless frequently been taken and
retaken.

Early in the present century, King Gezo (who came
to the throne in 1818) seized his opportunity, and after
hard fighting, finally drove out the warlike Oyos, who
were sinking before the Fula or Moslem movement in
the north,* and distributed the tribute amongst his
people,—one of his proudest achievements. He made
Kana a kind of *villagiatura* for the Court, free and easy
as such country quarters generally are, and resided in
it when his troops went forth to their lesser wars. The
remnant of the Oyo population was enlisted in his
army, and was well-nigh killed out during the attack
upon Abeokuta in 1851. And that the subjugation
of so terrible an enemy might not be forgotten by his
dynasty, Gezo—not his son, as the missionaries believe,

* See " Wanderings in West Africa."—Abeokuta, Chap. V.

—then instituted a sacrifice at Kana, which opens as it were the customs of Agbome. The victims are made to personate in dress and avocation Oyos, a pastoral and agricultural people.*

There is little to be seen at Kana, a wall-less scatter of huts and houses, thickening as usual around the palace and the market-places, and straggling over some three miles of ground. The population may at usual times amount to 4000, about one-third that of Whydah.† According to some enthusiastic travellers, the cultivation rivals that of the Chinese ; at present

* It is called Gezo's custom, and is performed at Kana, not at Agbome. Mr. Bernasko saw it in May, 1863 ; he describes it thus : " Near the second side of the (palace) wall were eleven platforms, erected on poles about forty feet high. On each of these was the dead body of a man in an erect position, clothed in the native style, each having in his hand a calabash or similar vessel, filled with oil, grain, or some other produce of the country. One was represented leading a sheep, also dead. All this was intended to illustrate that at Canna, of which they (the Dahomans) are now masters, they were once obliged to pay tribute." The Kana custom is described by Mr. Duncan, vol. i., p. 219. In his day the bodies had been exposed about two moons and a half, till the skin, from exposure, had turned nearly to the colour of that of a white man. " The vulture was industriously endeavouring to satisfy his appetite, but the heat of the sun had dried the skin so as to make it impenetrable to his efforts."

† No reliance can be placed upon native or quasi-native estimate of numbers, especially in towns. The traveller is reduced to the rude experiment of counting houses, and multiplying by what he learns to be the average household.

all such art has been lost. The situation is low; the air hot, humid, and unwholesome; the sea-breeze somewhat tempers the day, but the nights are extremely oppressive, and during the rains, fevers are rife.

About one mile to the south-westward of the English house is an old palace of a Dahoman king, by some named Agaja, by others Tegbwesun. It was in poor condition; in many places the wall was tattered, in others patched with matting, and the interior was a mass of bush and jungle. As usual, however, the entrances were kept in repair, and the ground before them was swept and sprinkled every morning by slaves established for that purpose. There is a tradition that the founder of this decayed palace lies here buried : if so, the remains have been removed to the great Agbome palace, where there is a single " family vault."

CHAPTER VIII.

THE PROCESSION.

ON Saturday, December 19th—Ember Day, it will be remembered—we prepared for the penance of reception. An early visit was paid by the King's chief physician and archi-magus, Buko-no Uro; a thin, dark, and somewhat castey-looking senior. He was close shaven, to hide the frostiness of his wool; simply clad in white shorts, and in a large silk cloth with none but the ordinary silver ornaments. He looked somewhat leaner than before, probably the result of his latest nuptials with one of the King's stalwart daughters. This personage came of course solely to renew old ties, to apologise for not having built a proper house, and to inquire about every one's health, from the most Exalted of the Empire to my humble self. The real errand at once peeped out : Harpagon* wanted a list of presents, and

* There is this kind of man at every negro court. The "Narrative of

was especially curious to know whether various items
specified to Commodore Wilmot, chiefly a carriage and
pair, were *en route*. After reading out to him the
official document touching these matters, he allowed for
a time the subject to lie, resolved to stir it up again at
the earliest opportunity. By way of showing friendship he announced that our reception would take place
to-day, and that on the morrow we should proceed to
Agbome : he also declared in an off-hand manner that,
even before presentation at the palace, we might walk
about when and where we pleased. Kana, I have said,
is country quarters ; the sort of state imprisonment
with which visitors are honoured at Agbome, is not the
rule here. He therefore graciously granted us no favour,
but our right, with which he departed, telling us to eat
and dress at once, as the King was preparing for our
reception.

I knew well from experience that these ceremonies
never take place, except in some emergency, before the
afternoon. Moreover, it is the first wish of every
Dahoman official to hurry "his strangers" as much as
possible for two reasons. The minor is, that by making

the Portuguese Expedition of 1798-99 " exactly describes Buko-no-Uró
in the person of " Fumo Anceva," at the Court of the Muata Cazembe.

white men, especially in uniform, sit for a few hours in the open air fronting a mud wall, called a palace, he enhances the opinion of his power amongst the people. The major is, his desire to make favour with the King, who when issuing from the interior wishes to be received by the visitors, and looks crookedly at the "minister" if they be not present. Something must be added on the score of African brain-looseness : these people have as little idea of time as of numbers.* The stranger, however, must be prepared to do battle with this nuisance from the beginning, and the struggle will endure unto the bitter end, when dismissal brings matters to a crisis. I ended by proposing that for the future a messenger should be sent direct by the King, not by the landlord as at present, to inform visitors that the hour of attendance was at hand. But, even should this be granted, the messenger will have, to some extent, the same inducements as has the landlord in discomforting visitors.

Under the then circumstances, So-kun, our guide, began, about 10 A.M., the systematic African worry-

* When Commodore Wilmot was at Agbome he gave silver watches to many of the chiefs. The main-springs were all broken at the first opportunity, but they did not the less "sport" these ornaments on all public occasions.

ing :* it was, however, of no avail, and we put off the evil
time till 1 P.M., which proved to be only one hour too
soon. The business of the day was to begin with the procession of Caboceers, a ceremony as old as the time of
Mr. Norris, who has left a notice of it. Followed by new
and handsome hammocks, we were conducted to the
Gbwe-hun-'li,† a clear space partially shaded with ragged
trees : it is about 100 paces N.N.E. of the " English
House," and for many generations it has been the seat
of these operations. Then ranging our sticks facing
northwards, we formed the focus of stare and gaze, the
smaller rabble being as usual conspicuous. Two Klan,
or Ai-hun-da-to,‡ jesters, came up, and in hopes of dole
did their best to amuse us. These African "Sutari"
are like the guiriots or buffoons, those Senegal profes-
sionals, who mingle in every crowd, and whose sole
object in life is to make men laugh. Ever racking their
wits to please, they evince the true negro poverty of
invention : there is a lack of variety in their tricks

* The African keeps you waiting with an exemplary *calme*: if you
keep *him* waiting he shows all the restiveness of a wild animal. This
is generally the case with barbarians ; I have remarked it in the South
of Europe.

† Meaning bush (gbwe), cotton-tree (hun), road ('li, for ali).

‡ Klan is a jester, a clown ; ái (heart), hun (drum), dá (play), to
(father).

which soon renders them lively as a professionally engaged mourner or a Turkish mute. Some of them take to the trade early in life, they are in fact born and hereditary buffoons. They are remarkable for their ugliness, to which they add by white-washing face, arms, and legs. The staple of their entertainment consists in " making faces," as children say, wrinkling foreheads ; protruding tongues, and clapping jaws like apes ; in a little rude tumbling,* in ugly dancing and agitating the clunes, in drawing in the belly to show emptiness, in smoking a bone or bit of cassava by way of pipe, in producing from huge bags † yams and maize paste, of which they bolted mouthfuls, or by pretending to be deaf and dumb—a favourite trick here. They offered us some provisions, and we had the laugh against them by accepting and passing them on to our servants ; and they imitated my notes by scratching a sweet potato with a stick. I need not add that they are bull beggars all.

* The "cartwheel" is here called " alogwe"; by the Egbas, " okiti."
† These wallets are of three kinds: the single bag of skin, called "glo ; " the large double pouch of the same material, known as " akpa-taklo ; " and the cloth sack named " vâté."

The History tells us that jesters used to amuse Agaja the Conqueror, by swallowing tubs full of frumenty, and that these men generally stuffed themselves to death in a few years.

Shortly after we had taken our seats appeared, borne
aloft on a negro's head, a table which was fated to be
one of our best friends in Dahome. It was a venerable article, once intended for cards, but the violent
hands of the *negraille* had long ago denuded it of green
baize, had stripped off its veneer, and had reduced its
single leg to a singularly smashed and shaky state. A
glance at it never failed to elicit a request for a new
"tavo," and a reminder that the Commodore had promised a *remplaçant*. After two or three had puzzled
their brains for a quarter of an hour with the intricate
problem of opening it, another would produce from a
calico-covered calabash sundry case and other bottles
of gin and similar spirits, sometimes wine, and always
tolerably pure water, from the palace. These elements
of endurance were supplied to us with a praiseworthy
regularity : hardly did we take our seats on any occasion
when lo ! the table. The King seemed to be pleased
by our appreciating the contents of his cellar : he
frequently sent us messages bidding us not to spare
them, and, though the Landlord frowned, I took especial
care to make our followers invariably empty whatever
was set before us. As a rule, the whites, even the French,
and the mulattos engaged in the *comercio*, are so over-

awed by the presence of one " whose smile is life and whose frown is death," that they would never venture upon such a liberty, consequently the King thinks that they fear him.

Presently a hum of voices from the north answered the first of the salutes. Under two tent umbrellas, one virgin white and the other figured,* and accompanied by two courtiers, walked the bearer of the royal cane, Bosu Sau.† He is a half-brother to the king; dark, not ill-looking, but showing no resemblance to the ruler. Followed by his band, drums and rattles, and by his armed escort, he advanced, snapped fingers with us, and presented the stick. We drank with him three toasts,

* In this land the umbrella is a rude kind of curiologics, faintly resembling European blazonry, and an armorist could tell the troops from the flag. In symbolism they precede Mexican writing. The newly-made Caboceer is presented with a virgin-white article of palace manufacture, and he is expected to illustrate it by his actions. The principal figures are knives and decapitated heads and faces, cut out of cloth and sewn on the alternate lappets of the valance. The knives are straight, and shaped like a butcher's, the handle blue, the blade red. The face is ruddy, with white eyes; and the head, which is clean cut off at the neck, wears an azure cap shaped like the East Indian ear-cloth.

† The king's eldest brother, Godo, is never seen in public. A tall, dark, and unprepossessing man, and a notable drunkard, he was set aside by his father, who, after the affair at Abeokuta, nominated his second son, Gelele, as the most likely of the family. In any Asiatic country such a senior brother would certainly be put to death, and in many the younger brothers would be either blinded or be rendered imbecile by medicines. So far Dahome is mild in her manners.

beginning with his master's health. A salute was then fired, and presently Bosu Sau and his chiefs sat down upon their tall Gold Coast stools placed on our left, and thus forming part of an oval opening north, where the saluters presented themselves.

Then the companies began to pass round, and first those of Whydah. In all these displays it is "funeral order," juniors first. A white umbrella, a pair of silver horns,* announced Nulofren, who, habited in the costume of the day, an armless tunic of red and yellow striped silk, was bestriding a little nag. After the latter had been led three times round us with a halter, and the equestrian had thrice waved hand to us as he passed the opening of the spectator-ring, he was lifted off by a pair of slaves. His fifty soldiers then formed line, whilst their commander advanced and bowed ; he then danced and fired a gun, the rest presenting arms ; finally, he snapped fingers, made compliments, and retired to the enjoyment of stool and umbrella. Such was the programme of the whole affair, whose resemblance to European tactics suggested imitation.

* Many are made of tin. There are two shapes: one, the thimble-formed, with lateral openings ; the other, somewhat like a small mushroom or a giraffe's horn, with ridgelets radiating from the centre of the domelet.

Nulofren was followed by Nuage, of Whydah, another half-brother of the king, a tall, dark, thin man, with a chief's silver armlets and thread pigtail depending down his dorsum. He rode past smoking a pipe.

The third was "the place"—meaning a confidential slave—of Wenu, who was unable to be present. He rode past, waved hands, danced, fired, and took his seat on our left; not however, like the caboceers, upon a chair.

The fourth was the Prince Chyudaton, a caboceer of note and influence, one of the king's many cousins, supposed to possess the ear of royalty, and lately appointed second Yevogan of Whydah. He is a young man, tall and well made, of coaly complexion, broad-faced, and with a prepossessing expression. The English subjects speak highly of him : the French, whose "landlord" he is, declare him to be cunning and interested. He certainly knows the habits of white men, and it was long ago proposed that he should visit England, the principal advantage being that after return he might venture upon the truth, which a meaner man would not dare before royalty.* When this was

* As will appear, the highest officials in the land (excepting only the blood royal) are *bonâ fide* slaves to the king, and therefore cannot say what they please.

mentioned to the King, he readily consented, declaring, however, that he must retain as hostages Mrs. Bernasko and her children. I much regretted not seeing more of this young man, but the jealousy of the " English landlord" managed successfully to isolate me. On the present occasion Chyudaton was smoking a bad Bahia cigar,—a bit of civilisation to be expected from one so conversant with " European society"; he wore a tunic of green silk, and his decoration was a pair of mushroom horns. He performed the decapitation dance, looking most amiable the while.

The French and English flags, preceding a company of dancing soldiery, announced the Yevogan, or viceroy of Whydah. In contrast with his lieutenant he is the old school of Gezo's officials, and he is perhaps the worst type. He was born at the hereditary little village * of his family, Dokon, about two miles to the east of the Kana Gate of Agbome. His appearance revolts: it is a compound of a bovine cerebellum, a deeply-wrinkled brow villainously low, a double prognathousness, massive lips with bad lines, thick-lidded, blear and yellow eyes, and the expression of a satyr. Mr. Duncan

---

* It consists of a number of thatches enclosed in a clay wall and surrounded by fine palm plantations.

found him an " excellent fellow," which in one sense is true. He is as bad as he looks, and his avarice is only to be equalled by his rapacity. If two strangers dispute at Whydah, 500 dollars for instance being the subject, and the litigants proceed to the Yevogan for justice; he at once confiscates half the amount in question to the King, that is to say, to himself; and a third quarter will certainly disappear amongst the caboceers and Fetishmen.* Until lately he has, like all the older officials, known white men only as slavers, and as the most abject order of traders. He treats every one with equal superciliousness. This insolence has more than once brought him into trouble, and in May last he was placed under arrest in his own house for incivility to strangers. Yet he is ever rude of manner, and requires to be treated in kind: " civil or rough," as

* The consequence is, that white men for the most part, and black men when they dare, take their own measures at Whydah. Before my arrival a merchant shipmaster having been robbed by a mulatto clerk, put him into the hands of a Brazilian slaver. The latter hung up the culprit by the thumbs and lashed his wrists tight to a pole, pouring upon them a powdered wood like sand, which caused the flesh to swell with intolerable pain. It reminded me of the days of 1724-25, when John Gow, the pirate, would not plead. " The judge ordered that his thumbs should be squeezed by two men with a whipcord till it did break, and then it should be doubled till it did again break, and then laid threefold, and that the executioners should pull with their whole strength."

the occasion requires, but much more of the latter than
of the former. On this occasion he wore, as a white
man, a felt hat, which he doffed to us thrice ; then,
dancing a few steps, he came forward to snap fingers,
and attempted, partly in jest but much in earnest, to
pull us from our seats.

The caboceers were followed by the companies,
of which the first was that of the Ahanjito or
singers and of the Hunto or drummers ; in fact,
the local bards, troubadours, or laureates, who are
not less powerful in Dahome than in other wild
lands, from Wales to Nepaul. The distinguishing
mark was the horse-tail " chauri," with a man's
jawbone above the handle. They were preceded
by nine " fancy flags," * adorned with all manner of
figures, animate and inanimate, cut out of coloured
cloth and sewn upon the plain ground. These were
followed by a truly barbarous display : eight human
crania dished up on small wooden bowls like bread-
plates, at the top of very tall poles,—a ninth remaining

* The favourite ornament of the flag, like the umbrella, is a blue-
handled red-bladed knife on each alternate valance-flap, the other being
occupied by decapitated heads wearing the East Indian kan-top, or ear-
cap, which the Egbos call " filla," having probably derived it from the
Fulas.

ominously ungarnished. After passing round in review without umbrellas, the musical warriors, who are *preux chevaliers* and extra-doughty worthies, formed line opposite me, and waving their " chauris," sang to a pretty tune certain words in my praise,*—

Burton (pronounced Batunu), he hath seen all the world with its kings and caboceers :
He now cometh to see Dahome, and he shall see everything here.

They were dressed in rich silks, and eleven of them wore horns. After dancing solos they sat down on our right, where before stood the common herd of gazers, chiefly boys.

Then, preceded by the Union Jack (why ?) and four flags, came the Akho-'si—" King wife,"—or Eunuch

* As these people have no written language, anything that happens in the kingdom, from the arrival of a stranger to an earthquake, is formed into a kind of song, which, rhythmless and rhymeless, is taught to professional men, and is thus transmitted to posterity.

The stranger, however, may find himself strangely named. European nomenclature not being pleasant to negro ears and tongues, every white man in the land has, as on the Gold Coast, a nickname. The Father Superior of the French mission is known as Nyan gli—" Padre Curto," opposed to a tall brother, Nyan gágá, " Long father." Another missionary, M. L——, being of highly nervous temperament, was dubbed Penan, or papaw leaf, which resembles the aspen. Mr. Beecham, being much addicted to meat, and walking about with rounded shoulders, became Kpon 'akra, the hunchback-vulture. I at once was known as Kwabna, Tuesday, from landing at Whydah on that day, and afterwards as " Ommoba," from a well-known Fanti character.

Company. There were three chiefs, two in black felt and one in horns; the corps, however, is no longer distinguished, as in the days of the History, by carrying bright iron rods. The head man presented the royal stick, whereupon I rose and drank to the King's health. He then informed me that he had been commissioned by the Chief Eunuch, the principal palace dignitary, to guide my steps.

The rest of the pageant was a rapid pass round of the *corps d'élite*. My Blue, or English escort of the last day, with their Colonel, Anaufen, in a cap of crimson velvet, followed an unfurled flag, fired, and saluted. The Achi, or bayoneteers, were headed by their commander in a man o' war's man's cap, about twenty in number; they were tall, large, and evidently picked men, dressed in blue cloth tunics, and armed with heavily loaded guns. They are recognised by a kind of eye on their conical caps, also of blue cloth, two horizontal parentheses of white, and a dark central dot.* Followed a few carbineers, whose half-shaven heads showed them to be slaves of the palace : they are

---

* The first bayoneteers were organised by the old Meu, or second minister, in the days of King Gezo: at first they were 200 in number. The reader will bear in mind that the *corps d'élite* and the officers in the Dahoman army are the same amongst the women as amongst the men.

known as Zo-hu-nun—" Fire at the foe's front." A white flag with a blue anchor at the end of a waving red stripe, denoted the Gan' u' nlan Company, the "Conquerors of all animals," so called from the size of their guns, which are expected to kill, not to wound :* forming part of the artillery with the Agbáryá,† or blunderbuss men ; they are chosen for size and strength, and much prefer themselves to the commonalty of the army. They followed a tattered Jack and a fancy flag, and their chiefs bowed to us, whilst the men, resting the butt upon the ground, fired resonant charges.

At 2 p.m., when the review was over, the Yevogan again came up, shook hands with us, and preceded by the most numerous of the companies, his own men, set out palacewards, leaving us to follow.

All our party then formed file, led by the youth Buko, carrying the King's cane which had reached us at Whydah, by So-kun, the English guide, and by the

* Gan'u (conquering), nlan (any animal). Thus I explain Mr. Duncan, vol. i., p. 236 : " Next came a regiment belonging to a country called Ginoa, commanded by a female of the same name. This regiment consisted only of 300 women. This corps make no prisoners, but kill all."

† This word must not be confounded with agbájá, a cartridge-box, which Mr. Duncan (vol. i., p. 226) erroneously writes agbwadya.

solemn eunuch De-Adán-de. Mr. Hilton preceded the hammocks with the flag of St. George, followed by the Reverend Bernasko, supported on both sides by Beecham and Valentine.* I went next with my armed Krumen in bright caps and "Pagnes ; " behind me was Mr. Cruikshank, then Governor Mark, and lastly the boy Tom. Between the ceremonial trees of Gbwehun-'li and the palace of Banyàmme,† the distance is about a quarter of an hour in hammocks : the different interruptions multiplied it by three ; at every 100 yards a 3-pounder ship's swivel fired a blank shot, and was carried on the shoulder of a single porter to the next station. The direction was north, with a little westing. A broad well-worn and carefully cleaned road—all those about Kana are the same—hard with water-rolled pebbles, wound through grass plots, scatterings of wild cotton heaps, and tufts of croton (*Croton tiglium*), between fields of maize and " thur" (*Cajanus indicus*), and

* Mr. Duncan (vol. i., p. 216) was " amused by the vanity of the old governor of Whydah," who showed a great anxiety to precede him, with a view of showing superiority, and, presently riding up, ordered to the rear his attendant, who seemed mortified. In Dahome the introducer precedes the presentee, but not with any idea of superiority.

† Or Banyañyamme, a strong name given by the builder, Gezo, when he was substituted for his eldest brother. It is not intelligible to my interpreters.

under the noble trees detaching the divers homesteads. An abundance of Fetish was also present.

Presently we struck upon the eastern angle of the palace. These buildings in Dahome are all made upon the same pattern : a swish wall of five courses or steps,* about 20 ft. high, forms the enceinte ; in many places it appears ruinous ; it shows patches of matting, and when new ground is taken in, a fresh palm fence denotes that labour is deferred to another day. The shape is an irregular square or broken oblong, and the circumference must be sufficient to contain the wives, soldieresses, and female slaves, composing the *personnel* of the feminine court. The gates vary in number; they are usually from eight to ten. They are thatched sheds about 100 ft. long, built against the clay wall, and 60 ft. to 70 ft. high ; though the roof ridge is tall enough for two stories, the deep and solid eaves rest upon posts barely 4 ft. tall, planted at 14 to 15 ft. from the back wall, and the two nearest the entrance are provided with earth benches.† The slanting roof

* In Dahome these swish steps are called "ko-hwe." The palace and the city gates are allowed five ; chiefs have four tall or five short, and all others three, or as the King directs. The singbome, or double-storied building, 30 to 40 feet high, and described by old visitors at Kana, no longer exists.

† Locally called "Pwé," the Abeokutan "Okpo."

of thick grass is kept in position by stout bamboo splints. Inside, the ground is raised about 1 ft. ; the material is a stiff red loam, in parts rudely pipeclayed. Outside the entrance there are invariably two stunted and pollarded trees, here as favourite a fashion as formerly in France ; and often a pole connecting them forms a gallows, from which jo-susu, vo-sisa, or Fetish calabashes, and other talismans depend. Each tree also has its bundle of Bo-sò, or Bo-sticks,*—truncheons, 3 to 4 ft. long, zebra'd or spotted with red and white, and at times inscribed with Moslem prayers ; they resembled on a small scale the barber's pole of old England and modern America. The external gateways act as guardhouses : in the interior, as far as can be seen, they correspond with the external, and the King always receives in these barn-like sheds. After the fashion of the old Whydah rulers, he is ever changing his sleeping apartment.†

* For an explanation of the Bo Fetish, see Chap. XVII.

† The only Englishman known to have been admitted into the king's sleeping chamber was Mr. Norris, who, in 1773, described it as a neat detached room, separated from the court in which it stood by a breast-high wall, the top of which was stuck full of human jawbones. The little area within it was paved with the skulls of neighbouring princes and chiefs, placed there that the king might trample upon them.

After a few minutes we arrived at the Akoreha,* or eastern market, where we were received by a consistory of Bo Fetishmen ; on their right were holy women in decent garb, petticoated to the ancles, and distinguished by flowers in the hair, and long necklaces of cowries. The chief carried by way of sceptre a wonderfully worked axe of bright brass, called by the people Asiovi, and known to the Portuguese as Facão de Bo. Lustily cheered we passed the several gates of the palace, each showing from one to three umbrellas of the guard, the captains on chairs, and the men on the ground sitting motionless with guns and blunderbusses pointed skywards, and like a picadil of spears. Turning down another open space, called Ajyako, we proceeded to the Addogwin, or western market. I did not recognise a place once familiar to my eyes : the palace fence of dry brown palm-leaves had disappeared for a bran-new dark-green matting, and the form of the clearing had changed : nothing recalled the old locality but a huge tree on the north side.

When opposite the western or main gate, the usual large barn-like thatched shed, supported on posts, we

---

* This is said to be a Whydah word, the name of a town " broken " by one of the elder kings.

dismounted, as is the custom, to make *congées*. On the right were two duck-guns, and a *machine infernale* with five bell-mouthed brass barrels, mounted on a dwarf bed,* and with a single flint lock : on the left were four wall-pieces, and one wooden case, which was probably empty. Twenty-four umbrellas, ranged in line, covered an equal number of the highest digni-taries in the empire. A somewhat lengthy description of this place will be required : it is the fac-simile in male of the feminine palace-interior, and it represents the soldiery of Dahome, minus the King, halted or encamped upon the line of march.

The army, or, what is nearly synonymous, the nation of Dahome, is divided, both male and female, into two wings—the Right and the Left.† They are so called from their relative position to the throne, which here was represented by the entrance dividing the captains and their retainers into two bodies.

The right or senior wing is commanded, *ex officio*, by the Min-gan,‡ the first of the two great Bonugan

---

* Apparently a favourite old weapon. Mr. Norris mentions, in 1772, a " blunderbuss with five barrels."

† There are no regiments, properly so called, as supposed by Mr. Duncan.

‡ Said to mean " we are all captains." The word is variously spelt Miegan, Minghan, and by the History, Tamegan. The Abeokutans call him the " Otton."

or civilian captains " of the outside." He is therefore the Premier of the empire amongst men ; * the she-Min-gan, being within the palace, takes precedence of him. He leads in the field the first battalion of the right wing, and, as head of the police, he is supposed to speak from the people to the King. Being *exécuteur des hautes œuvres*, he is also entitled " Men-wu-to, or man-slayer ; and, as he kills for the king proper, in the case of sacrificial or distinguished deaths he is expected to use his own hands, leaving the humbler sort to his assistants. The present " *M. de Dahome* " is a tall, dark, thin old man, by no means decrepid, with a neat and well-made small cranium, but decidedly the look of a headsman. I have said all Dahoman officials are in double pairs : his lieutenant is the Adanejan (by the English called " Adonijah "), the " King's Cousin," and a favourite at court. The woman Min-gan is Gundeme,† and she has an assistant.

* M. Wallon erroneously ranks the Mingan after the Meu. He makes the same mistake in saying that the Gau and the Po-su are equal. Mr. Duncan (p. 231) casually alludes to the " Me-gah, the King's principal jailer," and as wrongly tells us " the higher officers of the household are allowed to adopt their official titles as their family names (N.B., there are none), Mayho (for " *the* Meu ") being in the Dahoman language, Prime Minister."

† She is thus alluded to by Mr. Duncan, vol. i. p. 248 : " The head or commander of one of his majesty's female regiments, named Godthimay."

Under the Min-gan, or civilian Premier, is the Gau,* or leader of the second battalion of the right wing, and military Commander-in-Chief. He is, in the absence of the Min-gan, the head of the Ahwan-gan,† or war captains of the outside. The present officer is a tall and large old man, with a wrinkled forehead, nervous and ricketty : it is almost time that he should "go to sleep." His second in command is the Matro, brother to the present King. The corresponding officer amongst the Amazons is known as Khe-tun-gan,‡ and her deputy is the Zokhenu.§

The chief civilian Captain of the Left is the Meu,∥ who is the second subject in the empire. He speaks from the King to the people, collects the revenues, receives tribute, declares war, appoints, according to some, the Gau and the Po-su, and has the charge of all

* There are many ways of writing this word. Commissioner Forbes prefers Agaow, M. Wallon, Gao, and the History, Agaow, with a suspicion of derivation from the Turkish Agha!

† Ahwan (war), and gan (a captain). This rank includes all officers that can bring ten to a hundred dependants or slaves into the field.

‡ Meaning Khe (bird), tun (hammering), and gàn (metal).

§ The Zoheino of the History.

∥ The word is said to mean "his raiment fits him." It is spelt with more or less error, Mayho, Mayhoo, Mahu, Mehou (there is no aspirate, but a diæresis), and Mayo. The Egbas of Abeokuta translate the title "Osin."

strangers visiting the King. He also executes the
criminals of Addo-Kpon, the Bush King, an institution
which, with the reader's leave, I will explain at a future
time.* The present tenant of office was once celebrated for his memory, and could so class facts that he
never forgot name or event : with the poor mnemoni-
cal aid of a few beans or seeds he managed the complicated affairs of Dahome. In those days his power was
great, and he required to be bought at a high price.
He is now an old, old man,† with hollow cheeks and
toothless gums, which make his mouth appear lipless—
the only predicament which produces this phenomenon in
Africa. He easily forgets ; he appears to be half asleep ;
and he is manifestly becoming childish. The King has
occasionally hinted at his retirement; but the decrepid
senior clamours to be kept on, declaring, perhaps
truly, that do-nothingness would kill him : his exceeding rapacity and big eye ‡ would, if unglutted, certainly

* Mr. Duncan (vol. i. pp. 250—251), describes a horrible scene "in
which poor old Mayho, who is an excellent man, was the proper exe-
cutioner."

† Eight years ago, M. Wallon made him ninety. But negro longevity is
very uncertain in these lands, where, to sum up the almost diabolical
wisdom of the white man, people say "He knows his own age."

‡ Covetousness: a common Ffon phrase is, " E su nukun " (he has a
big eye). Mr. Duncan (vol. i. p. 217), calls him an " excellent old man,

cause his death.   But he has served as a " politic
blade" many a king.   At times he waxes bright, and
calls to mind the Captain Springatha so facetiously
depicted by the commander of the "Hannibal of London."
His favourite garb is an unclean shirt, an alpaca jacket
worn to rustiness, and broad silver armlets—Mr. Duncan's " silver gauntlets"—upon the brown sleeves, when
he manages to look exceedingly mean.   His lieutenant
is styled the Bi-wan-ton.*   Though not of royal blood,
he has lately succeeded to the name and rank of a
nephew of the King who debauched the twin princesses due in marriage to the Min-gan and the Meu.
The culprit is imprisoned, but, as a scion of royalty, he
receives food from his own house, and he is allowed
a single slave.   No intercourse with his wives is permitted.   Thus his greatest punishment is what we
administer to our convicts gratis.   The corresponding
officer among the Amazons is known as the Akpa-
dume,† and her deputy is the Fosupo.‡

and very different from the generality of uncivilised Africans, not having
that covetous and selfish disposition usual with them." Now it is
notoriously the contrary.

  * Bi (all), wan (love), ton (belonging to), meaning that the King's
love is over all those whom he has made.

  † Hence Mr. Duncan's Apadomey regiment, and Apadomey soldiers
(vol. i. pp. 232, 233).   ‡ The Phussopoh of the History.

Under the Meu, and related to him, as the Gau is to the Min-gan, ranks the Po-su.* He may also be described as the head war-man to the Meu, under the Commander-in-Chief. The present incumbent is by no means of prepossessing presence. He is a youngish warrior, black, lean, and muscular. The loss of an eye when Gezo attacked Abeokuta, adds to his scowling look. He appears ever sick or surly; and his wool, worn longer than usual, stands upright in little tufts and pigtails, like a thrum mop. His lieutenant is the Ahwigbamen, one of the King's brothers. Under the Po-su ranks the Ajyaho, the "Jahou" of the History, and there called "Captain of Horse." Though not a neuter, he is the chief of the eunuchs, whose offences he punishes. He swears witnesses, and he has medicines to elicit the truth.

These high officials, the Min-gan and Meu, the Gau and Po-su, or one of them, failing the Ajyaho, lead the four battalions which the Dahoman army numbers, in the field. The Amazons are, it has been seen, similarly conducted.

The third personage in the realm is the Yevo-gan,

---

* I have alluded to this dignitary in Chapter II. The name is written by Commander Forbes, Possoo, and by M. Wallon, Poissou.

whose functions I have described. By the state law of Dahome, as at Benin, all men are slaves to the King, and most women are his wives. The blood-royal is the only freedom in the country, and it probably does not exceed two thousand souls.

After the Bonu-gans, the Owu-tu-nun (royal attendants), and the Ahwan-gan, rank the Akhi 'sino,* or great traders, who pay over duties to the King. They are in fact the "merchant princes" of Dahome, and they certainly lead a more useful life than the Ahwan-gan, or military class, which will do nothing but eat and drink, dance, make war, and attend Customs. In the fifth rank are the petty governors and captains, to whom the King gives the insignia and the property of their predecessors, and who are degraded for the most trifling reasons—the neglect of some ceremonial, or the evil report of a messenger.

Returning to the western part of the palace, where sits the little host of high officials, we find them inspecting their retainers, especially the companies which had saluted us. These militia troops were marching round, singing, dancing, firing, and performing other evolutions distinguished by immense noisi-

* Akhi (market), si for asi (a wife), no (mother).

ness. We finished in hammocks our three official tours of the Addogwin market-place, each time stopping to salute the Sublime Porte. At 2·45 P.M., after the last salutation, we retired about a hundred yards, and, facing eastward, sat down till summoned to " the presence."

The heat was excessive, and the dancers' dust stained us red. After half-an-hour, a silver bell and a pair of horns hurrying up, motioned us to arise and advance. This person was the To-no-nun, or chief eunuch, whose functions, including those of his brother official, the Kan-gbo-de, must, at the risk of wearying the reader, be explained before I can hope to make the interior of the palace intelligible. So complicated are the various offices and the ceremonious receptions amongst these people, who own no other study in life !

The To-no-nun* is the chief of the Owu-tu-nun,† or body attendants upon the sovereign, the others being the Binazun, the Buko-no, and their followers. This head eunuch is the fourth personage in the realm—royalty not

* To (town), no (mother), nun (mouth), meaning that all must obey him. Commissioner Forbes writes the word Toononoo, and M. Wallon, who understood even less of the language, Tolonnou.

† From Owu (a body). These personal attendants are entirely distinct from the warriors.

included. He is the minister of the palace interior,
beyond which his authority does not extend ; he attends
the King's person, and on great occasions he interprets
between the women officers and strangers. Outside, he
commands the corp of eunuchs, who have an especial
residence in the city. During the late Gezo's reign, he
was on great occasions the organ of communication
between his master and the Meu ; it was also his duty
to rinse out the glasses in which toasts were drunk, and
to swallow the water, a custom now obsolete. The
present incumbent is very old, with a peculiarly baboon-
like countenance, and it is hardly possible to distinguish him from a senior of the other sex. He affects
silver horns and a blue broadcloth long coat, of quasi-
European cut, which, trivial as the comparison may
appear, forces upon the mind the idea of a magnified
bluebottle fly ; and he loves to buzz about as fast as his
emaciated limbs can carry him. He had a narrow
escape at the accession of the present ruler : properly
speaking, he should have accompanied his liege lord to
Deadland. Gezo, however, left express orders that he
must be spared, lest, in the hands of a young and
inexperienced king, the ceremonial of the Dahoman
Court might suffer let or change. He is now safe, as

he is held to have been re-emplaced by the Gbwe-wedo,* who is called To-no-nun or chief eunuch " for the present King." By the custom of this strange kingdom there is a chief To-no-nun, eunuchess " of the inside." She is called the Yavedo,† and her second in command, the sub-To-no-nun for the present King, is the Visese-gan.

The Kan-gbo-de ‡ is another personal attendant, whose duties, like those of the To-no-nun, do not extend beyond the palace gates. He is the chief of the royal huissiers, and inspects the guards at the several entrances. He wears round his neck a large silver bell, and his attendants have similar but smaller articles, to proclaim silence before the King speaks : they also precede the royal steps, to remove any sticks or stones likely to offend. The late dignitary attached to the old king used to present strangers ; he was,

---

* " Otton-iweffa," is the title of the second chief eunuch at Yoruban courts.

† Ya (they), vedo (think).

‡ Kan (rope), 'gbo (cut, or finished), and de (octroi, or town dues). This is an enigmatical title, after true Dahoman fashion, alluding to the official having command of the rear guard. When the rope which, stretched across the road, forms the turnpike of these regions, is removed by the master of the custom-house, all can proceed. Commander Forbes spells the word Camboodee, and M. Wallon translates it " Grand Chambellan."

however, permanently degraded for wilfully riding on
horseback up to the royal gate.. The present holder of
the office is a young man, and his assistant, forming the
normal Dahoman "happy pair," is the Kakokpwe, the
dignitary who met us at Whydah. The chief warrior
of the Kan-gbo-de is the Ko-ko'aje, who, having been
captured at the attack on Abeokuta, was bought by a
gentlewoman, and converted into a husband and Abeokutan "gentleman." The Dahomans swear that he must
be retaken.

The Bi-na-zon,* whom the missionaries, ever thinking of Pharaoh, call "chief butler" for the worst of all
possible reasons, is the King's head store-keeper. He
has charge of the royal cloth, cowries, and rum, and
thus he corresponds with our "treasurer." He is a subject, and not of the blood-royal ; but a pleasant fellow
withal. The corresponding officer of the inside, is
called the Vi-de-k'alo.

* Bi (all), na (I), zon (walk).

CHAPTER IX.

THE RECEPTION.

MARSHALLED by "Silver Bell and Giraffe Horns," we entered the royal gate, first removing our swords and closing our umbrellas, which may not appear before the King.* We were told to walk hurriedly across the

---

* The King's name in Dahome must be pronounced with bated breath. For in Dahome the King in his own person absorbs the undivided respect of the people. In England we adhere to the princely name; *e.g.*,

> Nana Sahib rest unsung,
> Let none speak of Badahung,

which is as correctly applied to Gelele as would be "Duke of Clarence" to William IV. after coronation. To utter it in his presence would, in the case of a subject, be death: once crowned, the King must forget his antecedents as an Adeling, and this is the common practice of African monarchs, even to the petty chiefs of the Congo. Many child princes, sons of the actual dynast, have been to my quarters, and have held out the hand for bread: and such a small boy the present ruler once was. Dr. M'Leod, however, errs in stating that the royal relatives, such as half-brothers and sisters, are slaves.

The word Badahung, or Badahong (which M. Wallon writes Budahou, and others Badahou and Badou), is properly Ba (bamboo), do (pushes or poles), hun (the cause): it is, therefore, not very dignified.

nearer half of the palace yard, and presently we halted
at a circle of pure loose white sand, where the ministers
prostrated themselves — silex, not mud, being Court
powder for the great in Dahome.   There we doffed hats
and caps, and waving them in the right hand, bowed
four several times to a figure that was sitting under
the chiar'oscuro of the thatch, and was, we were told,
returning our compliments.

   This preliminary over, we were made to advance
very slowly—the native officials bending almost double,
and uttering in drawn out unison " á—á—á ! " to warn
the Court that others besides the inmates of the palace
were approaching.   A few steps placed us close to the
King, who merits especial notice.

   Gelele,* also known as Dahome-Dadda—the grandfather of Dahome—is in the full vigour of life, from
forty to forty-five, before the days of increasing belly

---

* Gelele is, as we often find amongst kingly names in the Hwe-'gbe-
'ajya dynasty of Dahome, the initial word of a phrase—Gelele (bigness),
ma nyonzi (with no way of lifting). For the strong names or titles,
the curious reader will consult Appendix IV.

   As regards the dynastic name, first assumed by King Aho (Adahoonzou I.), Hwe-'gbe-'ajya, it corresponds with Osai (Osei) of Ashanti,
and may be broadly compared with the Egyptian Pharaoh. The meaning is, Hwe (a fish), egbe (will not enter), ajya (a weir); viz.: If a fish
shun the trap it will not be caught, so no one can do anything
against Dahome.

and decreasing leg. He looks a king of (negro) men, without tenderness of heart or weakness of head, and he appears in form and complexion the κάλλιστος ἀνὴρ of this black Iliad. His person is athletic, upwards of six feet high, lithe, agile, thin flanked and broad shouldered, with muscular limbs, well turned wrists and neat ankles, but a distinctly cucumber-shaped shin. The skull is rounded and well set on: the organs of locality stand prominently out; a slight baldness appears upon the poll, and the "regions of cautiousness" are covered by two cockade-like tufts of hair, mostly worn in Dahome for the purpose of attaching coral, Popo-beads, or brass and silver conelets. His hair, generally close shaven, is of the peppercorn variety, the eyebrows are scant, the beard is thin, and the moustachios are thinner. He has not his father's receding forehead, nor the vanishing chin which distinguishes the multitude : his strong jaw renders the face indeed "jowly" rather than oval, consequently the expression is normally hard, though open and not ill-humoured, whilst the smile which comes out of it is pleasant. His nails are allowed to attain mandarin-length : * the African king must show that he is an

* This length of talon probably suggested to elder travellers the idea

eater of meat, not of "monkey's food"—fruits and vegetables. Moreover, talons are useful amongst ragoûts,
in lands where no man has yet been called *furcifer*.
His sub-tumid lips disclose white, strong, and sound
teeth, the inner surfaces being somewhat blackened by
tobacco. His eyes are red, bleared, and inflamed,
betraying an opacity of the cornea which may end in
blindness. An ophthalmist might here thrive upon the
smallest display of skill. This complaint is not the
gift of rum, for the King is a very moderate drinker,
and prefers wines and beer, of which he has an ample
store, to rum and gin. The glare of the country, the
Harmattan winds, the exposure during the long reception hours, perpetual smoking, and lastly, a somewhat
excessive devotion to Venus, are the causes. The nose
is distinctly *retroussé*, quasi-negro, anti-aquiline, looking
in fact as if all the lines had been turned the wrong
way,—this mean and hideous concave is the African

of a poison-globule stuck under the nail of the little finger, which was
gradually protruded into the calabash or drinking-cup, when the venom
instantly dissolved. Captain Phillips was told by a caboceer of Whydah,
whom he had " well warmed with brandy and other strong liquors (here
the key of most secrets)," that it was brought from a distant inland
country, and that three to four slaves was the price of a single fatal
dose. But brandy has the power of heating the imagination as well as
the other faculties.

substitute for the beautiful, the sympathetic, and the noble convexity of the Caucasian,—but it is not much flattened, nor does it wholly want bridge. The lines of wrinkle subtending the corners of the mouth are deeply, but not viciously, marked : and the same may be said concerning the crumpling of the forehead during momentary excitement. According to some, he is afflicted with chronic renal disease. He has suffered severely from the small-pox—the national scourge— which has by no means spared his race.* The only vestige of tattoo is the usual Dahoman mark, three short parallel and perpendicular lancet cuts, situated nearer the scalp than the eyebrows, a little above the place where the latter meet the zygomata.

---

* We read in the History that the great Agaja was " pitted with the small-pox, or perhaps tattooed in imitation of it, as is customary in the country." And we are especially informed that at Whydah both sexes thus adorned their cheeks and foreheads—a practice now obsolete. The old Dahoman sign was a perpendicular incision between the eyebrows : the women marked the lower parts of the body with various devices. The modern is described in the text. Mr. Duncan (vol i. p. 266), wrongly asserts " the Dahomans are not marked at all, except such marks or tattooing as the parents may choose to inflict on the lower parts of the person by way of ornament." The Alladas used to make an incision in each cheek, turning up the flesh towards the ears, and allowing it to heal in that position—a hideous device also forgotten.

The sixth king, Sinmenkpen (Adahoonzou II.), died of small-pox in 1789. The late Gezo, after marching on Popo, is said to have fallen

M. Wallon, who probably never saw the present ruler, declares that he exactly resembles Gezo, whereas the latter was extremely dark-complexioned.* Also we read of his character : "*Rusé, tenace et très dissimulé, il est aussi plus intéressé que son père, et passe pour très cruel.*" But Gelele always disliked and distrusted Frenchmen—*en animam et mentem !* There can be no greater contrast than that between the sovereign and the ignoble-looking lieges, who, Hindu-like, after a certain age, either shrivel to skeletons or distend to treble bulk, and who, though rarely resembling the typical negro of the text book,† are not unfrequently black as ill-brushed boots. The pure reddish-brown of his skin, not unlike that of the so-called copper-coloured Indian, and several shades lighter than the lightest to be seen at his Court, confirms the general

from the *sequelæ* of the same terrible disease, which has thus killed two kings out of a total of eight.

* Mr. Duncan (vol. i. p. 224) describes Gezo, in 1845, as a "tall athletic man about forty-three years of age (he was older), with pleasing expression and good features, but the top of his forehead falling back rather too much to meet the views of a phrenologist."

† The same may be said of the typical John Bull, Johnny Crapaud, Paddy, and Brother Jonathan : we have selected an exception, a carica-ture. But such negroes do exist: I can point out a Yoruban family at Lagos which fulfils every external condition of the link between man and monkey.

report that his mother is a slave-girl from the northern Makhi:* others whisper that she is a mulatto from the French factory, Whydah.

Like Gezo, Gezo's son and heir affects a dress simple to excess. His head is often bare : on this occasion he wore a short cylindrical straw cap, with a ribbon-band of purple velvet round the middle. A Bo-fetish against sickness, in the shape of a human incisor, strung below the crown, and a single blue Popo-bead, of little value, was hanging to a thick thread about his neck. Despising the Bonugan-ton, or broad silver armlets of his caboceers, he contented himself with a narrow armil-

* In Mr. Norris's map the "Mahees" are placed west of Agbome. Their mountain-lands are to be seen rising due north of the capital : the tribes in the vicinity are subject to the King, the more distant are independent, and even court his attacks. Mr. Duncan, the only white man who explored the country, tells us (vol. i. p. 245), that "Makee is pronounced Mahee in the Kong mountains," and relates that the Dahomans there took 126 towns, making the greater part of the enemy prisoners. In June, 1863, the army of Dahome, after fourteen marches, probably short and circuitous, turned round upon a hostile clan, which defended itself so well that but few were taken. Indeed, I heard a report at Little Popo, that the King had been killed and the army destroyed by cannon sent up the Volta River.

The Makhi are a well made and comparatively light-complexioned people. Their tribe mark is now a black line raised, as amongst the Ejo of Benin, above the skin, from the hair to the root of the nose, but not extending beyond. Formerly, they cut three long oblique marks on one cheek, and a cross on the other. Their women are prized for matrimony: the mother of King Sinmenkpen was a Makhi girl.

and through the open entrance slave girls peeped at the proceedings. I regret to say that not a pretty face appeared, most of the "fair sex" had sooty skins, and the few browns showed negro features. They atoned for this homeliness by an extreme devotion to their lord and master : woman's position on earth, say Easterns, is to look up to somebody, and these certainly do, so far, their duty. It is no wonder that the King of Dahome's soul, like my "Lord Keeper's," lodges well. If perspiration appears upon the royal brow it is instantly removed with the softest cloth by the gentlest hands ; if the royal dress be disarranged, it is at once adjusted ; if the royal lips move, a plated spittoon, which, when Mr. Norris wrote, was gold, held by one of the wives, is moved within convenient distance ; if the King sneezes,* all present touch the ground with their foreheads ; if he drinks, every lip utters an excla-

---

* In Ffon, "nyin" is a sneeze ; manifestly, like ours, an imitative word. Almost throughout Africa, there is some superstition connected with this convulsion. In Senaar, courtiers turn the back, and slap the right thigh. Old authors tell us that when the "King of Monomotapa" sneezed, it became a national concern. Those nearest the royal person howled a salutation, which was taken up by the antechamber; and when the horrid cry had run through the palace, it was re-echoed by the whole city. In Europe the superstition is, that St. Gregory instituted a benediction upon the sneezer, because during a certain pestilence the unseemly act was a fatal symptom.

mation of blessing. This intense personal veneration reminded me of the accounts of Mohammed the apostle and of his followers left by contemporary writers. But without analysing too far, I suspect that in Dahome it is rather the principle than the person that is respected, the despotism more than the despot, the turban rather than the wearer : that were the King to be succeeded on the morrow, the same semi-idolatry would be heaped upon his successor. However that may be, the Dahoman King must only condescend to live, all, save what must necessarily be done by himself, is done for him. Such a life appears wearisome ; but kings are unlike common men, and the ways of princes are mysteries to the multitude. To this exceeding care only can be attributed the protracted reigns of a dynasty, whose eight members have sat upon the throne 252 years, thus rivalling the seven Roman monarchs whose rule extended over nearly the same period, and has caused them to be held fabulous or typical.

We walked towards the entrance down the clear lane' hedged by squatting Amazons, and we formed up in a group close to and opposite the King. The Meu, and his dependent the English landlord, who acted as it

R

were our sponsors, supported our right, the Yevo-gan and the Junior Min-gan our left, and all reclined upon the ground in the position of Romans upon the *triclinium*.

After the usual quadruple bowings and hand wavings, the King arose, tucked in his toga, descended from his *estrade*, donned his slippers—each act being aided by some dozen nimble feminine fingers—and advancing, greeted me with sundry vigorous wrings *à la John Bull*.* Still grasping my hand, he inquired after the health of the sovereign, the ministry, and the people of England, which he and his naturally suppose to be a little larger and a much richer Dahome surrounded by water. He then asked more particularly concerning the To-ji-'khosu† or Commodore, the Gau or Captain Luce, and the Amma-sin-blu-to or Dr. Haran, his last year's visitors. Gelele is said to have a right royal recollection of faces, names, and histories. A long com-

* His father used to affect with Englishmen a "familiar slap on the back with his open palm."

† To (water, especially the ocean, a pool, or a stream), ji (upon), 'khosu, for Akhosu by Synalepha (a king). "Gau," I have already explained. Amma (tree, or other leaf), sin (water, the compound word leaf-water meaning "medicine"), and blu-to (he who makes). Amma-bluto, or Amma-sin-blu-to, is the proper name for a doctor or surgeon; Amma-sin-kpele is the title of an officer, in whose charge is placed the King's medicine.

pliment was paid to me upon my having kept word in returning : I had promised on a previous occasion to apply for permission to revisit Dahome, and here to redeem a promise is a thing unknown. The King frequently afterwards referred to this trifle, attaching great importance to truth-telling, and assuring me that it made me his good friend.* It reminded me of—

> Beholde the manne! he spake the truthe,
> Hee's greater than a kynge!

He then finally snapped fingers with a will. Mr. Cruikshank wore a naval frock, which looked dull near a scarlet uniform, having no epaulettes ; his *accueil* was less ceremonious. Lastly, the Reverend received the greeting of a friend, and the King, before returning to his seat, kindly noticed the boy Tom.

Our stools were placed before the throne, and we sat whilst the materials for health-drinking were taken

---

* Truth, being a peculiarly rare article, is highly valued here. King Sinmenkpen said to Governor Abson (1803), who, being a resident of thirty-seven years in the country, had attempted a mild deceit, that " he wished the Englishman had not been so much of a Dahoman-man, as to make use of any artifice." I have myself been put to shame by hearing a Camaroons River chief declare to a Baptist missionary, who was palpably prevaricating, that had the truth been told, all would have been well. It must be a curiously self-sufficient brain that will enter into the lists of lying with an African.

from under a red calico cloth which lay upon a ricketty
table near the entrance, with legs once gilt. It is
not customary to address royalty, even though the
presentee be acquainted with the language.* The
sovereign's words are spoken to the Meu, who informs
the interpreter, who passes it on to the visitor, and the
answer must trickle back through the same channels.
It is evident the King will never hear anything
offensive, and that he will ignore all beyond his actual
inspection. I at once saw the necessity of attacking
the dialect, and, despite the nervous terrors of the hen-
hearted Beecham, who seemed to think teaching treason,
I had the satisfaction, before departure, of understanding most conversations in Ffon, and of being able to
join in a simple dialogue.

After *Sin-diyye!* and *Sin-ko!* we drank in three
several liquors to the health of the Sovereign, the
Commodore, and my humble self. After bowing and
touching glasses, the King suddenly wheeled round,
whilst two wives stretched a white calico cloth by way
of a screen before him, and another pair opened small
and gaudy parasols, so as completely to conceal his

---

* On the other hand, there is none of the ceremonial absurdity which
compels mere answers to a royal question or remark.

figure from our gaze. There was a prodigious outburst of noise. Guns were fired, "Amazons" tinkled
bells, and sprang kra-kra, or watchmen's rattles,
ministers bent to the ground clapping their palms, and
commoners bawled "Po-o-o" (i. e., "Bleo!"—"Take
it easy!"), cowering to avoid the dread sight, turning
their backs if sitting, and if standing they danced like
bears, or they paddled their hands like the forefeet of a
swimming dog. We were not expected to move.*

* Africans and some Asiatics are most subject to witchcraft when
eating and drinking; the Maldivian Islanders, for instance, eat alone in
the recesses of their houses, fearing lest some unlucky cantrip be played
with the victuals. Moreover, in most places, the King is too great a man
to eat, drink, or sleep at all. The origin of the idea is intelligible : it
could not have been imposing to see the august person of George III.
"at dinner on mutton and turnips." Hence the old kings of France
preferred to be served by knights on horseback. The Alake of Abeokuta
must be hidden even whilst he enjoys a *prise.* It was certain death to
see the petty King of Loango eat or drink, which he did in different
houses. When the cup was handed to him, an attendant struck together
two iron rods, the thickness of a man's finger : all who heard it buried
their faces in the sand till the sound ceased, and then clapped hands,
and uttered blessings. (Barbot : Supplement.) Also, no one might
drink in the presence except by turning back upon royalty, which is
also the case for all but white men at Dahome. The negroes of
"Ardra," we are told, used in friendship the same cup, showing that
the idea of dignity has done much towards surrounding the act with
ceremony.

Mr. Ditton has quoted upon this subject from the description of
Henry VII. and Elizabeth of York's coronation : first, "The Lady
Elizabeth Grey and Mistress Ditton went under the table and sat at the
Queen's feet, and the Countesses of Oxford and Rivers knelt on each

tribes of Asia, who fear the pen as they do the fiend.

I now proceed to portray the salient features of the King's levée. It was to me the most interesting scene in Dahome, showing more of picturesqueness and less of grotesqueness and tragedy than any other.

The long barn under which Gelele set was built against the eastern wall, which was clay ; fresh palm leaves, matted and planted as a fence, forming the other three sides of the oblong court. The regularity was relieved by a few poor sheds, and the only objects of remark in the yard were the familiar bundles of fetish sticks and a pollarded tree supporting an earthenware pot, with two pennons on tall poles. Along the shed, which was confined to the King and his wives, ran a line of four-and-twenty umbrellas, forming an extempore verandah. Those on the flanks were white, and mostly very ragged, sheltering the chieftainesses of the she soldiers : in the centre, denoting the place where the King sat, they affected the gaudish tulip tints, dazzling hues, variegated, yet in perfect harmonies — scarlet tender green, purple, white, and light blue : an especial favourite was red and yellow ; it is called in England Satan's livery, but when massed it excites the eye.

These richly tinted umbrella-canopies are forbidden to all save royalty, and the King takes no little pride in them.*

The only difference between the outer and the inner court is this—the former is a parade of the male, the latter of the female soldiers, and the first glance shows that both bodies exactly correspond. Mid-ribs of bamboo-palm (*Raphia vinifera*), in single line, lie on the ground separating the sexes ; this thin barrier no one is allowed to pass. The instrument of communication is the Mahaikpa, a princess who has not been seen for two years, and who consequently may be dead. Below the throne there is always one of her retainers, the " Dakro," a middle-aged woman, formerly attached to Gezo's Court, and a mighty stickler for ceremony. The Dakro bears messages from the King to the Meu, who passes on the words to the Min-gan, whence they find their way to the many. She walks out of the shed holding a war stick in her right hand, places it on the earth, kneels close behind the bamboo line, and resting

* They are manifestly made upon a European model. Mr. Duncan, who writes with the simplicity of a child, tells us (vol. ii. p. 271), that the King caused him to enter a memorandum of several patterns for canopies, desiring him to order a number of them to be sent from England. At the present moment (August, 1864) one of these umbrellas may be seen at the rooms of the Royal Geographical Society, London.

elbows on thighs, or sometimes with one hand on the
ground, whispers her errand, almost touching heads.
As a rule she goes on all fours to the Meu, and only
kneels to smaller men, who become quadrupeds to her.
A favourite gesture with both sexes here is to smooth
the ground before them with one or both palms, clearing as it were the place for prostration : it is the whit-
tling of the Yankee, and it serves to conceal thought.
The message is received by the minister in a similar
position, the feet resting upon the toes and the heels
supporting the posteriors.   After obtaining the answer
the Dakro rises, returns to within the barn, makes
obeisance, and placing herself on all fours—the nearest
approach to our brethren of the field since the days of
Nebuchadnezzar—either upon the ground or upon a
mat, before and close to the King, duly delivers it to the
royal ears.   Nothing but the prodigious memory for
trifles possessed by this people prevents a communication that travels so far from losing all its original sense.

Outside the bamboos, divided, as has been said, into
two distinct groups, stand the ministers.   All are in
their richest attire, gay with tunics of bright silk and
satin. The Min-gan wears eight necklaces, with a silver
ornament like a *fleur-de-lis* or trefoil, hanging upon his

breast. The Meu has doffed his alpaca jacket, displays
fine and valuable pink coral in long strings, with thin
thread pigtails lashed on to them, silver armlets adorned
with the British Lion, and with two quasi-human heads
which may have belonged to William and Mary ; whilst
the emblem of Christianity, in gold, depends from his
neck. But the crucifix is strangely altered, the crucified
being a chamelion, the venerable emblem of the rain-
bow-god. This is not done *par malice*, like the ass
placed by the irreverent caricaturist upon what is,
according to Dr. Rossi, the earliest known cross—it is
the simple instinct of a barbarous race. The Adanejan,
or assistant Min-gan, is more than usually gorgeous.
He is a huge Cyclops of a black, with a jetty face, at
least one size larger than his brain-pan, and a *faux air
de jeune homme*, effected by close shaving his stiff
whitey-grey beard and hair. Though long past " fright-
ful forty," he is much addicted to women, and he is ever
" chaffing " the Reverend about marrying a daughter to
him. A great trencherman, with a rollicking laugh that
quakes his fat sides, the big eupatrid is of somewhat
offensive presence ; he is moreover a professed beggar,
and what meets his touch never leaves it.

Non fuit Autolyci tam piceata manus.

The Gau is rendered conspicuous by his big brass bracelets. The surly Po-su wears four brass rings on his left arm, and his forehead is always ceremoniously marked with white sand or red earth. All the lesser fry are clad like their betters, in tunics of rich native cloth, and ornamented with horns, silver bracelets, armlets, crucifixes, trefoil-shaped articles, and necklaces, of which some wore as many as ten; Popo beads, large and small; coral, red and pink; blue and white glass beads; green, yellow, and variegated pottery; while some have neck-ropes of black and blue seed beads disposed in patterns.

On the King's proper right, in the wing presided over by the Khe-tun-gan (female Gau, or Commander-in-Chief), and outside the big barn, enthroned on a lofty chair, sat the Akutu; she is captainess of King Gezo's life-guards, called the 'Mman, or Madmen, the Bashi Buzuks, or *Enfans Perdus* of the Dahoman host. This dignitary is a huge old porpoise, wearing a bonnet shaped like that of a French *cordon bleu*, but pink and white below, with two crocodiles of blue cloth on the top, and the whole confined by silver horns and their lanyard. To the left of royalty, more in the open and under a tent-umbrella, upon as tall a seat as the Akutu enjoyed, is the Humbagi, the corresponding veteraness on the Meu's side. She is also vast in breadth, and a hammer-head in silver projecting from her forehead, gives her the semblance of a unicorn. As a rule the warrioresses begin to fatten when their dancing days are passed, and some of them are prodigies of obesity.

The flower of the host was the mixed company of young Amazons lately raised by the King; this corps, standing to the north of the palace yard, and on the right of the throne, was evidently composed of the largest and finest women in the service. Behind it stood its band, a Chingufu or African cymbal, two small tom-toms held under the arm, and four kettledrums of sizes, beaten with hand or stick. The newly-chosen company apparently contained two hundred, and the whole court certainly did not show more than one thousand. Some Amazons, however, are now absent, attacking, I have said, a village in the Makhi country, which distinguished itself by grossly insulting the King, by threatening to kill him and his army. They will have an easy victory.*

---

* It seems a peculiarity of climate in those lands, and the History can supply several instances, that compels individuals and tribes mortally and wantonly to insult a rancorous and hateful race like that of Dahome and then entirely to forget the injury, so as to take no precautions against

The gala-dress of the guardesses was decent, and not uncomely. A narrow fillet of blue or white cotton bound the hair, and the bosom was concealed by a sleeveless waistcoat of various colours, giving freedom to the arms, and buttoning in front like that affected by Hausa Moslems. The loin wrapper, of dyed stuff, mostly blue, pink, and yellow, extended to the ancles, and was kept tight round the waist by a sash, generally white, with long ends depending on the left. The body toilette was rendered more compact by an outer girth-ing of cartridge-box and belt, European-shaped, but home-made, of black leather, adorned with cowries; or of bandoleers, containing in separate compartments twelve to sixteen wooden gunpowder boxes, like cases for lucifer matches. The bullet-bag, with a few iron balls, hung by a shoulder-strap to the dexter

vengeance. The History tells us that the people of "Wemey," a petty village near "Porto Novo," that could perhaps muster one to every hundred Dahoman warriors, sent a challenge to one of the greatest of the kings, threatening, if not attacked, to march on Agbome. The king returned, as usual, an ironical answer, saying that he would soon dispatch his Gau with guns, powder, and iron (lead being here un-known), for the use of his brave foe; attacked the place, which he found unprepared, and "broke" it without the people making an effort at self-defence. So in 1728, Governor Testesole, of Whydah, exasperated by the insolence of the Dahoman traders, whipped one of their principal men at the flag-post, and said that he would serve the King (Agaja) in the same manner, if he could. That governor was, of course, murdered.

side, and was preserved in position by being passed under the cartridge-belt. All had knives, or short Dahoman falchions,* in shape not unlike, though smaller than, that most fatal—to the wearer—of all weapons, the old French *briquet*. The firelock, a good solid Tower-marked article,† was guarded by sundry charms, and protected from damp by a case of black monkey-skin tightly clasping the breeching, and opening to the rear. Many had long tassels dangling from the barrels.

The only other peculiarity in the court was a row of three large calabashes, ranged on the ground before and a little to the left of royalty. They contain the calvariæ of the three chief amongst forty kings, or petty

---

* Curious to say, whilst many of the central African tribes are adepts at smelting iron, it is an art unknown to the rude Dahoman; although the material abounds in the northern country, they import it from Europe. The blade is but slightly curved, one edged, and poorly tempered, about sixteen inches long, and 1·50 inch at the broadest part, which is the half nearer the point. The hilt or handle is only three inches long, and, like that of Abyssinia, too short for a good grip; it is of brass or other metal, of wood, ribbed or plain, covered with shagreen. Sometimes there is a single bar, as in the *briquet*, to guard the hand, and there is usually a brass knob for pommel. The scabbard is of black leather, with ferule of brass or white metal at the tip, a broad band at the top, and one or two round the centre; in some scabbards almost all the leather is concealed. The price varies from 1 dol. 50c. to 2 dols.: the silver-mounted fetch 8 dols.

† In Gezo's time the troops had mostly "long Danes," or "buccaneer guns."—Mr. Duncan, vol. i. p. 240.

headmen, said to have been destroyed by Gelele ; and they are rarely absent from the royal levees. A European would imagine these relics to be treated with mockery ; whereas the contrary is the case. So the King Sinmenkpen (Adahoonzou II.), after unwrapping an enemy's cranium, said to Mr. Norris, "If I should fall into hostile hands, I should wish to be treated with that decency of which I set the example." The first skull was that of Akia'on, chief of Attako (Taccow), near "Porto Novo," which was destroyed about three years ago. Beautifully white and polished, it is mounted in a ship or galley of thin brass about a foot long, with two masts, and jibboom, rattlings, anchor, and four portholes on each side, one pair being in the raised quarter deck. When King Gezo died his successor received a message from this chief, that all men were now truly joyful, that the sea had dried up, and that the world had seen the bottom of Dahome. Gelele rejoined by slaying him, and by mounting his skull in a ship, meaning that there is still water enough to float the kingdom, and that if the father is dead the son is alive. The second cranium, which also was well boiled, and which, like the rest, wanted the lower jaw,*

* The lower jawbone is coveted as an ornament for umbrellas, sword-

was that of Bakoko of Ishagga.   It was crossed at right
angles by four bars of bright brass ; a thin mask of
the same metal, rudely marked with eyes and unraised
nose, gave it a monkey-like appearance.   On the poll,
and where the bars met, was a brass bowl with a tip
like a calabash stalk, by which the upper half could be
raised, to serve as a drinking-cup : this, when viewed
in front, looked somewhat like a Phrygian cap, or a
knightly helmet.   During Gelele's attack upon Abeokuta, in 1851, the people of Ishagga behaved with
consummate treachery, which eleven years afterwards
was terribly punished by the present ruler.   Bakoko
was put to death, and as a sign that he ought to have
given water to a friend in affliction, men now drink
from his recreant head.   The third calvaria, also washed,
was that of Flado, an Abeokutan general, sent to the aid
of the Ishaggas.   Along the ridge crown of the head
ran a broad leaf in brass, to which was attached a thick
copper wire and a chain which can raise it from its
base ; the latter is an imitation in brass of a country-
trap ; whilst a small white flag and cloth are wound

handles, and other such purposes.   It is taken with horrible cruelty :
the muscles at each ramus are severed with a knife, and the jaw is
torn out with the left hand from the yet living victim.

round the stout wire.   This showed that Flado fell into
the pit which he dug for another.*

Whilst the soldiery of picked women danced and
sang, the deputation of four Moslems was brought in
by the Min-gan.   The captains who had charge of them
prostrated themselves upon the clay, not the sand-ring†
nearer the throne, and shovelled it up by handfuls over
their heads and arms, showing that they were of lower
rank than the ministers.   This is the ceremonial which
every writer upon Dahoman subjects finds so degrad-
ing, and with which the traveller meets in almost all
semi-barbarous societies, especially in negro and negroid
kingdoms, since the days of Leo Africanus.   The Itte
d'ai, or " lying on ground," is a strictly scriptural prostration,‡ and it corresponds with the "shashtanga" of the

* Gezo had also his three favourite skulls (Mr. Duncan, vol. i. p. 245).
That traveller, after seeing 2000 to 3000 crania, remarked that " several
were deficient of any suture across the upper part," in the proportion of
1 : 12, whilst those without longitudinal division were as 1 : 27.   He also
found the Makhi crania receding from the nasal bone, or lower part of
the forehead, to the top in a greater angle than those of any other
country

  † This loose white sand is brought from Diddo, a water to the north-
west of Agbome : it is quite as cleanly as the powder and other stuff
worn by our grandsires.

  ‡ See the cases of David and Abigail falling at his feet (1 Sam. xxv.
23) ; Mephibosheth (2 Sam. ix. 6) falls on his face and " does reverence ; " Absolom (Ibid. xiv. 33) bows himself on his face to the

Hindus, and with the Chinese "kow-tow." At the court of the Cazembe in South-Eastern Africa, and in the equatorial kingdom of Uganda, it is practised exactly as in Dahome. In the Congo regions, prostration is made, the earth is kissed, and dust is strewed over the forehead and arms, before every petty Banza or village chief. According to Barbot (1700), the interpreter of the " King of Zair," probably Boma, vulgarly Embomma, after rubbing his hands and face in the dust, " took one of the royal feet in his hands, spat on the sole thereof and licked it with his tongue." It is doubtless the origin of " sijdah " amongst Moslems, who hold a dusty forehead to be mubarak, or of good omen ; and the Shieh heresy rests the prostrated brow upon small flat cakes of the earth of Kerbela, much renowned for martyrs. The Mahommedans of Senegal have also learned to throw sand or earth with both hands over their own heads. Ibu Batuta has described the wallowing and dusting of the older Nigrotic Courts. Jobson remarked the same at Tenda, Clapperton at Oyo, and Denham amongst the " Musgows."

ground before the king; Bath-sheba (1 Kings i. 16—31) "bowed and did obeisance." But Mr. Duncan (vol. i. p. 221) was " much surprised as well as disgusted with such absurd abject humiliation." He apparently knew more of the bridoon than of the Bible.

over upon their bellies, or relieve themselves by standing "on all fours." When approaching royalty they
either crawl like snakes, or shuffle forward on their
knees. During the levee they must raise frequent cries
of *"Akhosu li akhosu!"* literally, "King all (*i.e.*, of
all) Kings!" and *"Akhosu te te le!"*—"Small, small
Kings!" meaning that before this mighty "Cham" all
other monarchs are boys. The messengeress, when sum-
moning a subject to the presence, says, "*Se iro we!*"—
"The Se, or spirit,* requires you!" When the King
has spoken, all exclaim "*Se do Nugbo!*"—"the spirit
speaketh true!" to which some add, "*moen de!*"—
"So it is!" an historical phrase often preceded by
"*nagboe!*"—"It is true!"

From these appearances a stranger, like Dr. M'Leod,
is apt to conclude that the Dahoman king represents,
like the Shahanshahs of ancient Persia, a kind of God
upon earth, and that he can daily act out, whenever he
is "i' the vein," even with the proudest in his dominions,
Henry the Fifth's "You are a liar!" with the speedy
conclusion, "By my head thou shalt lose thy head!"
This is far from being the case, as the more observing

---

* For an explanation of Se, see Chapter XVII. The King is called a
spirit, as having power of life and death.

former travellers well knew.* The ministers,† war captains, and fetisheers may be, and often are, individually punished by the King: collectively they are too strong for him, and without their cordial co-operation he would soon cease to reign. And this apparently perfect subjection of the inferior to the superior runs through every grade of Dahoman society. The " *Frippons*, or common scoundrel blacks," as the old writer calls them, kneel and clap hands before the patrician, as if the latter were their proprietor ; they listen to every order with religious attention, and afterwards they obey it or not exactly as they please. ‡ Except in the case of serfs, slaves, and captives, there is throughout Dahome, and I may say Africa, more of real liberty and equality—I will not add fraternity— than in any other quarter of the globe, and the presence of the servile renders the freemen only freer and more equal.

* So Captain Philips (1694) justly remarks of the King of Whydah: "Though his cappasheirs (caboceers) show him so much respect, he dare not do anything but what they please."

† Some except the Min-gan and Meu, which, however, is not correct.

‡ Barbot well hits off this trait. "Though the Whydahs," he observes, "tremble with awe at a word from the king, as soon as he has turned his back they seem to forget their great fear of him ; and not much regard his commands, as very well knowing how to appease and delude him by their lies."

The Moslems of the "Porto Novo" deputation resembled Bambarra men ; one, however, was fair as an
Arab. They wore white turbans over tall red caps,
large broad trousers, and the "Guinea fowl" embroidered robe of Yoruba. Behind them sat their
band, four co-religionists, in white calottes and meaner
robes. The only instruments were tom-toms. There
were also a few Kafirs, or pagans, that seemed attached,
probably as carriers, to the party. These men had
been sent by the King's brother, of, "Porto Novo,"
about which there was much excitement, to the great
disfavour of the French Protectorate.

Whilst the Min-gan who presented these men "made
obeisance," the Moslems sat gravely on the clay-ground,
at a distance from the King. Then one of the Alufa,*
with hands upraised in the prayer position, recited by
heart long, fluent orisons, concluded, as usual, by drawing the palms down the face. The introducer, who sat
with his back to the King, imitated every gesture of
the visitor. Although the Moslem countenance ex-

---

* Alúfá, probably a corruption of Arif, is the Egba word for a
Mullah, a Moslem theologian. Imále in Egba, and Málenun in Ffon,
both probably corrupted from Muallim, means the common Moslem. Hence
some of our older authors brought the *Malays* to Dahome.—See History,
p. 48, note signed "J. F."

pressed some awe at the apparatus in the palace, it well maintained before this heathenry the dignity of the Safe Faith.

Finally the Dakro woman at the foot of the throne brought in due form a welcome from the King to his brother's envoys. The heathen again powdered themselves with dust, and the Moslems bent towards the ground. This was a signal to the female attendants, who, after a startling clash and clang of cymbals, neckbells, and rattles, presented arms *à la Dahome*,— the guns being raised in the air. The mixed company of beauties performed sundry dances. Presents and drink, in sign of dismissal, were sent to the deputation ; the Moslems took the water, the Kafirs two flasks of rum, whilst two baskets (=20 heads, or £2) of cowries and five baskets of food were served out to the whole party. The gift was received by the heathenry crouching on the ground, and uttering a curious noise, likest to feline purring, whilst the True Believers again prayed for the King. The deputation was presently conducted to the palace-gate by their introducers, who bent, as is customary when leaving the presence, almost double, and went off at a hurried pace. It was then brought back, and the royal presents were placed upon the envoys' heads, only the four turbans being exempt. Salutes were again exchanged, and the Porto Novians finally left the Palace Yard.

The mixed company danced once more, and this time it was joined by a dozen razor women, who, defiling past the King from the she Meu's to the Min-gan's side, took their stations near the throne. These Nyekple-hen-to* seemed the largest and strongest women present, and they held their weapons upwards in the air like standards, with a menacing air and gesture. The blade is about eighteen inches long, and is shaped exactly like a European razor; it closes into a wooden handle about two feet in length, and, though kept in position by strong springs, it must be, I should think, quite as dangerous to the owner as to the enemy. These portable guillotines were invented by a brother of the late King Gezo, and the terror which they inspire may render them useful.

At the end of the dance, Ji-bi-whe-ton,† acting

---

* Meaning, nyekple (the weapon itself), hen (hold), to (one that does), French travellers call them "Les faucheuses."

† Ji (sky), bi (all), whe (sun), ton (belonging to), i. e., "all the sky belongs to the sun." The commanding officeress is Danh-ji-hun-to, meaning, the rainbow is the captain or governor of (viz., goes round the sky; that is to say, the King of Dahome rules the (black) world.

captainess of the Beauty Company, came forwards
with the usual affected military swagger, not without a
suspicion of a dance. She is, or was, a fine tall woman,
with glittering teeth, and a not unpleasant expression
when her features are at rest. She addressed a violent
speech to the male Min-gan, who repeated it aloud to
the King, with whom it found favour. Ending with
cutting off the head of an imaginary corpse upon the
ground, she retired to her command. Presently, for
the *cacoëthes loquendi* was upon her, she again advanced,
and spoke with even more gesticulation than before.
"Thus they would treat Abeokuta!" The sentiment
elicited immense applause.

Followed chorus, solo, and various decapitation
dancings of the mixed company, the weapons being,
as usual, grounded, the war-club seized, and the
shoulder-blades and posteriors being agitated to excess.
Even the performances of these figurantes, the cream
of the royal ballet, are not to be admired. They
stand most ungracefully—the legs, which are somewhat
slight for the body, being wide apart, and the toes
certainly turned in and probably up. When the

Mr. Duncan's "Dagbyweka," vol. i. p. 231, seems to be a confusion
between the two.

exercise ended, the razor and chopper women * bran-
dished their weapons, and all the line advancing,
" presented " with upraised muskets.

At the Dahoman Court, curious to say in Africa,
women take precedence of men; yet, with truly
Hamitic contradictiousness, the warrioresses say, " We
are no longer females but males ; " and a soldier dis-
gracing himself is called, in insult, a woman. It is
clear, therefore, that they owe their dignity to the
fiction of being royal wives. Wherever a she-soldiery
is, celibacy must be one of its rules, or the troops will
be in a state of chronic functional disorder between the
ages of fifteen and thirty-five.

After the Amazons, all the male caboceers, taking
choppers and peculiar bill-hook-like blades,† some iron,
others silver, danced tumultuously before the King, to

* The chopper is called anánun (confusion, or badness), wá (doing),
and hwisu (knife-sword, or dagger) ; meaning, the " cutting badly knife."
Strangers call it the blue-knife. It is a top-heavy blade four spans
long, bluff and broadening to one palm at the end like the old Turkish
falchion, and narrowing to two fingers at the hilt. The form is by no
means so exaggerated as the wonderful chopping-knives of the Gold
Coast. Down the centre runs a broad line, depressed and not polished
like the back and edge. These knives, being royal gifts, may not be
bought.

† Many of these end in a circle whose diameter is twice the breadth
of the blade ; sometimes the surface is worked and pierced like fish-
slicers. The bill appears to be ornamental, not useful.

the general song of the women on the right of the throne. Even the tottering Meu, who leaned upon a tomahawk long enough to act as a staff, joined in the movement. Presently Gelele sent a message to the Gau, declaring that this year Abeokuta must be taken ; the tall old man, standing up with a military air, swore that it certainly should fall, and the oath was repeated by his surly-looking junior the Po-su.

The King then addressed me through the Meu and Mr. Beecham, to the effect that this year Abeokuta must be as a mouse before the cat ; he also invited me to accompany him to sit behind the army and to see the sport. I replied that "Understone" had long ceased friendship with the white man. A little pleasantry ensued touching it not being our English habit to hang back when aught is doing ; and the King taking all in excellent part, we stood up bareheaded, and waved four salutations.

Among the remarkabilia of the scene was Adan-men-nun-kon,* right-hand Commander of the Blue

* Among the Dahomans are many mystic names, like Joshua, Isa, and others. These are mostly of the·Bo-fetish, a war medicine which prevents wounds (Chap. XI.). The words mean, adan (brave), men (man), nun (side, face), kon (upon). The title is explained in two ways. "I am brave upon another man's side," i. e., to take him

Guards, and a fine specimen of " Monsieur Parolles " in black. This man of loyal appellation is a tall, lean, sooty-faced fellow, with a large, whitish, and big-tasselled night-cap decorating his head, a pink pagne, and a baldric adorned with cowries. Rising like a warrior, with carbine and tomahawk, he assured me, in the midst of loud screams and violent gesticulatiohs, that at 'Gba * even the unborn child must perish ; and he strove to look as if he were doing it to death. His " brother " Zodome, acting for Chabi, the left-hand Commander of the Blues, confirmed the idea. The Voice from the Throne added, as is the habit, many an illustration of the speeches, concluding with the declaration that the Abeokutans must not only be beheaded, their bodies must also be cut to pieces.

There appeared two silver-horned fetish chiefs, of the Blue Company, who in the hour of battle personally

prisoner ; or, " however brave nations are, the king is the bravest of all."

* This is the Yoruban word Egba ; in Ffon it means " break." In Dahome the Egba race, from Lagos to Abeokuta, is called Anago at Whydah, and Nago at Agbome. J. F., the annotator of the History, says, " Of the Nago country nothing more is known than the name." The word has been greatly corrupted by old travellers : it is, however, extensively used in Brazil.

On the other hand, the Nago people call the Ffons, or Dahomans, Gunu.

attend upon the King. "Awafanfin," which was translated to me, "A fetish guide for Abeokuta," drew his knife, and declared that with the blade, not with a gun, he would attack the cravens who lurked behind their walls. The King cordially echoed this; and added that even if in England I should hear of his destructive deeds. His right-hand, or superior colleague, a good-looking youth, called Hnengada, a "King-Bo-fetish name" (interpreted to mean, "When the spindle turns cotton, it must become thread"), then stood up. He informed me, "The forest tree is strong with root and cordage, and is heavy with trunk and branch, whilst the wind is thin, and cannot be seen; but the gale lays low the loftiest of the green wood; and Dahome is that wind, whilst Abeokuta is that tree." This senti-ment was also explained by the King. The speakers kissed the ground, and rubbed earth upon their brows: then the chorus of captains sang—

> When we go to war we must slay men,
> And so must Abeokuta be destroyed.

The mixed company was now greatly increased by women, who had defiled in single line before the throne. There were bayoneteeresses, with blue cloth tunics and a white patch on the shoulder, white fillets like those of the men, sashes to match supporting their swords, and variously-coloured pagnes. The blunder-buss women, who were, like the former, sitting under the she Min-gan, distinguished themselves by scarlet woollen nightcaps. After they had danced and sung, their captainess, Ji-bi-whe-ton, advanced, and said that they would fire a salute for their old commander. With some difficulty two sides of a square were formed, fronting the south and west. The manœuvres consisted of an individual sallying out like the Arab " Mubariz," delivering her fire, and retiring to the ranks. All raised their weapons steadily, with left arms extended, and fired from the shoulders, not from the hips as the men do to avoid the kick; they returned with a kind of caper, and they did not flinch after the fashion of the Dahoman soldiers. The bayonet women, after firing, extended a single very *gauche* thrust. The blunderbuss soldieresses grounded the butts of their heavy weapons, and discharged them at an angle of 45 deg. After several rounds they again chanted:

We like not to hear that Abeokuta lives;
But soon we shall see it fall.

This was followed by the usual dance and chorus which concluded with a " present" of uplifted weapons.

· When the sun had set, a Dakro brought us directions to advance and bid adieu to the King, whilst sundry flasks and decanters of 'tafia and other liquors were distributed in token of dismissal. Approaching the throne, we made the usual " compliments." Gelele, wrapping his robe around him, descended from the *estrade*, donned his sandals, and, attended by his umbrella and a large crowd of the Kan-gbo-de's huissiers bearing lights and links, stalked forth towards the palace-yard gate, with a right kingly stride. Every inequality of ground was smoothed, every stick or stone was pointed out, with finger snappings, lest it might offend the royal toe, and a running accompaniment of " Dadda ! Dadda !" (Grandfather ! Grandfather !) and of " Dedde ! Dedde !" * (Softly ! Softly !) was kept up. Passing out of the gate, we found a swarming of negroes, whose hum during the whole audience had been heard inside the palace. They buzzed about like excited hornets. I know not if the manœuvre was done purposely to exaggerate the semblance of a multitude, but I can answer that it was a success.

* De! here means "softly," as " Bleo " is used on the Gold Coast.

The King accompanied us to some distance outside the palace—a compliment first paid to Commodore Wilmot.* His ministers were around him, and the Meu placed in my hands, according to ancient custom,† a handful of potsherd bits, showing the number of return guns expected at Whydah. Preceded by the Yevogan, we made for the English house. The road was crowded with fetish women, marching in full dress and single file to a queer song. Arrived at our destination, we gave liquor to the whole tail, and we were happy when we found ourselves in comparative solitude.

From the above description it is evident that the Dahoman possesses, to some extent, the ceremonial faculty. On such occasions the pageantry of African Courts is to be compared with that of Europe, proportionately with the national state of progress. But it is evidently the result of long and studious practice: Everything goes by clockwork; the most intricate etiquette proceeds without halt or mistake; and it ever superadds the element Terror, whose absence in civi-

---

* King Gezo accompanied Mr. Duncan almost to his dwelling.

† In the History (p. 124), Mr. Norris, after being saluted, was shown fifteen pebbles in a small calabash, which he "recollected was the number of guns that were fired on the preceding evening."

lised countries often converts ceremonial to a something silly. As, however, the reader has been warned, he has seen the best. The outside displays are wretched. Misery mixes with magnificence, ragged beggars and naked boys jostle jewelled chiefs and velvet-clad Amazons ; whilst the real negro grotesqueness, like bad perspective, injures the whole picture.

CHAPTER X.

THE King was detained at Kana, as we were afterwards informed, by sundry cases affecting human life.
Not less than 150 " Amazons " were found to be preg-
nant—so difficult is chastity in the Tropics. They
confessed, and they were brought to trial with their
paramours.* The King has abolished the " Brehon
judges " established by his father : the malversation of
these " justices in eyre " rendered reference to them
like " going," as the old traveller has it, " to the Devil
for redress." He now investigates each case personally,
often sitting in judgment till midnight, and rising
before dawn on the next day ; moreover, every criminal has a right of personal appeal to him.† The crime

---

* We read that in the reign of Sinmenkpen (Adahoonzou; II.), a
female conspiracy in the palace caused the sale of 150 men from the
villages near Kana, for dishonouring the King. Their innocence was
not discovered till too late.

† Mr. Duncan was present at two of these appeals (vol. i. p. 259).

was *lèse-majesté* rather than simple advowtry ; all the soldieresses being, I have said, royal wives. Eight men were condemned to death, and will probably be executed at the Customs. The majority were punished either by imprisonment or by a banishment to distant villages, under pain of death if they revisit the capital, and some were pardoned.* The partners of their guilt were similarly treated. Female criminals are executed by officers of their own sex, within the palace walls, not in the presence of men. Dahome is therefore in one point more civilised than Great Britain, where they still, wondrous to relate, "hang away" even women, and in public.

In the afternoon of Sunday, December 20th, we effected a departure from the English house. Sundry boxes were left behind, owing to the desertion of the carriers, who are fast learning bad habits : yesterday they stole an enamelled iron cup. The Court being at

---

* This leniency and amenity of discipline form a curious contrast with the horribly barbarous punishments which, according to Bosman and Barbot followed such an offence two and a half centuries ago. In 1845 Mr. Duncan was informed that the victims at the Kana sacrifice "had been guilty of adulterous intercourse with one of the King's wives, in consequence of which they were sentenced to be put to death by being beaten with clubs, and after death mutilated" (vol. i. p. 220). The object of the mutilation is here, I believe, wrongly stated.

Kana, bell-women were a nuisance on the road; at every five minutes the hammock-men huddled us into the bush. Arrived at the Akoreha, or eastern market-place, we sat down near the Buko-no's house, awaiting his escort. Here fetish women crowded upon us, clapping palms for a present. They were easily dispersed by their likenesses being sketched.

Already the sun began to cool,* though the sky was still all ablaze with golden glory. After half an hour's delay, the old Buko-no came up, leaning on the Bo-kpo,† or crutch staff, which wards off the evils of the way. Presently we remounted hammocks, and he, by means of a chair, climbed upon the back of his little *bidet*—a mare followed by a foal. The animals here are not larger than Shetland ponies, but they are generally, as is the Maharatta-land "tattoo," shaped like stunted horses, showing the remains of good blood. They have fine noses, well-opened eyes, and sharp ears. As in Yoruba generally, the tits are excessively vicious,

---

* Mr. Duncan twice asserts (vol. ii. pp. 260, 288), that "it is a custom in Dahomey for all strangers of note visiting that capital to arrive and depart as nearly as possible when the sun is at its meridian." The practice is now obsolete.

† Literally a Bo-staff. It is known by a litle petticoat called "Avo," or cloth, bound on below the crutch, and concealing the medicine.

and if approached by a stranger, they will fly at him
with a scream. This is doubtless owing to the brutality of their negro grooms. They are, when mounted,
invariably led, like donkeys, by a halter—the bridle,
like the stirrup, being unknown. The little jades are
almost hid in the local saddle, enormous housings of
blue cloth, padded, quilted, and worked outside with
white thread, while huge curtain tassels depend to their
knees. As a rule, the rider is lifted on and off by his
slaves. Whilst on horseback he passes his arm round
the neck of a man walking by his side, and his waist is
supported by the same attendant's near arm.*

The Buko-no was habited in the usual "Chokoto" or
little drawers, with a long shirt about his body, and a
black-ribboned Panama hat. His escort of thirty-three
retainers was that of a Dahoman noble on a journey,
and the common people on the road knelt and clapped
palms as he passed. He was preceded by nine
musketeers, who danced and sang the whole way with
unwearied energy. His fetish stick was carried before
him in a calico *étui* by a man in a long white cap like

---

* So King Gezo told off two attendants to hold Mr. Duncan, the
Lifeguardsman, on his horse, and was much surprised by a trot and a
gallop.

the extinguisher-shaped nightgear of our ancestors. The Buko-no rode under the shade of a large white umbrella, and was closely followed by his axe man, who gave orders as one having authority. The train was brought up by the band, chiefly boys, with three drums, a couple of tom-toms, two single cymbals, and a pair of gourd rattles : they kept up a loud horrid noise throughout the march. About a dozen carriers were scattered about the *cortége* bearing a pipe and tobacco bag, a Gold Coast chair, a footstool and calabashes, and bundles of clothes and matting.

From Kana to Agbome all is historic ground, and the land is emphatically the garden of Dahome, showing a wondrous soft and pleasant aspect. The soil is sandy, with the usual pebbles overlying red and yellow clays, and where grass is not, the surface is a succession of palm orchards and grain fields belonging to the King and his ministers. Many of the trees are pollarded as in Teneriffe, by removing the tops and branches to thicken the shade ; these are mostly observed round the frequent villages that stud the fair champaign. The road, six or seven miles long, separating the two capitals may compare with the broadest in England, and although to the eye it spans a plain, there is an imperceptible rise of about 694 feet, which extricates us from lowland Africa. For the convenience of the royal carriages it is carefully kept clear of grass, which would obliterate it in two months, yet the Africans, accustomed to nothing but Indian file, wear single paths in it like sheep tracks. It is a study of the national character to see each following his neighbour in goose line down a road upon which four coaches could be driven abreast.*

After a few yards we dismounted at a spot where a log placed transversely on the ground showed us the Kana 'gbo-nun,† or Kana Gate. It had the usual surroundings of fetish sheds and spaces cleared for worship, and all the natives when stepping over it

* In the "African Times," an ignoble sheet, which, I should hardly say "by permission," constitutes itself the organ of the African Aid Society of London, there has appeared for many an issue an advertisement headed "Aguapem Mountain Road," and sending round the hat in the usual style. This is no bad way to coax the British gold out of the British breeches-pocket. But beyond that nothing. Such a road, once made, would be buried in vegetation after a few months, unless kept clear at a great expense. Secondly, like that of Kana, it would be cut up into paths: the negro has no shoes, consequently he must tread, despite all our endeavours, on a place softened by those who precede him.

† Agbo (town-gate, or enceinte with wall and ditch), and nun (side, or mouth). A house-gate is called hon-to, from hon (a door), and if large, hon-to'gbo (big gate).

removed their caps. The next names were " Pakhi," so
called from an ancient chieftain slain by King Dako and
" Ekpwento " a " Bo " name—both holy places, with
barriers of the Thunder Fetish shrub stretching nearly
across the road. After half an hour we passed on the
left Legba 'si-gon,* a clearing with many dwarf thatches
where the Legba-priest comes forth and prays for the
King and for the largesse of white visitors. A few
yards further, and to the right of the road, was a
compound, showing only the tops of conical huts; this
is the Bweme, or country palace of the Agasun-no,†
here the Archbishop of Canterbury, who ranks at
Agbome next to the King. Rapidly we passed the
following interesting sites :—Brú-vodun, the fetish of
the " Bru " (blue) or English Company ; Arima, a fetish
of the same corps ; Aizan 'li, the road of Aizan,‡ a holy
place for the 'Mman or Gezo's Mad Company ; Bagidi-
Samun, so called from an old king of Adan-we ; the
Adan-gbno-ten,§ where the King halts when going from

* Legba (the Dahoman Priapus), si for asi (a wife, *i. e.*, a votary),
and gon (a place).

† For an explanation of Agasun, see Chapter XVII. No is " mother,"
the use of which word has been before noticed.

‡ For an explanation of Aizan, see Chapter XVII.

§ Adan (brave), gbno (swear), ten (place). Others pronounce the

Agbome to Kana ; and the Avrekete Loko 'li, or road of Avrekete * Loko tree. They are clean spaces, adorned with pots, sticks, flags, and tents : many of them have circlets of the Thunder Fetish shrub often surrounding a taller tree, and the latter is usually a giant Bombax, with the Azan or fetish-fringe round the trunk.†

About an hour of slow marching brought us to the Adan-we Palace.‡ It lies on the right of the road, a heap of matting half buried in trees. According to the people it was built by Tegbwesun (1727-1774) and the King still sleeps here when he leaves Agbome in the evening for Kana. Around it, but especially to the north, is the cradle of the Dahoman empire, the classic Uhwawe, corrupted into Dawhee by Mr. Norris, who calls it "the ancient residence of the reigning family, and the capital of their little territory before they emerged from their original obscurity." § The "Awawe people," though long subjects of the empire, still preserve, like the Agoni and others, their old name.

word Adan-blon-noten, and explain it, Adan (brave), blon (swear), and noten (stop).

  * For an explanation of Avrekete, see Chapter XVII.

  † For an explanation of this term, see Chapter IV.

  ‡ Said to mean Adan (brave), and we (white). Mr. Duncan (vol. i. p. 216) calls it "Adawie, three miles and a half from Canamina."

  § See also Chapter V.

Opposite the Adan-we is Addein, a village also conquered by the first Dahoman king, Dako.   Then came
the Akwe-janahan,* the market of these two settle-
ments, where a few women were sitting at sale ; it is
said to be the half-way place.

The road now was bordered with the Locust that
affords the Afiti sauce, by the Egbas called Ogiri.   It is
a tall irregular tree, with a leaf like a young fern ; the
fruit dangles to a long cord, and when ripe it is scarlet-
red, and about the size of a billiard ball.   Presently
the soft external substance falls off, leaving the core,
a green sphere not larger than a musket bullet, and from
it sprout long bright green pods curiously twisted.
When ripe the seeds are fermented to a mass strong as
assafœtida, and form in palaver sauce a favourite
ingredient, which however the stranger will not
relish before some time.   It is the " wild tamarind " of
Mr. Dalzel, and in the landscape it forms a most
effective feature.

Followed in rapid succession on both sides of the
path the fetish clearings of Daji, a princely worship,
Gá-sá-uhun † and Logun-aizan 'li, a Bo-name given by

---

* Akwe (cowries), janahan (if you have not got *scil.*, you can buy
nothing).

† Ga (bow), sa (throwing), uhun (bombax tree).

King Gezo. The next was a mud-house and a farm belonging to royalty : it is called Nyakho-gon, the place of Nyakho, the ruling chief, who was captured and slain by Dako. Another sacred place, Vodun-no Deme, a Fetish of the Fanti company of Amazons, led to a bifurcation of the road. The left branch is a short cut to the Jegbe Palace, of which more afterwards. Close to the junction are the little hut villages of Attako and Ishagga, named after the conquests of the present reign : when the King breaks a town he builds another, and is supposed to place there the poor remnants of his captives. A little beyond and in the road is the Ugo 'li :* here is the celebrated shea butter-tree, alluded to by every traveller, and apparently the only fruitful Bassia in the country. It is short trunked, twelve to fifteen feet high, thick branched, and mango-shaped, with a tender green leaf, at first of a dark colour, then waxing yellow and affording a dense shade, in which a small market is held. It is now flowering, and it will bear fruit in the rains. Then came a clear

L

* Ugo (shea butter-tree), 'li (for ali, a road). According to Mr. Duncan (vol. i. p. 285) this valuable tree was destroyed throughout the land at the suggestion of the Spanish and Portuguese slavers— which is incredible. He well describes the fruit and its various medicinal uses.

space on the left of the road, called Van-van from a Nago town conquered by Gezo. A "joji" * or tall gallows of thin poles, with the Azan fetish fringe to prevent the passage of calamity, then halted us : a wisp of grass was handed to each of us, and we were desired to throw it away to the fetish ; whom may Allah blight ! The land around is called Leflefun,† from the Nago people, whose chief, Cháde, was slain by King Gezo, and who were finally settled here. The eye dwells with delight upon the numerous country villages, like the 115 towns of the tribe of Judah, and upon the thin forest of palms rising from the tapestry of herbage, here waving, there cut short, which combine to make this spot the Fridaus or Paradise of Dahome-land.

Presently we arrived at another terminus or bifurca-tion, the left path leading to the houses of the Matro and the Adanejan, the Komasi Palace, and the Uhun-jro market. The next notable place was the Patin-'li, where the now grassy road widens out, and shows two ragged lines of figs, calabashes, locusts, and oil palm trees. This is also an Adan-gbno-ten or swearing-

---

* Jo (wind), ji (upon).
† The Leffle-foo of Commander Forbes (vol. i. p. 68).

place, where the King halts before entering Agbome
from Kana, to receive the oaths of fidelity, and to hear
the brave talk of his high officials, especially the
military. A heap of ashes,* the usual sign of entering
a great fetish place, points to a white village of
Bo-hwé, tabernacles,† or fetish hovels, under huge
cotton woods, beginning at about 350 yards from the
town gate. The guardian or Janus is Bo, who is Legba
on a larger scale. The nearest fetish huts are six in
number, and are disposed across the road; a neat
compound for spiritual meetings rising from the grass
on the right hand. The hovels contained effigies of
chamelions, speckled white and red; horses known
only by their halters; squatting men, like Day and
Night at masquerades, half mud-coloured and half
spotted; others brown all over, and grinning with
cowrie-teeth; and the largest a huge chalked gorilla,
intended to be human, and completely disgusting.
Beyond it, to the right of the path, was a single
swish room, a fetish place, where the King sits before
entering his capital; around it cluster dwarf thatches
sheltering attempts at leopards, and other holy beasts.

* Called Afin (ashes), zuru (heap), ji (upon).
† Levit. xxiii. 40.

Near the city gate is another village of fetish hovels,
where a trivia leads on the right to the Yevogan's
hereditary hamlets, straight in front to the capital, and
by the left to the Jegbe, the present ruler's country
palace.

We are now at the Dosum-wen Agbo-nun,* the
feature which gives its name to Agbome, the capital.
The word signifying the " town within the enceinte," or
" precincts ;" and it has the anomaly of being, and probably of ever having been, with gateways and without
walls.   The Agbo is a mud screen of five steps or
courses, like the palace enceintes, fifteen to eighteen
feet high, and about 100 yards long.   It is pierced with
two wedge-shaped gaps ; that to the right, as you front
it, is open for the public ; the other, and the larger, on
the left, is reserved for the ruler.   The latter is permanently blocked up with a stout hurdle, six feet high ; the
former is closed every night by a pair of similar fences,
tied to stout side-posts.   Before the wall is a shallow
moat, well worn by human feet.   Being pool-fronted
during the rains each more important gate is entered

* Meaning the town-gate of Dosum-wen, the name of the keeper. It
is called by Europeans the Kana gate. I have already explained the
meaning of Agbo-nun. Dr. M'Leod (p. 95), translates Abomey, by " Let
me alone.' (!)

by a clay mound or by two solid beams, overlaid with rough planks, forming a bridge. Beyond the passage, at the ends, the moat is dense grown with trees, especially with the thick and thorny acacia bush—in these lands one of the best defences,—and it is prolonged round the capital. It is never cleared. The outside grass is removed, lest in burning the stubbles the Zun[*] might catch fire. There are tunnels through the acacia bush where people may go to gather leaves and plants for simples : none of the lieges, however, are permitted, under pain of severe palaver, to cross the ditch except by the established entrances. There is a superstition touching these bridges. In former reigns, if any subject happened to fall when treading one of them he lost his head, even as in olden times happened to a dancer so committing himself or herself before the King [†]

Arrived at the Kana gate we descended from our hammocks, whilst all our attendants bared their shoulders, removed their hats, and furled our umbrellas,

[*] In all Yoruba towns the bush adjoining villages and towns is spared for defence and shelter: at Abeokuta it is called " abu-si," and here " zun."

[†] See Dr. M'Leod (p. 59). Mr. Duncan (vol. ii. p. 289), being lame, was permitted by the fetishman, on the King's order, to ride through the gate, " at which every man seemed much amazed."

as if it were part of the King's palace. Passing in, we found on the ground, at each side of the gate, a small black figure called a Bo-chio. A little higher up, and let into the clay of the gap-side, is a human skull,* with thigh bones and other amulets hanging about. Inside there are two guard-houses, leading to the Agbonun-'khi, or "gate market," one of the rude little bazaars scattered about the town. Beyond it, and placed to defend the entrance, are the remains of a broken-down battery. On the ground, to the right of the road, lie thirty-six, on the left thirty-five old guns, with their touch-holes rivalling their muzzles, and with trunnions in many cases knocked off, showing the insolent security of the place, and giving it already the aspect of a ruin. Behind the right-hand battery is the residence of the Gau, behind the left that of the Po-su ; so, in the city of Great Benin, the "Captain of War's" establishment is at the entrance. Both are the usual masses of huts, enclosed in the normal clay wall. The establishment of the Commander-in-Chief is called Gau-sra-men ;† it is backed by "Gau-hwe-gudo," an open

---

* Skulls are also nailed to doors, in token of respect for some dead enemy

† Sra means the slaves' quarters, near the master's house.

space of grass and dwarf corn plants, and that quarter
of the town is still known as Agbo-kho-nun,* the site
of the old gate which Agaja the Great removed to its
present position. It is evident, at the first glance, that
Agbome is built less closely than Whydah ; and that
the open spaces and gardens, even in the thickest part
of the town, have greatly the better of the houses.

The blacksmith's quarter, a field dotted with open
hovels, leads to the large enceinte of the old Meu : it
contains a prison for minor offenders, and the walls are
defended by a *chevaux de frise* of sharpened sticks.
We then arrived at an open space with a few trees to
the eastward of the "mighty carcase," called the
Agbome Palace. The *place* was bounded on the north
by the usual entrance to a Dahoman royal abode, a
huge barn-like shed, built by Agaja, the fourth king,
and called " Agrin-go-men"—" In Agrin's Quiver." †
On the west is the Ji-hwe, or Lofty Abode, by strangers
called the Cowrie-house. It is a two-storied barn

* Agbo (the enceinte), kho (old), and nun (side, or mouth).

† Others say by Aho (Adahoonzou I.) the second king. It is related
that when he importuned for more land Agrin, a petty chief of the
place, the latter exclaimed, " Wouldst thou build in Agrin's quiver ?"
He was duly slain, and the gate was erected according to his words.
The etymon is too like that of " Dahome " (Chapter V.) not to excite
our suspicions.

under a heavy thatch. The red-clay walls are split
from top to foot, and almost all of the thirty-eight
windows, or rather holes, in the frontage sides, and
four in the short ends, are shored up with sticks. Long
lines of cowries are suspended from the windows during
the Customs, to astonish the weak minds of the lieges,
and these "bawbees" are afterwards removed.

Having learned my ceremonial by heart, I positively
refused to dismount at this place, and I found afterwards that it was a mere impertinence on the part of
the Buko-no. We passed along the southern wall of the
Agbome Palace, our direction being from N.E. to S.W.
On the summit were a few rusty iron skull-holders, an
upright spike to pass through the cranium, with a ring
as handle, and in the lower part a thin crescent-shaped
bar for the base of the head to rest upon. There was
only one human relic, a great alteration since the days
of Sinmenkpen (Adahoonzou II.), who, though six
slavers were awaiting their loads at Whydah, excited
the admiration of his subjects by taking off 147 heads
to complete the "thatching of his house."* The

* According to the History, the war-order of the King to his Gau
was to "thatch his house," and in those days human skulls were placed
on the roofs of the sheds at the palace doors. None of the natives knew

custom is evidently dying out, and Agbome will soon ignore what the Persians would call her "kalleh-munar." *

After passing a huge unrepaired rent in the Palace walls, whose miserable tattered aspect was an emblem of the decaying Empire, and after hastening from its dirty drains, mere holes with a bright shrub springing from a foul pool, we came to a second barn-like shed. It is called the Agwaji Gate, and was built by King Tegbwe-sun (Bossa Ahadi). Turning an angle we debouched upon the palm leaf fence, denoting the new gate of the present king, which, according to custom, he is expected to complete. Near it is another large shed, known as Agrin-masogbe.

We then reached the *Grande Place* of Agbome, the scene of Gezo's displays and receptions, but neglected by the present king. The aspect reminded me of the History's description, "An assemblage of farmyards with long thatched barns." Of these there were about a dozen, large and small, intended to shelter the

the phrase, which is perhaps obsolete. The Komasi Palace, built by Gezo, is quite free from this manner of ornamentation.

* A skull minaret. After a massacre, the heads were built up with lime into a kind of tower, the Oriental modification of our cotemporary hanging in chains.

soldiery.   As usual, a few shady trees, chiefly the
thick-leaved ficus, relieved the baldness of the view.
On the N.E. side, springing from the enceinte, was the
Singbo, or two-storied house built by King Gezo, and
his favourite place of residence. Covered with a pent-
roof thatch, the walls were of clay, whose redness
blushed through the thin coat of chalk acting white-
wash, and the front was pierced for eight windows with
large shutters of pale-green, and small wickets.   The
doorway was un-European, a dwarf barn of Dahoman
fashion, and we found there three umbrellas, white, blue,
and pink, the former belonging to the Governor of the
Palace.

This dignitary is an old servant of Gezo, once the
kan-gbo-de, or King's store-keeper, but degraded, as has
been said, for presuming to ride up to the royal gate.
He is now known as Kpon-ne-mi—" Look for me ! "
According to custom we dismounted before this palace.
The fat old man, in brass bracelets and pink checked
cloth, prostrated himself in front of the gate, whilst we
stood and bowed to it.   He then snapped fingers, and
returning to the half-opened door, whispered in con-
sultation with some of the female inmates.   Presently
he returned with the formula, " That the King's wife,

having inquired about every one in England, desired us to go and eat, after which we should have her message."

Leaving the Singbo, we passed on the right another huge barn entrance to the enceinte, supported by fourteen mud pillars, and called Adan-jro-'ko de.* It shelters the two howitzers presented to the late Gezo by the French Government ; they are not better treated than the English presents at Abeokuta. Under a tree in the square-centre is a curious relic of the past—a fine brass gun, gone in the touch-hole, and bearing as inscription, " Dordrect, 1640—Coenraet Wegewaert me fecit." It is therefore almost coeval with the Dahoman kingdom.

The broad road on the south of the Agbome palace was now lined with gazers, and the Court being at Kana we did not suffer from the bell-women, the peculiar plague of the place. Advancing, we turned another abrupt angle, and facing west, passed on the left the roomy and comparatively comfortable house of Prince Chyudaton, where the luckier French lodge. A

* Adan (brave), jro (likes), ako (family, tribe), de (any one). Meaning, if any people be brave and like (to fight, let them come and take Dahome). Commander Forbes spoils all this fine sentiment in his "Dangeh la Cordah."

few doors further placed us at the Buko-no's establishment—cow-houses, ultra-Arcadian in their simplicity—
of which the first sight was enough. These people so
dearly love domesticity that they make their houses
prisons to all inside, where there is no possibility of
privacy. From within you see only tall red walls, with
perhaps a few tree tops, and thatch roofs above and
beyond it, making the saddest impression upon a lover
of liberty. On the other hand, every word uttered can
be heard throughout the building, thus securing, as in a
ship, the two greatest and opposite undesirables. It is
evident that the King, unlike him of Ashanti, does not
visit the strangers' quarters and drink palm-wine with
them.*

The establishment lies to the west of the Agbome
palace, insulated as usual, and the parallelogram of
about 300 ft. each way is not quite square with the
cardinal points, our principal room fronting E. S. East.
The enceinte is bisected by a high wall with a single
door, which is carefully closed at night. Our landlord
and his many wives are to the eastward of us; we
could hear the laughter of these merry dames, but only

---

* Nor is it at present "etiquette" for the King of Dahome to visit
even his highest officers.

one old specimen ever leaves the house by that door.
We occupy the western half, lately vacated by Sedozau,
a son of the King, and the first item of two sets of
twins presented to royalty by the she-Yevogan, who
thus took the initiative in making him a father.   We
entered by a southern gateway with the customary
thatch : in aftertimes the King's Dr. Dee was ever
hanging it with his superstitious frippery.   The door
was a screen of bamboo fronds with native hinges, a
pole working in wooden cups.   This entrance led into
a kind of outer court, containing only a shed for the
hammock-men, who left it uncleaned for two months.
An opposite doorway opened upon the backyard, a
mixture of filth and fetish of which more presently.
Another adit through a wall to the right led to our
private quarters : it had fortunately a stout wooden
planking, which we closed when privacy was desirable.

Our lodging was a barn 45 feet long, by 27 feet
deep.   A thick thatch, like the East Indian chappar,
descended within 4·50 feet of the ground, and rested
on a double line of strong posts buried in the earth.
The north-eastern angle of the roof formed a kind of
false gable, or single pavilion wing like the Kobbi of
Abeokuta, here called " kho-zwe," or house-corner.   The

verandah had an earth-step, some eight inches high, to
keep out the rain, with a descent to the floor of tamped
earth.   The low ceiling was of rough sticks, plastered,
like the walls, with native white-wash.

After the verandah we entered the " hall," an apartment 20 feet by 10.   On the left was an earthen
estrade, about thirty inches high, a sleeping platform for
domestic servants.   In front was a small dark room,
hot to the last degree, as are all places in this country
where the wind cannot penetrate.   I at once knocked
a window through the back wall of clay, which was two
feet thick, provided it with a shutter made out of a
claret case, and turned it into a tolerable study.   Attached to it was a dark and windowless store-room,
whence the " drivers " sallied out once a week ; having,
however, a door, a lock, and a key, it saved us many a
gallon of rum and bag of cowries.   On the right of the
hall and study were two small dark rooms, and, lastly,
an open verandah occupied the whole depth of the
house under the false gable ; it had in one corner a
raised earth-rim for a balneary, and a drain to draw off
the water.   Opposite this verandah a strip of courtyard
was divided by a jealous party wall from the Buko-no's
quarters.

The front court, facing to the E. S. East, commanded a view of the top of a pollarded calabash, and a blasted tree upon which the early vultures prospected for carrion. The back yard * contained sundry heaps of offal, the "cook-houses," and the *lares* of the young prince, who had been given by his father to the Buko-no, with the object of learning medicine, and perhaps of preventing poison. I must describe them at some length to show the intricate practical worship of this people. Shortly after my arrival, hearing my *velléité* for curiosities, even under sacrilegious circumstances, two fetish youths made their appearance in the evening, knelt down before the domestic altar, prayed, broke some of the images, and went away declaring that they had called out the fetish, and that I might, after this *evocatio deorum*, do my worst. Similarly we removed all the fetish from the lodging-house, and the Buko-no only laughed—this was *en règle :* of course we could not have turned it out of his.

The roof of the Bo-kho, Bo-temple, or *Lararium*, had been allowed to fall, exposing the worshipful inmates to every weather. There were two sets of grotesque

* Here called " Kho-gudu," the " Ipaka " of the Egbas.

figures ranged in a row opposite one another.   That to
the south numbered six.   1. A bit of iron-stone clay
stuck round with feathers, and planted on a swish clay
step a couple of inches high.   2. A little Bo-doll, in a
cullender or perforated pot.   3. An earthenware basin
with a circular base, surrounded with the Azan or
fetish palm-girdle, and the Asen (Sein ?), or Twin-iron*
stuck in the ground before it.   4. A Nlon-gbo, or
Sheep fetish, very easily confounded with—5. An Avun,
or canine, provided with any number of claws.   Finally,
No. 6 was an awful looking human face in alto-relief, flat
upon its base, a swish square, with a short stake planted
behind it, three small earthen pots rising from its
wrinkled forehead ; its huge gape of cowrie teeth, and
eyes of the same, set in red clay, were right well
calculated to frighten away, as it is intended to do,
witchcraft from the devotee.

The other set occupied three sides of the dwarf roof-
less hut ruin, and embraced everything necessary for
man's welfare.   A red clay kpakpa, or duck,† with a line

* It is formed of two iron cones, cymbal-shaped, and very like the
extinguisher of a candle, fastened to a single stem six inches long.   It
is generally planted in a lump of clay behind the Hoho pots, which will
presently be explained, and thus forms a domestic altar.

† Clearly an onomatopœtic word, like our " Quack."

of feathers round its neck, and an artificial tail, if duly
adored, makes the prayerful strong. A Bo male image,
half black half white, even to the wool, and hung with a
necklace of beasts' skulls ; with a pair of Hoho-zen, or
twin pots, two little double pipkins of red clay, big pipe-
bowls, united like the Siamese twins, and covered with
white-washed lids to guard the water offering, would
protect Sedozau and his brother from the ills to which
twin-flesh is heir. There was also a So-hwe, or " stick
beat," a wooden stump eighteen inches high and eight
inches in diameter, wrapped in old palm-leaf and dirty
calico, with a string of cowries hanging from its sooty
summit, and an Achatina shell on the higher of the two
dwarf steps forming its base. If a stone be struck upon
the top of this invaluable article the enemy certainly
sickens and dies. Defence against disease was secured
by a clay parallelogram, puddinged half with cowries and
half with pottery-bits stuck edgeways, and supporting
an Asen-iron and an Asiovi or fetish axe; by a red clay
Bo-man with a beard of poultry feathers and the left
side stuck with fragments of earthenware ; and by a
Bo-pot containing a heap of black earth rising to a ball,
and supporting a fetish iron. Proper respect for the
rainbow was shown by the presence of its favourite

ceramic,* containing a clay snake, with two small red
feathers for horns.   Finally, there was a pair of
" Iro " or philters, which, rubbed on after the bath,
obtain from man loan of moneys, from woman the *don
d'amoureuse merci :* the one was a pot, the other a calabash, full of filthy-looking grease, capped by the skulls
of a dog and of some other animal, one to each.

For the distances and other peculiarities of the road
between Whydah and Agbome, the reader is referred
to Appendix I.   It may be observed that the length
of the journey has shrunk, with wonderful regularity, to
the present year.   Mr. Lamb (1724) gives 200 miles
from the port to the capital ; Mr. Norris (1772),
112 miles ; Mr. Dalzel (1793), 96 miles ; Commander
Forbes (1849), 90 miles ; Commodore Wilmot (1863),
65 miles ; the general opinion being 75 miles.†   I found
(1864), by meridional observations of Sirius, a direct
distance of $51\frac{1}{6}$ geographical miles between the beach-
town Whydah and the English house, whilst my sketch
map gave 62 to 63 indirect miles.

* For a more detailed notice of these pots—each deity has its own—
the curious reader will consult Chapter XVII.

† M. Borghero (1861) made 150 indirect kilomètres to Kana, but he
passed round the longer Toffo road.   M. Jules Gérard (1863) reckoned
fifty indirect English statute miles from Whydah to Kana.

CHAPTER XI.

OUR arrival at the unpleasant domicile which was to be our home for nearly two months, was a signal for the Buko-no Uro to begin operations.* This *belle tête de mort* craved an audience, and, after the customary "ambages," requested me to open before him the four boxes of presents forwarded by Her Majesty's Government. His object was to secure the first news for the royal ears, hoping thereby—excuse the phrase—to curry a little favour. The boxes had been stored in his own magazine ; however, I of course refused to touch them, except inside the palace, and I told him to meddle with them at his peril. He pleaded usage, and the custom of the country. I rejoined that it was a false plea, the present being the first mission from Her Majesty's Government to the King, consequently that

* The second is a Bo name, belonging to his father.

there could be no precedent. Hoping, however, thereby
to exert some influence in the matter of human sacrifice, I read out my " Message," as instructions are
locally called, and regretted to receive only the ste-
reotyped replies.   The Buko-no, however, was duly
warned, that if any attempt was made to put to death
victims in our presence, it would be the signal for our
return to Whydah.   Which was, of course, duly
reported.

The next day, December 21, was to witness the
King's ceremonious return to his capital.   At noon, a
dusty-browed messenger rushed in, saying, that royalty
was approaching ; and we heard cannon-shots, denoting that the King was halted at the Adan-blon-
noten, receiving the homage of his war chiefs.   The
Buko-no ordered out his horse and " tail," and presently
came in a green sheet to fetch his strangers.   I was
taken in for the first, and not the last, time before the
day of our dismissal.   The fact is, this veteran so
believed in the usage of Dahome, that he considered
us to be, like other white men, during our residence at
the capital, mere slaves of the King.   I flatter myself
that when we left he had greatly modified that opinion.
On this occasion, our uniforms having been left at

Kana, we were compelled to wear the ordinary mourn-
ing attire of Englishmen when they want to be merry.
As the King approved of this proceeding, I resolved
for the future to confine uniform to the more ceremonious occasions within the palace.

We rode in our hammocks by a short cut, instead
of down the broad south-western road, flanking the
Agbome Palace. The sun was deadly, not being
tempered by the sea-breeze, which, at this season,
rarely blows before 3 P.M. We then turned southwards, along a large thoroughfare, towards the Ako-
chyo-'gbo-nun gate.* These streets are formed, like
those of Whydah, by the walls of the habitations,
thus giving them a populous look : they are, however,
mere shams, and forest-bush rises close behind them.
On the right there is an open space, with a 10 iron-
gun battery scattered upon the ground. We furled
our umbrellas, and, dismounting, marched through the
gate, a gap in an incontinuous wall, like that before
described. It opened upon the Uhun-jro † market, a
broad space, whence the huts had been cleared, and

* Ako (tribe, family), chyo (all), agbo'nun (gate) ; meaning, that all
the world must come to visit Dahome.

† Uhun-jro, or Uhun-jlo, is derived from the fact that a bombax from
a conquered place was there transplanted by Gezo.

where men were raising a scaffold of tree trunks, barked, and rudely squared. On the other side was the tattered wall of the royal precincts : the lowest of the five courses of mud masonry was much injured by contact with the ground. Passing under a scatter of trees, where women were seated, vending edibles, we remarked a man standing, gagged,* in front of a drummer, and we were told that he was a criminal, left for execution at the next Customs. Here the pace was quickened (it is not respectful to pass the Palace except in a hurry), and a summons from the King must be obeyed with ostentatious alacrity. On the left of the road, and distinguished by the careful sweeping of the space in front, is a large fetish-house, a long shed, called Nesu-hwe, and dedicated to Nesu, the peculiar Dahoman fetish, the tutelary numen of the empire.

Turning to the south, we dismounted, as the rule is, at the south-eastern corner of the Komasi Palace, built, as I have said, by King Gezo. We passed the Komasi gate, the usual barn, with twenty-seven wooden

* The instrument is a Y-shaped stick ; the sharp end touches the palate, whilst the fork embraces the tongue, so that the criminal, however much he may suffer, cannot cry out. The gag is used, because, if a man speak to the King, he must be pardoned.

posts, and with the two stunted and pollarded trees forming, with a bamboo, the *forca*, common to every palace gate. To the cross-pieces hung the normal Jo-susu, a little square mat, with narrow perpendicular stripes, alternately red and black, and a calabash, painted in ruddy and whitey-red speckled sections, like those of a melon, and by bundles of Bo-so, freshly painted Bo-sticks or truncheons, at each side, completed the defences of the entrance. From this the ruler will issue to perform the Customs, and his seat will be a little to the proper right of the door.* At the time only a few men and women soldiery, with tall white bonnets, like Sepoys' shakos in former times, lounged at the gate. Thence, guided by the Buko-no, whose band was never silent, we went to a tall tree, near the Agwaji, or southern gate ; a large thatch, with sixteen mud pillars ; and we placed our stools under its thin shade, witnessing the usual dancing.

The space about the Palace is clear, as in Great Benin ; but here there are no strews of skulls and skeletons. The only fragment of a man was a cranium, nailed together with a white flag to the trunk, under

* I thereby mean the left side, as one stands opposite it.

the lowest boughs of a large tree opposite the Komasi gate. As usual in Yoruba towns, where they build loosely to avoid the fires which annually devastate elbowing Lagos, the open space in which the multitude will gather for the Customs was scattered over with palms, calabashes, and figs, with a natural ablaqueation, their roots having been bared by rain. There were, besides two mean fetish-houses, only three remarkable objects in it. The first was a scaffolding, gradually rising, opposite the palace. The next was the Adanzan, a round house, with rough posts, supporting a conical thatch roof, capped with a white pennon. The two opposite entrances were each flanked by two small sentinel huts, with clay walls, and shaped somewhat like old bee-hives. The interior showed two flights, each of eight mud steps, barred against intruders, and the interior was concealed by screens of matting. Before campaigning, the King here swears, in the presence of his soldiery, what he will do, and listens to their terrible boasting of valour. On such occasions, the roof and screens are removed.* The third was a

* This was a ceremony introduced by King Gezo. I was told that the present King keeps it up, but during my stay at Agbome it was not performed.

fine Bombax, enclosed in a dwarf mud wall, and called Bwekon-uhun, the Bwe-kon cotton-wood, under which Gezo used to sit before he built the Komasi Palace. The name Bwe-kon,* meaning a happy or auspicious spot, is also applied to the large southern and detached suburb, divided from the royal house by the open space, and by three wall-less sheds, where the troops sit. It contains the Bwe-kon Hwe-'gbo, or big house, built by Agongoro (Wheenoohew). The other tenements are those of men about Court, and many Aja and Takpa † captives are settled here. Beyond Bwe-kon, again, is the Jegbe Palace, of which more hereafter.

We observed the place narrowly, on account of its connection with the coming executions. Long strings of people, especially women, who apparently do little else, were passing to and fro, carrying on their heads monstrous baskets and calabashes, " wide as the old Winchester bushel," with food for their mistresses the soldieresses. Shortly after 1 P.M. two umbrellas, white and pink, preceded by musketeers, announced the arrival of Agbota, senior Governor of Whe-gbo, and of

* Bwe (happy), kon (living).
† Chapter XXI.

eastern road,* formed in masses at the other end of the open space, somewhat as in a theatre. Then, with the braying of trumpets and the beating of drums, they began to pass round in review order. The right shoulder is presented to the King's gate, the Pradakshina of the Hindus, opposed to the Arab Tawaf, or circumambulation, which turns the left side to a venerated object ; and we shall observe this in all future processions. The Captains danced and skipped like the Salii, their attendants firing and skirmishing before them. As is customary, the juniors came first, five warriors and worthies of the King leading the rest.† They were followed by the Po-su, the " place " of the Matro, and the Gau, in a black felt, riding a "tattoo," and accompanied by his agminal umbrella, of red, blue, and buff colours. Followed three caboceers,‡ and two of the King's half-brothers, Bosu Sau and Nuage. The 15th was Assoyon, under a white umbrella, with twelve men dancing and sham-fighting before him ; followed by Assogban and Akhokhwe, a half-brother of the King, with a fancy umbrella and

---

* The southern entrance is sometimes preferred.

† *Viz.*, the Aloghan, Akpi, Dokhenun, Akati, and Ahwibame.

‡ *Viz.*, the Kade, Jogbwenun, and Apwejekun.

an escort of seventeen men. Two other caboceers[*]
preceded the place of Chyudaton, who was sitting with
us, and the 21st[†] umbrella ushered in the Bi-wan-ton,
a man with a pleasant expression, whose escort was a
fancy umbrella and ten men. The Adanejan, habited
in a red and blue tunic, and riding, woman-like, a
little pony, was preceded by sixty men, firing and
dancing, accompanied by plain red and white fancy
flags, and followed, like most of the others, by his big
drum on a man's head, another beating it from behind,
as if braining it.

After a short pause, the old Adukonun, a brother
of the late king, advanced, followed by the Tokpau, a
war chief, who fired his gun from the shoulder, under
an umbrella speckled white and blue. The 26th party,
that of the Awobi, preceded the Yevo-gan of Whydah
with a French tricolor, a white umbrella, and an escort
of fifty men : he rode, and waved hands to us as he
passed. Four other worthies ushered in the highest
official of the empire, the senior Min-gan. His dress
was a war-tunic and a Lagos smoking-cap; with pipe

---

[*] *Viz.*, the Akho, with a fancy umbrella and fourteen men, and the
Ukwenun, with a white umbrella and nineteen men.

[†] *Viz.*, the Tokonun-vissau, who was on horseback.

in mouth he rode a nag handsomely caparisoned, under a white fancy umbrella. He was numerously escorted, and was followed by a big drum, and by rattles, discoursing hideous music. Being a man of the old school, he studiously avoided looking towards us, lest he might be compelled to salute.

The lesser chiefs, after passing once round the square, if I may so call it, crossed, and formed a line of umbrellas opposite the Komasi gateway. The high dignitaries performed their circuits in the order before described, the Min-gan immediately preceding the 33rd party, which was that of the King.

The royal *cortége* consisted of about 500 musketeers and blunderbuss men : it was preceded by skirmishers, under the command of Adan-men-nun-kon, "Blue" Captain. They were accompanied by one skull standard, and eight flags, white, red, anchor-marked, and fancy ; and they were followed by two gorgeous umbrellas. Immediately in front of the King were borne two leather shields, sections of cylinders, white, with black patterns, upraised horizontally at the full length of the bearer's arm. They are a remnant of the old days, when the Dahoman soldiery was armed with muskets, cutting swords, and shields ; the latter carried ɪ boy squires, of whom one was told off for training each man-at-arms. The weapon is now looked upon ᷉ a kind of ægis. Near the shields stalked two big bold dragoons," in brass helmets and huge black ɔrse-tails.* They had guns as long as spears. Be-nd them, in a white calico case, and capped with a ɪowy plume, the iron Bo-fetish stick, called " kafo," ınounced the presence of royalty. The King rode ᷉der four white umbrellas ; and three parasols, yellow, ᷉urple, and blue-red, were waved and twisted over him,) act as fans. When he passed before us, exchanging ɪlutes, there was the usual " Tohu wa Bohu," a frantic ᷉sh, filling the air with red dust, a swarming of men round him, " riotously and routously," and a *feu 'enfer* from their weapons. Following a huge fetish ᷉e came the band, mostly boys, whose thirty rattles, ᷉irty cymbals, and dozens of drums, added their din) the wildness of the spectacle. A crowd of slaves ᷉en appeared, laden with large Gold Coast chairs, ᷉xes and baskets of cowries, bottles, decanters, and ᷉her articles : in fact, it was the commissariat, with a

* Mr. Norris mentions a troop of forty women, with silver helmets : ᷉ch wealth has long disappeared. A French merchant presented to ᷉ng Gezo 100 brilliant casques of *pompiers.*

suspicion of *bakhshish* or largesse.   The rear was
brought up by two shabby war-umbrellas, white and
blue, whilst a tattered flag announced the *arrière-garde.*

The King went round twice, in an antiquated red-
lined vehicle, a mongrel between a cab and a brougham.
It was drawn by men, who, at the third circuit, raised
it upon their shoulders :—the African labourer will do
the same with his wheelbarrow.   The fourth and fifth
tours were made in a Bath chair, a late present from a
committee of English philanthropes ; the sixth time it
was carried aloft, like the carriage.   The royal circuits
are usually three ; the extraordinary number was possibly intended to afford me an opportunity of "book-
ing" the procession ; besides which, the ruler, being
young, is, as will be remarked throughout the Customs, fond of change.   The King pressed his mouth
with a thick kerchief, to keep out the dust.   As an
old traveller says of the Whydah monarch, "he
seems of a good free temper, and full of mirth and
kindness, especially when he intends to beg a boon."
This day he looked wearied and cross, an expression
not unfrequent upon the brow of royalty in all lands.
We must consider, however, that he went a total of
ten circuits of the square, representing some five miles

' dust and din. We were afterwards informed that
℈ had been slightly indisposed at Kana ; but had
ꞇsitively refused to break an appointment with his
white friend." Illness is rare with him : M. Wallon
ιys he was sickly in youth ; despite reports he shows
ꞇ traces of debility now. It is wonderful to see the
ꞇount of labour which he endures in the form of
leasure, and the cheerfulness which he maintains
ꞇder his enjoyments : he seldom misses a day in
ublic, and he ends by tiring out the whole Court.

When the male chiefs and soldiery had made their
xth round, they joined the line of umbrellas on the
ꞇuth-east of the square. The King then transferred
imself and his most gorgeous canopies to the Ama-
ꞇury, which was massed at the mouth of the eastern
ꞇad. Presently, preceded by skirmishers, firing, and
ꞇnging their sharp bells, the women, forming three
ꞇrps, that they might appear the more numerous,
ashed into the square. The first brigade was that of
ꞇe she-Mingan, four white umbrellas and two flags :
ꞇme were in parade uniform, others in their travelling
arb—brown tunics. This small party was followed
y its band, and, at a short distance, by the twenty-
ne umbrellas and the five flags of the she-Meu's troop,

concluding with their music. After three turns, dancing, singing, and firing muskets and blunderbusses, they
retired to the east of the palace.

The royal body-guard, called the Fanti,* now appeared upon the stage. Their skirmishers, young
women in high training, performed with great agility.
Then came twelve fancy flags, escorted by half a dozen
razor women, who were followed by a platter, containing a calabash adorned with skulls. Immediately before
the King were two crimson leather shields, held up as
the others were by the men. The Monarch was carried
by twelve women, in a hammock of yellow silk, hanging
from a pole, about thirteen feet long, black, set with
silver sharks, and shod at both ends with brass. Three
royal umbrellas, blue, red, and yellow, defended him
from the sun, and he was fanned by three parasols,
which were not the same as before. Again we remarked amongst this people the inordinate hankering
after change, novelty, and originality, even in the most
trivial matters, and the failure which results from their
poverty of, or rather their deficiency in, invention.
After the royal hammock came the bands—rattles,

* Or Gold Coast Corps, in somewhat better discipline than the late
unlamented G. C. A.

cymbals, and drums—with two white umbrellas ; and
the rear was brought up by the baskets and baggage
of the commissariat, and by the flags of the *arrière-
garde*.

After the King had made four circuits, the beginning
of the end was shown by the old To-no-nun crouching
near our table.   " It " was dressed in a blue velvet
cap, a blanket jacket, and cotton tights, and " it "
looked more like a guenon than a human.   Gelele
halted opposite us, and sundry of the elder Dakros
brought for us four large coloured decanters of rum,
and small bottles of trade liqueur, which were received
by the chief eunuch.   Strangers are sometimes addressed personally at the end of these parades.   On the
present occasion, fatigue, souring temper, abridged
ceremony.   The King and Fanti *cortége* then stood
aggrouped to the west of the square, where a heavy
salute of blunderbusses was fired.   They finally passed
round to the east, and slowly defiled through the
Komasi gate, folding their umbrellas, in token that the
" play " was done.   The men soldiers indulged in a
frantic *carrousel* opposite the palace, furiously dragging
the empty old brougham round and round, shouting,
screaming, and firing their weapons like madmen.   We

waited till the square was clear of women, and at
5·45 P.M. we retired from the Laus-Perennis of row
and riot, with the usual finale to a Dahoman parade—
a headache. Our guides, the Buko-no and the Prince
Chyudaton, retired to *breakfast*.

CHAPTER XII.

THE PRESENTS ARE DELIVERED.

AT night a violent tornado, whose sheets of flying water could hardly be called rain, and a heavy shower in the morning, convinced our hosts that we were " good men, whose palaver would be soft as water, not hot as fire." The next day (December 22) ought to have been one of rest, but the King could not curb his impatience to see the presents sent by Her Majesty's Government. A final attempt to make me open the boxes was vainly made by the Buko-no, who then forwarded them under protest to the palace. I could see, however, by his face that the absence of certain highly coveted articles had been reported, and had excited royal dissatisfaction. Our offerings* to the

---

* We presented to the King:—
    1 picture.
    1 box French perfumery.
    2 pieces merinos.

And to the English Mother:—
    1 fathom silk kerchief.
    1 piece figured calico
       (Madras).

King and to the English mother*—whom, by-the-by, I have never seen—were at once shown and given over to the Buko-no, as a matter of little moment.

At 10·15 A.M. we set out to the Komasi Palace, and placed our chairs opposite the Agwaji gate. Presently Prince Chyudaton, after prostrating, shovelling dust, and kissing the ground, before the Komasi entrance, under the tree with the ominous fruit, joined us. The party was completed by the Buko-no, who issued from

1 piece crimson silk.
1 silk kerchief.
1 case curaçoa.
1 dozen coloured glass tumblers.

Mr. Bernasko gave to the King :—	To the Buko-no :—
1 carpet.	10 yards silk.
1 case of liqueur.	1 piece Madras.
1 piece blue Danes.	2 silk kerchiefs.
	1 pair razors.

Sundry other presents of cloth must be given to the landlord and the chief officers. These, however, I reserved for the exit.

* At the Court of Dahome every man must have at least one mother, and she may be twenty years his junior. The King's actual parent is now alive; when she departs, he must supply her place by selection. For each monarch in the dynasty there is, as will be seen, an old woman mother. The " mothers " of the high officials are the corresponding honours. For instance, the she-Min-gan is popularly called the " he-Min-gan's mother." Many have two " mothers," an old one for the last, and a young one for the present reign. Visitors communicate with the " mothers " of their several nations. As will be seen, " mothers " is the official title of the " Amazons "—hence the custom.

the palace, by the fat Adanejan, and by the Bi-wan-
ton, or junior Meu, who acts as the Master of Ceremonies in the absence of his principal. These worthies
were in poor "Hausa tobes," showing that we were
not likely to see royalty that day.

After waiting causelessly half an hour, we received a
summons to enter. Removing our uniform caps, we
passed through the Gate of Tears into a deep, gloomy
barn, so dark that we could hardly distinguish the two
characteristic features, women selling provisions on the
right, and on the left Gezo's immense war-drum,
chapletted with skulls.* The inner court, which we
were fated to learn by heart, bore a family resemblance
to that of Kana. Here, however, the westerly side
was a partially whitewashed royal store-house for cloth,
cowries, and rum—the notes, silver, and copper of the
country. At its northern extremity, a rough ladder
led to an immense boarded-up window in the second
story, and giving to the whole the appearance of a

---

* This, the national oriflamme, is called Nun (with a very nasal N,
sounding like Nú, a thing), ú (that), pwe (able), to (he that does). It
is a title assumed by King Gezo, and meaning, "He is able to do anything he likes." As will be seen, it was first taken by him when he
imported from England a carriage and horses, and it is applied to a
cloth, and to other articles of Dahoman vanity.

grange. At the bottom of the court was the usual
thatched barn, like the men's guard-house outside ; and
four white, with three tulip-tinted, umbrellas, showed
the King's place. The square was scattered over with
trees and fetish. On the right side were five Legbas
under one little thatch. To the left rose four fetish
huts, each containing a dwarf whitewashed idol. The
most remarkable figure, a Janus, composed of two
naked bodies joined *à tergo*, was made of dark clay,
with glaring white eyes, and two pair of antlers, bending
inwards. Probably this " Auld Hornie " has been borrowed from the Portuguese idea of Sathanas.

The list of presents has been given in the Preface. I
may be allowed to say of them a few words.

1. The tent was found to be too small, and, indeed,
to sit under it for an hour would have been hardly
possible. We were obliged to pitch it with our own
hands, which evinced complication, and, in a land of
white ants, metal, not wooden, pegs were required, as
Mr. Edgington, whose cards fell in a shower from the
boxes, should have known. The article was handsome,
more so, perhaps, than anything belonging to the King ;
yet the only part of it admired was the gingerbread
lion on the pole-top.

2. The pipe was never used, Gelele preferring, for lightness, his old red clay and wooden stem.

3. The *belts* caused great disappointment : all the officials declared that *bracelets* had been mentioned to Commodore Wilmot. Africans are offended if their wishes are not exactly consulted, and they mulishly look upon any such small oversight as an intended slight.

4. The silver waiters were very much admired, and their use was diligently inquired into.

5. The coat of mail was found too heavy ; and, as it will certainly be hung up, fired at, and broken by the King, a common cuirass would have been better. The gauntlet was too small, and, like the former article, not galvanized.

But what about the carriage and horses ?

I vainly, for the dozenth time, explained the difficulty of sending them. It was disposed of at once with consummate coolness. Carriages had been brought, and could come again. If the horses died upon the beach at Whydah, no matter. King Gezo, after obtaining an equipage, had taken the strong name Nun-u-pwe-to, and the son burned to emulate the sire. My hints touching the propriety of some concession, on their part, in the cause of humanity, were as cavalierly ignored.

A few words touching presents to African princes, the sole object of whose foreign friendships is to obtain them, and with whom those who pay the highest are, and ever will be, the most powerful. I have already mentioned one requisite for contenting them, namely, attending to their wishes. A second and a third are, that the gifts should be rich and showy, or, at least, well *assortis*,* and that they should not come too often. It is commonly supposed in England, that anything is good enough for a barbarian ; and I have seen presents sent out which a West-African chief would hardly think of giving to his slave. The old days of the *traité* familiarised the higher ranks with a kind of magnificence, and they have not forgotten it.

At Dahome, everything given to the King is carried

* In Dahome, for instance, at the present time : A silver liqueur-case, with six bottles, each labelled, and a dozen strong and ornamented glasses ; a pair of portable mahogany tables, about three feet in diameter ; a dozen good chairs for guests : they must be of iron, or they will be broken in a month ; a strong lantern for night use ; English Union Jacks, and other flags—the bigger and gaudier the better. On one occasion the King sent me a message, that he vehemently wanted some large banners inscribed with Her Majesty's august name. Finally, all these African kings, from Gelele to Rumanika of Karagwah, are delighted with children's toys, gutta-percha fans, Noah's Arks ; in fact,

to the palace during the hours of darkness, and is concealed with care from the multitude. On the other hand, the meanest article presented by him, after being paraded round the squares, that the King's munificence may be known to the whole world, is sent in state to the happy recipient's house. Under these circumstances, it is some satisfaction to know that the " dash " in these regions, like the bribe in Asia, is omnipotent.

On the present occasion, the King never even uttered an expression of gratitude. His disappointment soon pierced through his politeness, which was barely retained by a state of feeling best expressed in our popular adage,—" Better luck next time," especially in the matter of an English carriage and horses.

When the tent had been pitched, the other boxes were carried by three juvenile captainesses under the King's barn-verandah, and we were summoned by the old slave women to open them. Despite their respect, and almost adoration, for the royal person, all the barbarian officiality present made trial of the pipe and the gauntlets. They asked us to do the same, when I

what would be most acceptable to a child of eight—which the negro is. Unfortunately, I could find none upon the coast, where they are used only in the Batanga ivory trade.

informed them that such was not our idea of respect to crowned heads. The young Amazons presently bore the gifts into the interior, carefully closing the door,—a huge, rudely cut board, carved into a human head, with stripes for hair, a face, and a knife, with other Fetish objects, stuck about it. The messengers brought us water and Akansan bread,* which my companions mixed with the element. A bottle of Medoc was produced from the royal cellar : it was lukewarm, and far too sour to drink. Yet I have no doubt but that it was bought with gold. This is the inevitable result of trading with slavers, who sell the worst of everything for the highest prices ; the refuse of European markets for a cargo which, if successful, fetches ten times its cost price. Upon this subject the Dahomans have not been blinded ; but, like children, they want to eat and keep their pudding, to combine the profits of illicit with the benefits of licit commerce, and the constant formula is, that what white men have done, white men must undo.

Presently the young women returned, bearing the royal request that we would withdraw to our former

* See Chapter V. This custom of placing a table before the visitor with " plenty of refreshment, both of solids and liquids," was practised by King Gezo.—Mr. Duncan, vol. i. p. 243.

place under the thin tamarind. This was to enable the
" King's wives " to inspect the tent without approaching
too near us. The Amazons again disappeared to report, and they soon brought back a dismissal decanter
of rum, with the evil tidings that my " Message "
would be heard at another opportunity.

At 1·15 P.M. we retired, after the unusually short
corvée of three hours. ˙ The rain-sun was dangerous
when it broke through the clouds, despite occasional
puffs of cool sea-breeze. We entered the house in
time to escape a heavy storm from the east, rising
against the lower wind. It had all the characteristics
of a tornado, rattling, crackling thunder, with prolonged electric crepitations ; vivid, rose-coloured, forked
lightning appearing to lick the earth with the tip of
its fiery tongue ; and gusts, that tore the thatched
roofs from the houses, and sounded like discharges of
artillery. Parenthetically, we hardly ever had a shower
without these displays of electricity, and the Whydah
men characteristically complained that I had brought
them too near heaven. Rain fell in lozenges, like the
cross-hatching of engravers' shadows, and afterwards
in perpendicular torrents, that flooded the clayey ground
in a few minutes. The mass of storm shifted gradually

to the north, and cleared away after two hours, allaying for as many days the vehement plague of dust.

I will conclude this chapter with a few words touching our landlord, who holds much the same position, in respect to King Gelele, as did Dr. Dee to Queen Elizabeth. He is, I have said, the son of the last ruler's pet mediciner, and for many years he was a man of little note. Having attached himself to the actual monarch when the latter was a cadet, and by no means a favourite son, he predicted to him a crown ; whence his present influence. He soon exchanged his little huts, which many at Agbome remember, for a large establishment, and he was enriched by the usual process. When the King desires to honour a subject, he gives him a larger, or a smaller, gang of slaves. By selling these, and applying them to palm oil, Fortunatus obtains wealth, without which, in Africa, there is no true nobility.

I soon had a conversation with the Buko-no, on the subject of his specialty, the Afa * divination. It is a profitable trade ; every one in the country who can afford it

* The Dahoman form of the Ifa of Egba-land, the god of wisdom and prophecy. His origin is from the mythical city of Ifè, or Fé, as the Ffon contracts the word. I have given rough outlines of the worship in " Wanderings in West Africa,—Abeokuta," chap. iv.

" gets Afa," as the phrase is. Even English and other mulattos consult the oracle, without, however, owning to the belief. The master and student must repair to sacred, retired, and shady spots, scattered about the fields and bush.* After long ceremonies the diviner finds out the sign or symbol representing the features of the neophyte ; he then demands a heavy initiation fee; ten heads are the minimum required even from a poor man, whilst the rich would pay a hundred. The pupil then receives sixteen palm-nut counters, and is taught their use. As he cannot learn much of so dark an art, he must take professional advice on all important matters ; but the subsequent fees are light, being chiefly presents of fowls and provisions. Finally, the neophyte is taught by the " Master of Afa " what to abstain from—beef or mutton, brandy or palm-wine, like the Rechabites obeying their father Jonadab. Afa begins before the Dahoman's birth, informing his parent what ancestor has sent him into the world ; it is his intimate companion and councillor throughout life

* I have sometimes found them so engaged. It is an ancient practice. So Cain and Abel sacrificed in the fields (Gen. iv. 8); Isaac meditated, or prayed, in the country (Gen. xxiv. 63) ; Elias on Mount Carmel; John the Baptist in the Desert of Judea; Jesus in the Garden of Olives; and Mohammed on Jebel Nur.

until he reaches the grave which it has predicted to him.

The Buko-no ignored the Yoruban triad, Shango, Oro, and Obatala ; but he agreed with the Egbas about Afa. Seeing that I had some knowledge of the craft, he produced from a calico bag his " book," a board, like that used by Moslem writing-masters, but two feet long by eight inches, and provided with a dove-tail handle. One side of this *abacus* contained what are called the sixteen " mothers," or primary, the other showed as many children, or secondary, figures.* Each

* The following note will explain the use of the palm-nuts, and the names of the figures :—

In throwing Afa, the reverend man, or the scholar, if sufficiently advanced, takes 16 of the fleshy nuts of a palm, resembling the cocoa-tree ; these are cleared of sarcocarp, and are marked with certain Afa-du, or Afa strokes.

When Fate is consulted, the 16 nuts are thrown from the right hand to the left ; if one is left behind, the priest marks two ; if two, one (the contrary may be the case, as in European and Asiatic geomancy) ; and thus the 16 parents are formed.

The 16 are thus named and made :—

1.   ¨¦¨ Called Bwé Megi : it is the Mother of all.
        ‖
        ‖
        ‖

2.   ∣ ∣ Yeku Megi.
      ∣ ∣
      ∣ ∣
      ∣ ∣

was in an oblong of cut and blackened lines, whilst at the
top were arbitrary marks—circles, squares, and others,
to connect the sign with the day.   It began with the
Bwe-Megi, the figure, assigned to Vodun-be—fetish day,

3. ‖ ‖ Wudde, or Odé-Megi.
    | |
    | |
    ‖ ‖

4. | | Dí-Megi.
    ‖ ‖
    ‖ ‖
    | |

5. | | Losu Megi.
    | |
    ‖ ‖
    ‖ ‖

6. ‖ ‖ Urán Megi: an inversion of No. 5.
    ‖ ‖
    | |
    | |

7. | | Called Abla Megi.
    ‖ ‖
    ‖ ‖
    | |

8. ‖ ‖ Akla Megi; or Abla inverted.
    ‖ ‖
    ‖ ‖
    | |

9. ‖ ‖ Sá Megi.
    | |
    | |
    | |

10. | | Guda Megi: an inversion of No. 9.
    | |
    | |
    ‖ ‖

or Sunday,—whose mnemonic symbol was six dots in a
circle ; whilst Monday had a sphere within a sphere.
It was a palpable derivation from the geomancy of the
Greeks, much cultivated by the Arabs under the name
of El Raml (الرمل), " The sand," because the figures

11.   ‖ ‖   Turupwen Megi.
        ‖ ‖
        | |
        ‖ ‖

12. | | Tula Megi.
        ‖ ‖
        | |
        | |

13. | | Lete Megi ; or Tula inverted.
        | |
        ‖ ‖
        | |

14.   ‖ ‖   Ká Megi.
        | |
        ‖ ‖
        ‖ ‖

15. | | Ché Megi.
        ‖ ‖
         |
        ‖ ‖

16.   ‖ ‖   Fú Megi : considered the Father of all.
        | |
        ‖ ‖
        | |

These 16 parents may have many children. Nos. 13 and 2, for
instance, make | |
                | |
                ‖ |
                | |

—and so on, showing an infinite power of combination.

were cast upon the desert floor. " Napoleon's Book
of Fate " is a notable specimen of European and
modern vulgarisation. The African Afa is not, as in
Asia, complicated with astrology ; and no regard being
paid to the relative position of figures, it is comparatively unartful. Two details proved to me its Moslem
origin : the reading of the figures is from right to left,
and there are seven days, whereas the hebdomadal
week is beyond the negro's organisation.* The Buko-
no, however, is not bigoted ; he is more knave than
fool. Before his retainers he must keep up the farce of
faith ; but in private he freely owns that the Afa, by
which a tree can be destroyed and the hour of man's

---

* When travellers talk of an African week, they unconsciously allude
to the great markets, which give their names to the days, and which
recur at different intervals in different places. Here there are four.
The first is the Ajyahi, in Agbome : it was Ajyahi day on Saturday,
February 6, 1864. The second is the Miyokhi, a large market at
Kana; also the Uhun-jro, in Agbome : Sunday, February 7, 1864,
would be called Uhun-jro day. The third is the Adogwin, at Kana, and
the Fousa, a little provision market, near the Dahome Palace. The
fourth is the Zogbodomen, near Agrime ; also the Ako-de-je-go, near
the Gau's house at Agbome. The word means Ako (family), de (one),
and jego (tuck up clothes to fight). All these old names are mysterious,
and little known to the people—the missionaries call them " parables,"—
and they admit of many interpretations. Some explain it by, " If
the King leave his crown to one son, the rest must obey him ; " others
by, " If any people boast their valour, let them come to Dahome and
see."

death can be predicted, is merely the means of livelihood—the King's Afa always excepted.

This rationalistic admission, however, did not prevent
the Buko-no at once making a sacrifice to his god, for
having brought a "good stranger" to the King. The
dancing and singing in his "compound" lasted till dawn,
and in token of the favourable issue of his divination,
he sent us next morning a dish of palm-oil, stained
yams, stewed with pieces of boiled goat. This, con-
sidering his habitual parsimony, was going far.

The Senior sets out on his nag, with his suite, to the
palace, at 6 or 7 every morning. He squats or stretches
himself, dozing, smoking, chatting, eating, and drinking,
in one of the outside sheds, ready to be summoned at a
moment's notice within. Sometimes, but rarely, he
revisits his house for an hour about noon, when he bar-
ricades the door, and is not "at home." The post-
meridional are spent like the morning hours, and he is
rarely dismissed before dark, often not till deep in the
night. These people seem hardly to take natural
rest; the drum and the dance may be heard at his
quarters until dawn, and he delares that if this mode of
life were changed he should fall ill. Like the Dahoman
dignitaries in general, he must be sober, under pain of

"King's palaver." He cannot be said to have an hour's liberty, or to be his own master for a day, whilst the King is in the city. He leads the life of the East Indian Dhobi's dog, "Na ghar ka, na ghat ka."* Such is the routine of a Dahoman noble. What an existence to love!

The Buko-no has lately married a young princess,—

" Blythe and buxome at bedde and boarde,"

with whom Love is yet the Lord of all : we shall presently meet her in the palace. According to etiquette, he must prefer her to all his other spouses, of whom he has eighty. He is perpetually begging us for aphrodisiacs ; † and on one occasion his wives, overhearing the request, loudly accused him of taking away their good name. He is very jealous of these ladies, and

* " A washerman's dog, neither of the house nor of the ghaut" (where the master washes).

† Similarly, Captain Phillips relates to us that the uxorious old " King of Whidaw," when about to marry (probably a 3000th wife), applied to him for a rundlet of brandy, as a Christmas present for the bride's friends and his " cappashiers," and for a " strong-back medicine" for himself. He sent the ship's surgeon, who gave him a dose of cantharides, " which so heated the old man's reins that he became, as it were, a youngster once more," and on the next morning related to the strangers various impertinences.

often declares that a woman is the only thing which a
man should not share with his friend. We constantly
hear them singing, chattering, and quarrelling within ;
but they rarely appear ; and on one occasion he accused
my Krumen of making too free with our "fair"
neighbours. They are mostly black, rarely brown ;
like Shakspere's waves, they "curl their monstrous
heads" into the semblance of a prize cauliflower, and
their dress is a long white sheet, extending to the
ankles, passed under the arms and over the bosom. At
times the faster lot play at bo-peep, when *le brutale* is
away ; but as they are never alone, matters cannot go
too far.

Christmas here was distinguished by a violent storm
of thunder, lightning, and rain, the latter, as the old
traveller says, "more like fountains than drops, and
hot, as if warmed over a fire." Our modern copy of
the ancient Saturnalia opened with a cool, grey morning, almost as cloudy and sunless as could be expected
in the Black North. We duly drank to the land we
live out of, and the day ended with a heathenish
dance of the hammock-men, to whom rum had been
issued. The Mission servants joined, and the boy
Richard Dosu distinguished himself by the activity of

a rat, the cunning of a fox, and the impudence of a London sparrow. The next day was a half Harmattan, which made the natives don warm wrappers, lose appetite, and shun the bath. We, un-Ascians, delighted in the cold, dry air, accumulating positive electricity, and throwing off the negativity of the humid plain-heat. We bade adieu to anorexy, felt " *hinc sanitas* " now, and were ready to hymn, with holy Mr. Herbert,—

" Sweet day ! so cool, so calm, so bright."

Our first passage of arms with " Pantakaka," the old Buko-no, occurred on Christmas eve. The King has virtually abolished the custom of cribbing, cabining, and confining visitors till the Message is delivered.* To my request that the landlord would provide us with a guide, as we purposed going out shooting in the morning, he returned various frivolous excuses. I at once sent an interpreter to the Prince

* Dr. M'Leod, who had made himself obnoxious, received a message, when applying for permission to depart, that he was to become a *King's slave*, meaning, not one who had actually to labour, but a state prisoner. This, which he justly calls the " bleakest prospect imaginable," was a mere temporary act of caprice.

Chyudaton, who, in reply, begged pardon for the old man's folly, and requested me not to act before his visit. He came to us in the morning, heard my complaint, and went with it to the palace. In the evening, the Buko-no met us with an ample apology, a quarter of beef, a promise of a guide, and an offer of introduction to the " princess."

The King usually supplies his guests with pure water : in our case, however, the courtesy was neglected. We had forgotten—future travellers will not— to take a large dripstone filter, and we were beginning to suffer from the white, clayey stuff brought to us by our lazy hammock-men and servants. The element is here about as scarce as in Thorold Square and Hollybush Place. *Sin dagbwe diyye !*—" Good water this ! " is a cry ever heard in the streets, and pots full are sold in every market. We therefore engaged four Sin-no or " water-mothers," as they are called, to supply us with a sufficiency for the day. Unfortunately, as soon as they could collect a few cowries, they would stay at home for a week.

To reduce our establishment, I sent back five of the Mission boys to Whydah, with orders to wait for and return with our letters. They would do nothing : their sole efforts were confined to eating and talking, in which two pursuits, but in these only, I must own that they displayed all the Anglo-Scandinavian energy and competition. As is usual in the land, every one was afflicted with " a paralytic distemper which, seizing the arm, the man cannot but choose shake his elbow : "— they gambled from morning till night. The favourite game is Aji-do ;* probably the most ancient form of *tabliers*, or tables ; but here it is far from the civilisation of "*evangiles de bois.*" It is played on a board, with twelve cups, the antagonists taking the six nearest to them ; four *tesseræ*, dropped into each, are moved round from left to right, until the last cowrie falls upon two or three of the adversary's, and takes them. There is another, and a somewhat more complicated game, called Sigi-to.†

On St. John's Day (December 27), Mr. Cruikshank, when returning from the palace, where he had been

* From Aji (the Guilandina Bonduc seed, which was originally used in it), and dò (a hole). The game is the Sa' Leone " Wari," the Ashanti Warra, the Fanti Wal, the Egba's Ajo, and the Bao of Usawahili and Zanzibar : it is played in a great variety of ways.

† From Sigi (the dice with which it is played), and tò (a town). The dice made in Agbome are very rude ; but manifestly an imitation of the European.

treating an Amazon for a deeply-seated inflammation
of the eye, saw the war-chiefs arriving at the capital
from the last out-stations, and parading before the
palace.   This was a hint that the Customs would com-
mence at once.

CHAPTER XIII.

OF THE GRAND CUSTOMS AND THE ANNUAL CUSTOMS
GENERALLY.

THE word "Custom" is used to signify the cost or charges paid to the King at a certain season in the year. It is borrowed by us from our predecessors on the West African Coast—the old French—who wrote *coûtume*,* and the Portuguese *costume*, meaning habit or usage.

The Grand Customs † are performed only after the death of a king. They excel the annual rites in splendour and in bloodshed, for which reason the successor defers them till he has become sufficiently wealthy. The "History," which was not written in the days of details, gives cursorily some terrible accounts of the

---

* So Barbot (i. 4) speaks of *La coûtume* (the tax) *de Parmier.*

† Dr. M'Leod (p. 59) distinguishes them as double customs, opposed to single customs; but he is singular in this.

slaughter and of the barbarities which accompanied it.
" In the months of January, February, and March
(1791), the ceremonies of the Grand Customs and of
the King's coronation, took place ; the ceremonies of
which lasted the whole three months, and were marked
almost every day with human blood.   Captain Fayrer,
and particularly Mr. Hogg, Governor of Appolonia,
were present ; and both affirm that not less than five
hundred men, women, and children fell " victims to
revenge and ostentation, under the show of piety.
Many more were expected to fall ; but a sudden
demand for slaves having thrown the lure of avarice
before the King* he, like his ancestors, showed he was
not insensible to its temptation."

The curious reader will find at the end of the present volume a paper by the Rev. Mr. Bernasko, who
was present at the last Grand Customs performed in
November, 1860, by the present sovereign, to honour
the manes of his sire.   Although the horrors of this
rite were greatly exaggerated, with ridiculous adjuncts,†

* Agongoro (Wheenoohew), the grandfather of the reigning sovereign.

† For instance, the Europe-wide report that the king floated a canoe
and paddled himself in a tank full of human blood.   It arose from the
custom of collecting the gore of the victims in one or two pits about two
feet deep and four in diameter.   See Appendix III.

ı Europe, it is clear that very little change has taken lace, especially in the number of victims, during two-hirds of a century.

The yearly Customs were first heard of by Europe n the days of Agaja the Conqueror (1708-1727), lthough they had doubtless been practised many years ıefore him. They form, in fact, continuations of the ırand Customs, and they periodically supply the de-ıarted monarch with fresh attendants in the shadowy vorld. They are called by the people Khwe-ta-nun The yearly head thing," and Anun 'gbome* "Going ıo Agbome in the Dries." The number of victims ıas been much swollen by report. Mr. James, at the ıeginning of the present century, found the maximum ıf three several years to be sixty-five. Commander Forbes, who writes feelingly, owns that, in the later ıears of King Gezo's reign, not more than thirty-six ıeads fell. I have laid down a total of at most eighty luring the time of my mission, and of these none, ıxcept the criminal part, were Dahoman.*

* Literally, anun (in the dries after the rains), 'gbomen, for Agbomen we will go to Agbome). The other name is khwe (year), ta (head), nun thing).

† So Mr. Duncan states. "The people thus sacrificed are generally risoners of war, whom the king often sets aside for this purpose . . . .

The season of the Customs, which combine carnival, general muster, and *lits de justice*, seems to comprise the whole year, except the epoch of the annual slave-hunts,˙ here dignified by the name of "wars."   For instance, at present the King purposes to set out on his marauding expedition in February, and to return in March or April.   He then lodges at the Jegbe Palace, "spreads a table" (in other words, gives a banquet), and purchases the captives from his soldiery. The next move is to the country-quarters at Kana, where, about May, he will perform the Oyo Customs,* and then take his rest—a happy murderer.   In November, when the rains are ended, he will summon his chiefs, sleep at the Adan-we Palace, and on the next day make a ceremonious entrance into his capital, like that which I have just described.   This year various delays have put off the rites till December.

The annual Customs are of two kinds.   The first— which happened, for instance, in 1862-63—is called Atto-ton-khwe, or the Atto† year, from the Atto, or

Should there be any lack of these, the number is made up from the most convenient of his own subjects."   Such, however, is not, I believe, the custom now.

* See Chap. VII.

† Pronounced Attaw.   In the History there is mention of four plat-

tform, in the Ajyahi market, whence the vic-
is are precipitated.   Of its peculiarities we have
etches by Mr. Norris (1772) and M. Wallon (1856-
), finished descriptions and poor drawings by Com-
mder Forbes (1849-50), and, later still, an official
count by Commodore Wilmot.*   The second is the
-sin-khwe (1863-64), the " Horse-tie year," and the
ison of the name will presently appear.   As yet, no
iveller has, I believe, described the ceremonies of the
-sin, which, however, differ but little from those of
e Atto.

ms, raised stages of rough timber, covered with cloths and provided
:h seats for the King and his visitors. Gezo reduced the number to
:, and his son has again excelled him by doubling it.
* See Appendix III.

CHAPTER XIV.

THE KING'S "SO-SIN CUSTOM."

SECTION A.

First Day of the King's Annual Customs.

EARLY on the Day of the Innocents (December 28th), a discharge of musketry near the palace and a royal message informed us that the Customs had begun, and that our presence at the palace was expected. We delayed as long as was decent, and, shortly after noon, mounting our hammocks, we proceeded by the usual way to the Komasi House.

In the Uhun-jro market-place, outside the Ako-chyo Gate, and not attached, as it used to be, to the palace-wall, stood a victim shed, completed and furnished. From afar the shape was not unlike that of an English village church—a barn and a tower. The total length

as about 100 feet, the breadth 40, and the greatest
eight 60. It was made of roughly-squared posts,
ine feet high, and planted deep in the earth. The
round-floor of the southern front had sixteen poles,
pon which rested the joists and planks supporting the
ent-shaped roof of the barn. There was a western
ouble-storied turret, each front having four posts.*
he whole roof was covered with a tattered cloth,
lood-red, bisected by a single broad stripe of blue
heck.

In the turret and the barn were twenty victims.
All were seated on cage stools, and were bound to the
osts which passed between their legs ; the ankles, the
hins under the knees, and the wrists being lashed
utside with connected ties. Necklaces of rope, passing
ehind the back, and fastened to the upper arms, were
lso made tight to the posts. The confinement was not
ruel : each victim had an attendant squatting behind
im, to keep off the flies ; all were fed four times a
ay, and° were loosed at night for sleep. As will be

---

* We find in the History (print, p. 130) a single thatched and open
ted, with twelve men sitting on the ground : their hands are lashed as
ow. The late king added a turret of one story, and the present ruler a
econd stage. In the old illustration there are twelve horses tied to the
inder posts, we saw but three.

shown, it is the King's object to keep them in the best
of humours.

The dress of these victims was that of state criminals.
They wore long white nightcaps, with spirals of blue
ribbon sewn on, and calico shirts of *quasi*-European
cut, decorated round the neck and down the sleeves
with red bindings, and with a crimson patch on the
left breast. The remaining garment was a loin-cloth,
almost hidden by the " camise." It was an ominous
sight ; but at times the King exposes without slaying
his victims. A European under the circumstances
would have attempted escape, and in all probability
would have succeeded : these men will allow themselves
to be led to slaughter like lambs. It is, I imagine, the
uncertainty of their fate that produces this extraordinary *nonchalance*. They marked time to music, and
they chattered together, especially remarking us. Possibly they were speculating upon the chances of a
pardon.*

We dismounted, as usual, at the palace corner, and
the Harmattan sun made us take refuge under one of

---

* Exactly the same thing is observed in the History. " The unhappy
victims, though conscious of their impending fate, were not indifferent
to the music, which they seemed to enjoy by endeavouring to beat time
to it."

the sheds. A procession was walking round the square—a mob of followers escorting the Sogan, or Horse Captain,* who was riding bareheaded under a white umbrella. This high official, who is under the Meu, opens the Customs by taking all the chargers from their owners, and by tying them up, whence the word "So-sin." The animals must be redeemed, after a few days, with a bag of cowries.

A gun, fired inside the palace, warned us that royalty was about to appear. A corps of "Amazons" streamed from, and formed a rough line in front of, the Komasi Gate. The King, under a gorgeous umbrella, and the usual parasol upheld by his wives, stalked down a lane through the thick crowd towards his own proper So-sin. This was a shanty fronting, and about 150 paces from, the palace. It resembled the Uhun-jro, or market-shed to the N.N.East, but it lacked the turret. Thirty barked and badly-dressed tree-trunks, and a strong scantling of roughly-squared timber, supported the first-floor, which was without walls. The thatch of the pent-roof was hidden, as in the other So-sin, by a glaring blood-red calico, with long black stripes along the ridge and eaves. Splints of bamboo frond were

* So (horse), and gan (captain).

occupied a kind of couch, strewed with handsome home-made cottons; in front of him, upon a mat, crouched a Dakro, or messengeress, and behind him stood and sat a semicircle of wives.

On the King's proper right was a larger shed, somewhat like a two-poled tent. The mat and thatch were covered with cloth, parti-coloured at the sides and at the roof, whilst elsewhere it was of white calico, adorned with grotesque shapes. Unlike its neighbour, it was closed all round except at the entrance, which had for verandah two white umbrellas. Inside, at the bottom, was a kind of divan, and on the ground before it sat a small black child in red, and two women with white caps and vests, and blue pagnes, with four or five others hardly distinguishable. The double posts supporting the entrance were clothed with red and pink silk; about their middle hung a dozen abacot caps, and under the verandah squatted a woman with a gun placed on a stool before her.

This tent contained the relics of the old King. His ghost is supposed to be present, and all bow and prostrate to it before noticing the present ruler.

To Gelele's extreme right was planted a white flag, with a blue cross; around the staff a group of armed women gathered. Immediately near the King, but leaving a square space in front, were the Amazons, at squat, with their gun-barrels bristling upwards ; there were amongst them many young girls in training for military life. A half-naked boy lay on the ground within a few feet of the royal umbrellas, and children are allowed behind the bamboos. On other occasions, juveniles, wholly nude, wandered about, heedless of re-proof, and I have seen two of them fighting before the throne. Even the lowest orders crossed the presence with an air for which, in Asia, their feet and calves would have disappeared under the bastinado. The barbarous nature of the African everywhere pierces through, whatever be the disguise.

On the left of the King were the Amazon drums and rattles. In the open space between the throne and the bamboos lay the three calabashes supporting the three chieftains' brass-mounted skulls. On two large mats of palm-fibre were ranged shallow baskets, which acted as saucers to calabashes some 2·50 feet in diameter. Three of them were adorned with silver crescents and stars, whilst all were covered above and below with various coloured calicoes—red, blue, yellow, pink, and striped. Periodically, knots of eight or nine women came from the palace with larger or smaller gourds of provisions, which they disposed upon a third mat in front of the King.

In a much shorter time than it has taken the reader to peruse this *mise en scène*, the caboceers and their followers, who were scattered over the square, gathered into a dense semicircle near the bamboos. The dignitaries sat or lay on the ground, unarmed, under their white, blue, and fancy umbrellas. The little people were on foot behind them, and the women and girls stood aloof, peeping as they best could. The total number present, including about 300 children, might have amounted to 2500, and I never saw at Agbome a larger gathering.

The day opened with various preliminaries. Ten unarmed men were dancing in line before the Komasi Gate when the King came forth. The sally of the Amazons was succeeded by long and loud firing. After all were seated, the old Yevogan led us up to the bamboos, where, fronting the King, we exchanged salutations,—this was an invariable part of the ceremony. The senior then conducted us to a place on the left or Meu's side of the male semicircle, close to a very strong band, whose two chiefs wore Phrygian bonnets of red and blue velvet. A hole was dug in the ground and a large white umbrella was planted over us for shade, the "earth being beat tightly round it, similar to a large mushroom." Presently the Meu brought up a flask of gin and a calabash of Atá, or bean-cake, wrapped in plantain leaf, with a royal message that the "white-man's captain" had sent, according to custom, this food to the King, and that he shared it with us (*formula*); whereupon we bowed our acknowledgments.

Gelele then rose, and came from out his shed. His dress, besides the usual *braccæ* and a dark silk kerchief round his waist, was a blue-flowered damask shirt, a table-cover, in fact, and this was knotted on his left side. He formed an effective picture : a fine tall figure, with shoulders towering above his wives, the head bent slightly forwards, and his hands clasped behind his back. There were hushed murmurs of applause, and the faces of his subjects expressed unaffected admiration.

Sundry of the King's wives accompanied their lord, and stood or sat upon the ground behind him. None were handsome, but some had the piquancy of youth. Their strong point, as in the Italian and Spanish women, was the *pettinatura.* The prettiest of the hair-dresses was a short crop, like lambswool, sometimes stained blue, as with indigo. The plainest was the melon-stripe, where the short hair was plaited in lines, exposing the scalp between. The most grotesque was the semblance of pepper grains, or of cloves stuck in a ham, formed by twisting up single little wool spirals. Another peculiar *coiffure* was the tuft, varying from one to four, some small as thimbles, others large as the Turk's-caps on lamp chimneys ; they rose sharp and solid from the clean brown scalp, and seemed made of black velvet, burned reddish by the sun. The princesses wore the hair like a fez, bristling stiff to the height of six inches, and looking compact as ebony wood. A few had bear's ears, two tufts upon the "region of cautiousness ;" others wore the scarlet feather of an oriole stuck in their sable locks.

Immediately behind the King stood three wives— one with the head shaven and naked, the second with long hair, and the third with a princely "fez." They sheltered his uncapped poll with three gorgeous tent-umbrellas of cotton velvets, whilst a fourth protected him with a gay parasol. The first was a parody upon the *Sacré Cœur*—which the Dahomans admire, probably because it suggests tearing out the foeman's heart. Each lappet of the valance was alternately green and crimson ; in the upper part was a larger cross, red or yellow, with a black or white border, and below it, of the same hue, an object manifestly intended for a human heart but broken into crockets. In the centre of this was a better shaped heart with a small white medial cross ; and both were disposed apex downwards. The second showed an upper line of white crosslets on black velvet ; below it was a blue shark, edged white and yellow, with a red and purple eye, resting upon crimson or claret-coloured velvet, which was lined with a binding like that of the animal. The third, and the most splendid, was capped with a very heraldic wooden lion, painted the brightest saffron. The lappets showed the king of the beasts grasping in the dexter paw a white scimitar, and below it a biped, very negro, with dazzling white knickerbockers and no legs to speak of, vainly upholding a blue sword blade. Both figures were on red ground, *parsemé* with little white crosses. This umbrella was equally grandly lined, whereas the two former were white inside. The diameters varied from six to ten feet, rendering them unmanageable in windy weather. The poles were seven feet long, and instead of wires they had square rods connected by strings, probably brought by the Portuguese, and easily to be distinguished from the rude native stick frames. They were kept open by a peg passed through the upper part of the handle.

Before the speech began, four bundles of palm-matting, which lay inside the bamboo barrier, were opened by the women. Each contained a lamp-black drum, the largest three feet high, all with skin-heads lashed tight to about a dozen large pegs projecting a few inches below the top. They were decorated with small squares of red stuff in front, with white, blue, and black cloths behind them, like four aprons of different sizes. These are called Ganchya 'hun.* The word applies especially to its peculiar sound or beat, and, by inference, to the song of which it forms the accompaniment.

The King having hitched up his body-cloth, began an allocution in a low tone, as if " nervous." Men and women *huissiers* and heralds, standing on the right, and the youths calling themselves the "Donpwe," proclaimed attention by loud and long cries of " Ago ! "

* Hun, or uhun, is the generic name of a drum.

Audience !—or " Oyez ! " *   On the left a sharp double
tap was struck on the cymbal, and all obeyed.   The
King spoke with the head a little on one side, assuming
a somewhat *goguenard* air.   His words were many and
oft repeated ; the genius, or rather the poverty of the
language necessitates verbosity.   In so artless a tongue
it is only by " battology " and frequent repetition that
the finer shades of meaning can be elicited.   The sense
is short to relate.   " His ancestors had built rough and
simple So-sin sheds.   His father, Gezo, had improved
them when ' making Customs ' for the ghost of Agongoro (Wheenoohew).   It is good to beget children who
can perform such pious rites.   Therefore, he (Gelele)
would do for his sire what he hoped that his son would
do for him."   And some score of men sat listening—
about to die !

Presently, the women in attendance placed the
drums before the King, and handed to him four hooked
sticks.   Upon these he spat, beat two of the instruments, and spoke during the intervals of drum ming
The " Ganchya," I was told, is a new ceremony.

---

* The general word for " silence ! " is " nágbó ! " Both at Abeokuta
and at Agbome it is used when entering the house, so as not to take the
inmates by surprise.

After listening to loud applause, and being saluted with discharges of musketry, the King retired behind the curtain held by his wives, and whilst he drank the subjects went through the usual ceremony.

After resting awhile, Gelele stalked to the fore. In his left hand was a Kpo-ge,* or singer's staff—a silver-headed and feruled stick, two feet long. To the upper part was fastened a square of silk kerchief, striped red and purple, and folded into a triangle. The apex was passed through silver-lined eyelet-holes, like those that in former times, amongst us, held the "beau's" cane tassel. The King also wore the bard's insignia—double necklaces of beads, disposed like cross belts over the breast, and with the usual pigtails behind. After singing for awhile, to the great delight of the listeners, he danced, first to the men's, then to the women's band. He is, unlike his father, a notable performer, and though the style is purely Dahoman and barba-rous, the movements are comparatively kingly and dignified. He was assisted in this performance by a " leopard wife " † on each side, dressed in white waist-

---

* Kpo (a staff), and ge (thin).

† In the Ffon, kpo (a leopard), and 'si (a wife)—here usually trans-lated tiger-wives. They are the youngest and the fairest of the harem.

coats, and striped loin-cloths extending to the feet. In their hair was a kind of diadem of silver pieces, bright as new sixpences. At this sight the people vociferated their joy. A herald, in a huge felt hat and bright bracelets, and a jester, conspicuously ugly, with a tattered " wide-awake," a large goat-skin bag under the left arm, and chalked face and legs, rose to their feet, and pointing at the King—a peculiarly disrespectful action to European eyes—declared, in cracked, shouting voices, that he was " Sweet, sweet, sweet as a white man ! " Then followed a chorus of soldieresses, and from the crowd loud " Ububu," * made by patting the open mouth with the hand. On the women's side the " King's birds " † chirruped and twittered to justify their names.

Before sitting down, Gelele advanced to the front rank of male spectators, and removing, with his right fore-finger, the perspiration from his brow, scattered it with a jerk over the delighted group. He was then

* This is the " kil " of Persia and the "zagharit" of Egypt. Here it expresses wonder and pleasure, and is mostly confined to the men.

† A select troop of musicians known as akhosu (king), and khwe (bird). They are of both sexes; but the sound generally proceeds from the women. The male " king-birds " are attired, like Moslems, in white petticoats.

cooled by his wives, who rubbed him down with fine yellow silk kerchiefs, and vigorously plied their round hide fans,* coloured and embroidered.

Then, rising again, like a refreshed giant, the monarch danced to six modes. When the time was to be changed, a chorus of women gave the cue to their band by repeating certain meaningless technical terms, ending with frequent repetitions of " Ko ! ko ! ko !" till the musician has learned the right measure. Presently, two, and, at a short interval, three wives danced on each side of the King, keeping an eye upon him, and so preserving excellent time. The fourth dance was more animated, and as the monarch showed shortness of breath, an old Amazon addressed him, " Adan-we !" † He resumed his labours to the words, " Agida 'hun-to Ko-'hun !" ‡ and he advanced, stooping towards the ground, and rolling one elbow over another, to show that he was binding captives.

Followed a little change of scene. The King, propping his elbow upon the bard's staff, and bending low

* In Ffon, known as "Afafa ;" in Abeokuta, "Agbebbe."

† Meaning, " O brave white !"

‡ Explained thus: Agida (the bent drum-stick), 'hun-to (drum beater), ko-hun (beat the drum), kaya (turning or wheeling about); viz., Drummer, use thy drum-stick, and we will turn about.

whilst his wives surrounded him, sitting on their hams, sang, and was responded to by what appeared a laughing chorus, but which was a dirge — a single cymbal making melancholy music. Then rising with uplifted staff, and turning towards the larger shed-tent, he adored, in silence, his father's ghost. This new and startling practice was twice repeated.

Decorations were distributed — a pair of singers' staves to a male and a female, who received them with cries of " Tamulé ! " * The King then brought out by twos half a dozen double-pigtailed necklaces of yellow beads, interrupted by red. Three were handed to the Meu, the Yevogan, and a favourite singer, who put them on in due form. The rest were given to the highest she-dignitaries, whose lips were white with kissing the ground. Gundeme, the woman Min-gan, is white-haired and tottering. Egbelu, the " Meu's Mother," has grey hair, sharpish features, and broken front teeth. Na-dude Agoa,† the female Yevogan, is a huge, middle-aged woman, brown, and rolling in fat. Her hair is still black, and her features not quite uncomely ; her

* A corruption of the Fanti " Endamenen," O brave man !

† Explained by, " I eat one thing not, right" ; *i.e.*, I cannot eat or embezzle anything.

voice is strong and clear ; moreover, she speaks well.
This is the officer who bare two sets of twins, first girls,
then boys, to the King. The two former, according to
the ancient usage of the empire, were betrothed' to the
Min-gan and the Meu, when the wicked cousin' won
their *prémices.* Formerly, the royal ladies had only
temporary husbands, visiting' all men who pleased
them. As this caused great scandals, the King has
forbidden polyandry ; but the husbands, as a rule, must
confine their marital attentions to the blood-royal. On
marriage, the daughters receive each a dowry of eighty
slaves, male and female, but the aged sons-in-law are
expected to " spend money like water."

Presently, Gelele, who was sitting in front of the
feminine Court, handed sundry rolls of blue and pink
cottons to the Meu. The high dignitaries all rose
excitedly, unfolded, and, standing at a distance,
stretched each cloth to show that it was an entire
piece. A white umbrella, opened and waved about by
the Min-gan, a caboceer's stool, bran new, and sundry
heads of cowries were placed before the presence. This
was the ceremony of raising a captain to the rank of
Ajyaho,* and, to the wonderment of all, Chabi, a young

* See Chap. VIII.

man and Left-hand Commander of the Blue Guards,
therefore under the orders of Adan-men-nun-kon, was
raised to the sixth rank in the realm.

The "Grandfather of Dahome" has ever been, I
have said, the heir of his subjects, whose widows,
slaves, and all moveable property must be carried to
the palace. It is probable that the goods do not leave
the lion's den without yielding considerable "heriot" as
the lion's share. As a rule, the eldest son, or, if he
be judged unfit, the successor to the vacant office,
inherits the deceased's wives and makes them his own,
excepting, of course, the woman that bare him.* This
was practically proved to us. A file of fourteen
women, two with babies on their backs, twice issued
from the palace, carrying big native boxes, grass-
cloth bags, old muskets, silver armlets and bracelets,
home-made stools, hats, pipes, sticks, umbrellas in
ragged cloths, and similar valuables. Twice the
new wives and slaves crouched humbly before their
proprietor. Soon afterwards, forty-three male "chat-
tels" of the deceased crawled on all-fours from the

---

* Especially in the royal family. So in 2 Samuel xii. 8 we read
that Nathan gave David's master's wives unto David's bosom. In that
barbarous state of society women are inherited like cattle.

left past the King, and did homage to their "live lord."

When the King's silver-mounted pipe had been lit behind the *tente d'abri* extemporised by the wives' clothes, and had been handed to him, we produced our cigars, and applied ourselves to the old liqueur-case. We persevered in distributing the contents amongst our Krumen and followers—they are expected to drink kneeling—although the Buko-no showed manifest disapproval of such waste. Presently, the cracked-voiced Min-gan rose and explained what things had been done by the King to the *novus homo,* and when supported by the Tokpo (a captain, but not of royal blood), he committed himself to a recapitulation. All gave the ruler that full feed of flattery which his soul loves. He may be said to breathe an atmosphere of adulation, which intoxicates him. The wildest assertions, the falsest protestations, the most ridiculous compliments, the ultra-Hibernian "blarney"—all are swallowed in the bottomless pit of poor human vanity, and midnight will often see him engaged in what ought to be a very nauseous occupation.

Echili, the fourth caboceer of Whydah, then rose and performed the part of a skull at the Nilotic feast. The

Ajyaho, he said, rarely lived for more than a year, and if Chabi, like those before him, should die of poison, the crime must be punished. Then the fat Adanejan declared, in his bull's voice, that he and many caboceers had proposed for the Ajyahoship another person, but that the King had chosen one trusty and brave ; moreover, that all poison would now be detected.

Whereupon the lucky man stood up, puffed like a pouter-pigeon by the new clothes which the ministers had bound about his upper half; his hair was brickdust red after much shovelling, and his right hand nervously, methought, fingered his musket muzzle. After his " portrait " had been duly taken, he spoke till the sun burned crimson above the western horizon, even through the fringes and valances of our portable tent. He had been raised from a simple captain to the position of a high caboceer ; he would soon achieve an act of loyalty and bravery : with much boasting on the same pattern. After sundry prostrations, and other speeches to this purport, he publicly assumed three new " strong names " : 1. Azon-kpo má-jí-won ; 2. Achoroko ; 3. Sevi kanyena-ma-se-gbo-'gbwe.*

---

* The caboceers, like the kings of Dahome, assume a first name or names after any remarkable action or event. Those in the text are

A chorus of plaudits received these distinguished sentiments. The Ajyaho danced under his unfolded umbrella, and, backed by his fresh gang of slaves, raised muskets and war-clubs to salute the King. Presently, Ago! from the women, and the cymbal-taps from the men, proclaimed silence for royalty.

The King, still sitting amidst his female group, then addressed the Ajyaho, who stood up reverently in the front centre of the caboceer's semicircle. He added emphasis to earnest words by often shaking the forefinger —as is done in North America to men, and in England to naughty boys—at his last promotion, whom he exhorted to be brave and loyal, and whom he warned not to obey any dignity except the Min-gan and the Meu. Hereat the people clapped their hands. Silence being again enjoined, the Ajyaho was once more strictly cautioned not to be deceived by his brother chiefs.

Ensued the promotion of another captain, whose

taken from the Bo-fetish jargon, and are not intelligible to the vulgar. The first was thus interpreted: Azon-kpo (a training stick), má (not), jí (afraid, synonymous with si, or khe-si), won (portent, evil omen, especially a child); *viz.*, (I am) a club not afraid (to slay), portents (that menace the king). The second was explained, "I will punish all who will not serve my king." The third means, Sevi (an evil-doer), kanyena (a bad thing), ma-se (never listens), gbo (dont! or leave off!), 'gbwe! (emphatic, *e.g.*, gbo-'gbwe, I tell you to leave off!); *viz.*, "People plead for offenders, but I will not suffer this if any one harm the king."

name was changed from Koikon to Hon-je-no.*
Before all the ceremonies could be concluded, the
wood became dark, and the store of provisions strewed
before the King was distributed. The Dakros placed
the calabashes outside the bàmboos, whence they were
removed by the several recipients. Suddenly, as is his
wont, Gelele rose, and came towards us. After snapping fingers, I thanked him for the spectacle. He
showed me the rum for our hammock-men, and our
share of provisions ; after which we were all three
told that we must dance, sing, and drum—the latter
accomplishment, unfortunately, has not received from
me the attention which it deserves. Dr. Cruikshank
and I willingly consented to dance with the King,
knowing it to be the custom, and that he greatly enjoyed it. We pleaded, however, successfully for Mr.
Bernasko, who, being a Reverend, could only sing.
Gelele showed much delicacy in the matter, often
threatening but not calling upon us to perform, lest
our nerves might be startled by so great an event, and
saying that he would choose evening time, as the sun
does not suit white men.

* It is a Bo-fetish name, interpreted to mean " The man in charge of
the King's door." Hon (door), je (waits), no (within).

Whereupon we withdrew. The provisions, which accompanied us, caused a tumult till near dawn. *Pain et spectacles* are apparently the cardinal wants of these people; they sing, drum, and dance all the day, and they fight for their wretched prôvision half the night. When not engaged in these pleasures they are plundering the wherewithal to procure them. Hence the melancholy state of the land.

Nothing could be poorer than the display above described ; any petty hill rajah in India could command more wealth and splendour. All was a barren barbarism, whose only " sensation " was produced by a score of men looking on and hearing that they are about to die.

I again sent a message to Chyudaton, officially objecting to be present at any human sacrifice, proposing that lower animals be substituted for man, and declaring that if any death took place before me I should at once return to Whydah. He replied that there would be no necessity for the latter measure, and, with respect to the victims, that many would be released, and that those executed would be only the worst of criminals and malignant war-captives. With which crumb of comfort I was compelled to rest satisfied. Hitherto the gang of victims has been paraded round, under tortures, before the visitors, and in later years they have been cruelly gagged; moreover, the executions took place within hearing, and often within sight of the strangers.* It is, therefore, already something to lower the demoralising prominence of the death scenes.

SECTION B.

The Avo uzu 'gbe,† or Second Day of the King's So-sin Customs.

December 29th was again a *dies non.* The vile water had affected us all, and the Reverend was in bed of a Harmattan. The King, therefore, kindly deferred for a day the grand spectacle with which he intended to surprise us. At 2·25 P.M., December 30, we mounted hammocks and proceeded to the market-shed.

The picture was as follows. To the west of the

* See Mr. Duncan (vol. i. pp. 250-252). The people say of him that he was a good war-man, as he used to walk up to, and to inspect the corpses.

† Avo (cloth), uzu (change), 'gbe (to-day).

Uhun-jro, the broad open space opposite the gap which acts as gate, was another cloth-covered tent, with wings of upright matting. A clean entrance led up to the former, near which a tall flagstaff held a yellow flag with a broad blood-red cross. The wings were railed off for the royal wives by the usual Dahoman fence of palm sticks and bark rope. The erection was flanked by two large trees, about a hundred yards apart, and they were connected by a semicircle of bamboos, bulging to the front and forming the boundary between the sexes. To the north was the ominous victim-shed, with its steeple-like turret, and with its score of wretches gazing at the *fête*.

Our chairs were placed on the men's side, or a little to the left of the tent entrance line, and on the opposite side of the square near the gate. Presently a motley group passed us three several times, moving as usual to the right. First appeared the old To-no-nun and his six eunuchs, who carried with difficulty a huge package, like a bagged tent. Followed a hunchback, whip in hand, clearing the way. Visese-gan, the sub-chief eunuchess, preceded about a score of women, carrying upon their heads coarse palm-mats; they were followed by an escort, bearing calabashes and baskets, each filled with about twenty bundles of tightly-rolled cloth, stuck upright and compacted by an outside wrapper. The total represented 120 bearers, but of these ten had no burden. Valuing the minimum at 2 dols., and the maximum at 5 dols., and assuming 3 dols. to be the medium, the value shown to us was about 1320*l.* ($110 \times 20 = 2200$ cloths $= 6600$ dols.). The rear was composed of a corps of "leopard wives," with silver-studded hair, and by a large band of women who, as they passed by, openly "chaffed" us. After the third circuit the mats were spread and the baskets were deposited at the entrance of the tent, when thirty women, coming from the wings and opening the cloth bundles, began to build the "Avo lilli," * cloth heap or divan.

Meanwhile, preceded by singing and dancing musketeers, the high dignitaries passed before us, riding, under their umbrellas, the horses which they have now ransomed, and followed by noisy bands. The two schools showed themselves at a glance. Our friends, the Anlin-wa-nun,† who is the "King's place," when

* Avo (a cloth), and li or lilli (smoothen!).

† This is a Bo name, and imperfectly understood. The words are Anlin (a hole in the ground), wa (make), nun (a thing).

royalty does not go to war, the Binazon or treasurer, the Bi-wan-ton or Junior Meu, the Abo and the Matro, uncle and brother, by the father's side, to the present King, either bowed smiling or came up to us and danced. The Matro, who holds the high dignity of lieutenant Gau, is a fine, tall young man; he was habited in a Moslem skull-cap, a large white body-cloth and canary-coloured shorts. When his band and musketeers had formed an oval opening opposite us, he danced with a face expressing great glee, instead of the usual serious and inanimate look. Two of his re-tainers, a jester and a soldier, conspicuous by his gloria of monkey skin, rising from a band of cowries, shouted in mediæval phrase, " A Matro! A Matro!" As the excited chief took a musket and manœuvred with it, his people bawled out " Da-mon." * The honour was great, but the dust and the heat were excessive.

The unfriendly " umbrellas," namely those who dis-like foreigners, as the Min-gan, the Tokpo, the Woto, a small dark senior of royal blood, and others rode by either affecting to ignore our existence or suddenly looking the other way. We were much amused by the

* Da (fire!) mon (as you are), *i.e.*, " May you fire straight!" said in praise to one of high name.

peculiarity of the other groups, which either prowled
or rushed about outside the bamboos. The old To-no-
nun and his fifty men went round the half ring, passing
right and left, singing, dancing and clapping hands,
taking aim with muskets, and waving their long knives.
Then came the Pani-gan-ho-to or Gong-gong men, four
in number, and carrying single and double cymbals,
whilst a corresponding female band promenaded the
space within the bamboos. Twenty singers also walked
about, preceded by a peculiar drum borrowed from
Ashanti and called Ganikbaja. At intervals stalked
before us the Men-ho-blu-to,* or "Company of Boast-
ers." These are a score of local and negro Radcliffes
and De Courcys who by especial permission wear
in "the presence" their broadbrims or white nightcaps and their dirty cloths over their shoulders.†
Moreover they are allowed to smoke long pipes, of which
one was on the tomahawk principle ; and all over the
square there were independent groups drumming and
dancing violently as if to throw off the exuberance of

---

* Men (man), ho (great), blu (do), to (he who does).

† Throughout Yoruba and the Gold Coast to bare the shoulders is
like unhatting in England. These men were exempted from the
necessity by a mere caprice of the King, not because they have in any
respect distinguished themselves.

their animal spirits. So at Aden I have seen a Somali, when walking quietly down the road, seized by some unintelligible influence and fall to capering like a dancing-master demented.

Meanwhile the Amazons, thròwing a stratum of loose cloths and covering them with a finer piece outspread, had built up a circular divan 12 feet in diameter by 5 to 6 feet high.* Most of them were of European manufacture, many were made in the palace, and those that surmounted the heap were the best silks, of brightest colours—pink, yellow, red and tender green— which sound outrageous but which look side by side beautiful as a rainbow or a butterfly. All this finery is carried back after the ceremony to the palace, and is not, as I was assured, given to the people.

At 4·5 P.M. an increase of bustle and hubbub announced the approach of the King. Preceded by boys and musket-men, cheering and presenting arms, came the *Cœur de Marie* umbrella, shading the fox-like features, the black face and the ignoble white nightcap of Adan-men-nun-kon. After an interval followed the royal

---

* To the north of this divan, outside the bamboos, a small heap of silks was raised upon mats, in honour of Addo-kpon, of whom more presently.

escort—three male caboceers, a " Gobbo," and a woman
captain, marching before a female host. The King wore
a straw calotte with a brilliant striped cloth, and was
toujours la pipe à la bouche. He sat woman-like on a
little dingy nag, with a bell, and led by a chain halter.
Behind his lion-umbrella and parasol trouped chanting
soldieresses and a strong band, with seven skulls
mounted on fancy flags, followed by a dozen " leopard
wives" and a rearguard of old women and small girl
recruits. The King passed three times in thirty minutes
round the market-place, waving hands to us, and the
" Ububu" rang and guns banged in all directions.

When the procession was over, Gelele took his seat in
the pavilion, with his wives on the right, and on both
flanks a bevy of musketeer women squatting motionless
as statues. The male caboceers saluted, touching the
ground outside the bamboos with their foreheads and
twice shovelling up dust. A troop of men spread a
thin line of single mats from the victim-shed past the
bamboo semicircle and southwards towards the
Komasi Palace : the extent was about 350 yards, and
the breadth proved to be 12 to 13 feet. On each mat
was placed a pole 14 feet long, tipped with a short and
blunt iron fork. Presently the six eunuchs brought up

and opened what had appeared a tent bag. This is the Nun-u-pwe-to* cloth belonging to King Gezo, a patchwork supposed to contain a specimen of every known manufacture, native or European. The pieces vary in size from 1 to 10 feet, the colours are blue, yellow, green, pink, red, and purple, and the patterns checked, striped, zig-zaged and barred. This the King will wear about his person when Abeokuta has been taken. How he is to support 1050 feet of stuff no one could explain, but the investiture it appears has been deferred until the Grecian Kalends.

As the King issued from his tent at 5.4 P.M. the long cloth which had been placed on the mats was upraised at arms' length by the attendants with the blunt iron forks passing through eyelet-holes. Thus exalted, it stood more than twice the height of a man. When the novel screen had been placed between the men and the women, Gelele passed up and down the inside and the outside, waving hands when opposite us. This exhibition of untold wealth excited the people, as their fearful noises testified.

* The word has already been explained. Mr. Duncan also describes this "noble piece of patchwork," making it 600 yards by 2; and in another place 1000 yards by 8 (vol. i. p. 264; and vol. ii. p. 27).

The "Able-to-do-anything" cloth having being removed, the King ascended the divan by a five-rung
ladder covered with calico, picked out with pink reliefs.
He was accompanied by four wives.   One held a
parasol, which was repeatedly changed, and this she
constantly twirled.   The second was the spittoon
bearer, who also fanned the King with a yellow silk
kerchief, assisted by the more substantial hide circles
of other women who stood below and around the heap.
The other two opened and piled upon the divan the
green, blue, pink and speckled muslins with which
Gelele would "change cloth to-day."   It was waxing
late, and royalty had become fatigued and impatient :
the King testily snatched the bundles from the hands
of his wives, and worked at them in double quick
time.

Presently Gelele mounted the platform and there
disrobed, retaining, however, his shorts, which were of
satin yellow-flowered on a dark ground.   From his
left shoulder hung, by a long sash of crimson silk, a
short silver-hilted sword.   He first put on a toga of
what appeared to be green netting, like a mosquito bar,
and took in his right hand a large bright bill-hook
ending in a circular bulge.   He formed a most effective

figure, his swarthy stalwart form being thrown out against the glowing western sky.

The various dances, all of them in the decapitation style, performed by the King, corresponded with the number of "drums" or bands. On the male side, sitting in the Meu's or the minister division, were about twenty men and youths with "tabl," or tambourines, under their left arms ; they were habited in scarlet coats and queer bonnet-caps of red and black cloth. Within the bamboo, was an equal number of women, similarly clad. I will not trouble the reader with the names and details of the several corybantic saltations, comprising the first set of eighteen and the second of one dozen. The King performed only a few steps of each, and then, outstretching his left palm towards the *musique* with an imperious gesture, he caused it to stop. Still the labour was severe, as the free use of the forefinger, the yellow silk, and the hide fans proved. The thirteenth dance of the second set was called "Agbata," a performance borrowed from the "Nago" people, and much admired for the kicking and jumping which are its elements. It drew down unusual applause : generally, however, shouts of joy, murmurs of wonder, and discharges of musketry and cannon accompanied the whole performance. The eunuchs and the caboceers made courtier-like speeches, the "niggers" stolidly admired the grandeur of a king who can defray the expenses of such exhibitions, and a wild group of frontier bushmen, who act as guides to the army when on the war path, hailed and bellowed their own melodies. These roughs were all armed with muskets, and they were led by two chiefs in dingy red tunics, whose thick beards and straw hats, which they did not remove before the King, rendered them conspicuous.

The *brouhaha* was infernal. There was a momentary hush as the King, having girt on with a cartouche belt a toga of white muslin, armed himself with a lion-stick, and a musket, which he pointed at his subjects pretending to fire. At this burst out a glorious shout of real African laughter—yep! yep! yep!—whilst guns were fired in all directions. The din increased when the brass-set skulls of the three kings * were severally handed to the conquering hero. With these trophies of his own peculiar prowess he toyed, and played various childish antics, to the intense delight of the *mobile*, placing them under his left arm, hiding them beneath his cloak, stretching them out for better view, resting his

* Described in Chapter IX.

elbow upon them, and waving them to us as we bowed.
He then loudly addressed the Po-su's party, which stood
on the left of the semicircle.*   They replied with noisy
greetings, which he acknowledged by a crab-like movement, advancing and retreating sideways, with his left
elbow akimbo, and jogged to the fore ; this expressive
action is called "ago," and means "I undertake to
do it."   The King then tossed off a bumper of rum
from the brass cup on the crown of "Bakoko's" head,
and sent it to us that we might pledge him : it was at
least as civilised as Lord Byron's drinking cranium ;
and more so than the "bony goblet"—"apparently not
long before it had been useful to the original possessor"
—out of which Mr. Duncan † caroused with King Gezo.
I was allowed to sketch the three calvariæ, and to
handle the royal sticks and caps.   One was of the Fanti
Company, a loose calotte of purple velvet, with a yellow
line on the crown, and a narrow band of white silk with
a border round the lower part.   The second had a
white shark on a puce-coloured velvet ; and the third,
a cap of the Blue Company, resembled in shape a
Moslem "Takiyah," but showed a green lion eating a

* Mr. Duncan (vol. i. p. 247), saw King Gezo perform similar antics.
† Vol. i. pp. 239, 240.

claret-coloured porcupine, fretted over with quills of yellow stitching. These animals were all very heraldic and unintelligible.

The vociferous rapture of the subjects knew no bounds as the King danced with his sword between his teeth, and exulted over Bakoko's skull and the breaking of Ishagga. The Buko-no eagerly asked me, if all the world o'er I had ever seen so grand a sight ? I have had to answer similar queries in far more civilised countries; and I have ever found that there is nothing easier than to convince people who already believe.

Presently the King began to hand down decanters of rum, a sign that he was weary of pleasure—he had danced thirty two dances. At 6.15 P.M. he descended from the divan, and mounted the smaller heap, whose cover was a white cloth powdered with little ochre-coloured lions. Here the King assumed his fetish war-dress, a body-pagne of chocolate-coloured netting, and a dark blue indigo-dyed cloth, passing from the left shoulder low down the right side : it was studded with charms and amulets in small squares, stained with dry blood, and bordered with cowries.* His umbrella

* Cowries may be remarked in the musket stocks. According to
C C

was equally gloomy, and his large crooked Bo-stick was swathed with alternate blue and white bandages. After motioning with this weapon, he danced to the songs and instruments of the fetishmen, and seized a musket, which he levelled but did not discharge. He then came forward, and we advanced : after the usual greetings, I requested him not to forget his English coat of mail, which hint was whispered in his ear by the timid Beecham, who dreaded the fetishry. After a little chatting, and being requested to return on the morrow, we made for home with much pleasure,—there are none of Rimmel's perfumed fountains here.

Mr. Duncan (vol. i. p. 261), they are an honourable distinction, given as medals to civilised armies. The stock is repeatedly smeared with the victim's blood, coat after coat, till its thickness is sufficient to form a setting for the shell, around which it soon dries. Although only one cowrie is given per head, some old soldiers have their weapons entirely covered over with them. This custom, of course, stimulates murder, and excites perpetual jealousies in the service. I have heard the same said of a certain modern English decoration.

END OF. VOL. I.

BRADBURY AND EVANS, PRINTERS, WHITEFRIARS.

Printed in Great Britain
by Amazon

50137979R00239